*D*ialogic Civility
in a Cynical Age

SUNY series in
Communication Studies

Dudley D. Cahn, editor

$\mathcal{D}$ialogic Civility
in a Cynical Age

Community, Hope, and Interpersonal Relationships

Ronald C. Arnett
and
Pat Arneson

Foreword by
Julia T. Wood

STATE UNIVERSITY OF NEW YORK PRESS

Production by Ruth Fisher
Marketing by Patrick Durocher

Published by
State University of New York Press, Albany

© 1999 State University of New York

For information, address State University of New York Press,
State University Plaza, Albany, NY 12246

Library of Congress Cataloging-in-Publication Data

Arnett, Ronald C., 1952–
    Dialogic civility in a cynical age : community, hope, and interpersonal relationships / Ronald C. Arnett and Pat Arneson ; foreword by Julia T. Wood.
        p.   cm. — (SUNY series in communication studies)
    Includes bibliographical references and index.
    ISBN 0-7914-4325-6 (alk. paper). — ISBN 0-7914-4326-4 (pbk. : alk. paper)
    1. Interpersonal communication. 2. Interpersonal relations. 3. Civil society. 4. Cynicism. I. Arneson Pat, 1961–   .
II. Title. III. Series.
HM1166.A76 1999
302–dc21   99-26607
                                                                          CIP

10 9 8 7 6 5 4 3 2 1

Contents

Foreword   xi

Acknowledgments   xvii

PART I. INTERPERSONAL PRAXIS: FROM COMMUNICATIVE CRISIS
     TO NARRATIVE ACTION   1

1. Introduction: Beginning the Conversation   3
     An Overview
         Horizon of Significance
         The Conceptual Key

2. Voices of Cynicism and Hope   11
     Routine Cynicism
         Interpersonal Suspicion
         Language Disconnected from Action
     Listening to Two Sides of Cynicism
         Routine Cynicism as Debilitating
         Cynicism as Survival Tool
     The Wedding of Cynicism and Hope
         Pain and Joy
         Hope within Limits

3. Historicality and Presence   29
     A Foundation for Communicative Change
         Historicality
         Missing the Historical Moment

Meeting the Historical Moment
Dialogic Limits
  A Dialogic Perspective
  A Practical Dialectic
  Interpersonal Praxis as Historical Common Sense
  Interpersonal Commonplaces

4. Common Ground: Interpersonal Narrative   51
  Opening Narrative Structures
  Narrative Background
    From Metanarrative to Therapeutic Culture
    Historical Mismatch—The Therapeutic Metaphor
    An Overextended Metaphor
    Walter Lippmann's Warning
  A Narrative Ethic for Interpersonal Discourse

PART II. INTERPERSONAL VOICES   79

Section 1. Narrative Decline: Interpersonal Dialogue and Self

5. Carl Rogers: A Voice of Pragmatic Optimism   83
  Introduction
  Significance of Carl Rogers's Life and Practice
    A Founding Voice
    Scope of Carl Rogers's Influence
  The Quiet Revolutionary
    Communicative Focus
    Historical Grounding
    An Optimistic Listener
  Central Concepts in Carl Rogers's Work
    Self
    Innate Wisdom of the Human Organism
    Relationship
  Historicality and Dialogic Civility

6. Abraham Maslow: Science, Values, and Additive Change   103
  Introduction
  Significance of Abraham Maslow's Science/Values Project
    Additive Approach to Science

Additive Education
Self in Service to the Other
Central Concepts in Abraham Maslow's Work
A Science of Interpersonal Health
Human Values
Self-Actualization and Earned Self-Esteem
Peak-Experiences
Historicality and Dialogic Civility

Section 2. Narrative Confrontation:
Interpersonal Dialogue and Crisis

7. Martin Buber: Attending and Response Between
   Persons   127
       Introduction
       Martin Buber's Common Center: The Between
           Horizon of the Between
           The Existential-Phenomenological Nature
               of the Between
           Ambiguity, Story, and Guidance
           A Communicative Poetic
       Central Concepts in Martin Buber's Work
           The Great Character
           Dialogue
           Focus of Attention
           Authenticity
       Historicality and Dialogic Civility

8. Carol Gilligan: Gender and Moral Voice   149
       Introduction
       Historical Context: A Window for Cynicism
       Moral Voices
       Central Concepts in Carol Gilligan's Work
           Female Adolescence
               Disconnection
               Re-Connection and Care
               Responsibility in Relationship-Grounded Caring
               A Dialectical Dance

A Morality of Care
Voice and Inclusion
Historicality and Dialogic Civility

9. Paulo Freire: Dignity and the Limits of Inclusion   167
Introduction
Interpersonal Pedagogy
Humility
Praxis
Affirming the Other
The Limits of Inclusion
Central Concepts in Paulo Freire's Work
Rejecting a Culture of Silence
Narrative Sickness
Critical Consciousness
Dialogue
Historicality and Dialogic Civility

10. Sissela Bok: Crisis and Ethical Imagination   189
Introduction
Ethics and Postmodernity
Communication without Ethical Coherence
Central Concepts in Sissela Bok's Work
Lying
Secrets
Peace
Common Values
Historicality and Dialogic Civility

11. Viktor Frankl: Meaning, Displacement, and Courage   207
Introduction
Lived Life as Thoughtful Action
Central Concepts in Viktor Frankl's Work
Pragmatic Spiritualism
Meeting Disappointment and Suffering
Discovering Meaning
Tripod of Meaning
Tragic Triad
Freedom

Problematic Assumptions
    Self-Actualization
    Contrary to the Pleasure Principle
Choosing Meaning
Historicality and Dialogic Civility

Section 3. Narrative Construction:
Interpersonal Dialogue and Story

12. Nel Noddings: Re-Storying an Ethic of Care   233
    Introduction
    Re-Storying Ethics
        Missing Stories
        Caring as Story
        Moral Education
    Central Concepts in Nel Noddings's Work
        Reducing Evil
        An Ethic of Caring
            Caring in Relation
            Risks of Caring
        Intuition and Interpersonal Reasoning
            Intuitive Capacities
            Complementary to Reason
            Meaning and Story
    Historicality and Dialogic Civility

13. Robert Bellah: Re-Storying Broken Covenants   255
    Introduction
    The Practices of Identity
        Individualism
        Therapeutic Limits
        Characters of Modern Life
    Central Concepts in Robert Bellah's Work
        Broken Covenants
        Tacit Understanding of a Problematic Story
        Communicative Background—The Common Good
        Inviting Community
    Historicality and Dialogic Civility

PART III. DIALOGIC CIVILITY   277

14. The Interpersonal Praxis of Dialogic Civility   279
       From Privatized to Public Discourse
       A Minimal Foundation for Dialogic Civility
       Respect and Civility
       Civility and the Other
           A Call for Dialogic Civility
           From Unreflective Practice to Praxis
           Our Historical Problematic
           Practical Philosophy of Dialogic Civility
       Conclusion—Dialogic Civility

Works Cited   305
Index   323

Foreword

I t is a rare pleasure to read a scholarly book that offers a realistic basis for hope about the possibilities for enriched communication. *Dialogic Civility in a Cynical Age: Community, Hope, and Interpersonal Relationships*, written by Ronald C. Arnett and Pat Arneson, aims to inject hope into a historical moment burdened by pervasive cynicism. In this book the authors offer hope—hope for human thought and action and, most especially, for human communication praxis. No naive scholars, the authors do not advocate a romantic optimism that springs more from idealism than a realistic awareness of problems and constraints. What they advance— even insist upon—is a realistic hope, one that is aware of, but never defeated by disappointment, cynicism, and what they refer to as "the mud of everyday life." Their hope is informed by the work of preeminent philosophers and social thinkers as well as by the authors' original theorizing.

The problem that this book addresses is the pervasive and untempered cynicism of our era, which undermines the possibility of thoughtful dialogue. The authors suggest that the currently ubiquitous cynicism has two primary wellsprings: cultural emphasis on radical individualism, which prioritizes the self over others; and the abandonment of a once assumed (however unreflectively) collective identity in favor of alignment with fragmented social groups, which too often are solipcistic and narcissistic. Without advocating a return to a grand metanarrative or a falsely universal collective identity, the authors steadfastly insist on the importance of the common good, of a commitment to an "us" as well as a "me."

This book attempts to answer the question: How do we get along with others and create relationships with them in an era marked by social diversity and the absence of a compelling, consensually embraced metanarrative?

Their answer is that we do so by approaching communication with a commitment to *dialogic civility*, which requires respect for topics, others, multiple perspectives, and the given historical moment. This answer reflects the wisdom of two scholars who have devoted their careers to studying and theorizing ethical bases for human communication. The answer also reflects a sophisticated understanding of the tensions between social communities and the common good, between hope and cynicism, and between individualism and collectivity. This book provides a thoughtful foundation for developing communication theories, principles, and praxis that are capable of meeting the urgencies of the present era.

It will come as no surprise to those familiar with the authors' previous work that they draw upon interpersonal communication theory to develop an ethic for social interaction. The respect that ideally guides private discourse becomes civility in the realm of public communication. Civility does not require individuals to alter private attitudes, but it does require them to be motivated by a pragmatic goal to keep the conversation going, something that is unlikely to happen when civility is absent. Terming their framework a "public interpersonal model," the authors propose ethical commitments that foster civil communication between individuals and groups that associate themselves with a range of experiences, values, and narratives. When enacted, these minimum commitments preserve a space for engagement among diverse people, especially engagement about differences.

Their model does not rely primarily on individuals' private dispositions, preferences, or moods. Instead, it begins with civility in the public domain, which reflects a commitment to something beyond the self and which fosters dialogue. The minimum condition for dialogic civility is an attitude of respectfulness toward others, topics, different and sometimes inharmonious perspectives, and the given historical moment.

For the authors, attention to the given historical moment is paramount. They offer an extensive and uncommonly thoughtful analysis of the current historical moment and its implications for communication. This moment, they assert, is suffused with a habitual and unreflective cynicism that bespeaks a loss of hope. Cynicism paves the way for mistrust, defensiveness, and rejection of whatever does not reflect or meet the individual's goals and values. In turn, allegiance to only individual priorities and narrow identifications with specific social groups discourages engagement across groups and across differences.

Although occasionally useful and appropriate, cynicism is morally vacuous when it is a habitual attitude. Routine cynicism is morally impoverished because it cannot generate a basis for a communicative life in which self and others engage. The authors do not counsel denial of cynicism. Instead, they encourage communicators to acknowledge the rampant cynicism of our era and to meet it with hope and a desire to move beyond the barrenness of unremitting doubt and skepticism. A delicate marriage between hope and cynicism, the authors argue, avoids both utopian idealism and banal negativity.

Pervading the book is an insistence that effective communication requires meeting others within their commonsense worlds and respecting their narratives, which often differ from our own. The central importance of historicality leads the authors to point out that all models of communication are grounded (often implicitly) in particular temporal, geographic, material, and social contexts. A model that was appropriate in the 1960s and that met the demands of that era should not be assumed to be appropriate on the brink of the twenty-first century. They argue that the therapeutic model of interpersonal communication that ascended in the 1960s and 1970s is unable to respond to the current era. That model's emphasis on the self, in general, and self-actualization, in particular, is incapable of cultivating productive dialogue among widely diverse individuals who make up society today.

To replace the therapeutic model, the authors propose a model grounded in historicality, which is best understood as a willingness to meet the demands of a particular moment. Reflecting the authors' long-standing commitment to a dialogic approach to communication, the model they advance respects the preferred stories of all communicators. The model assumes that each individual's previous or established story moves into dialogue with the stories of others, as well as the constraints and commonsense questions of the present moment. Respectful dialogue that opens self and other to the possibility of change is fostered when all communicators embrace the authors' proposed narrative of dialogic civility—with narrative understood as a story held in the public domain by a group of people.

As I have already suggested, the attitude of hope that the authors advocate is not utopian. Rather, it is a pragmatic hope that arises from awareness of and respect for multiple voices and the experiences that inform them. On its own, cynicism degenerates into chronic negativity; on its own, hope is doomed to be overcome by inevitable disappointments and shortcomings. Yet, when hope and cynicism inform and temper each other, one result is the possibility of civil communication that keeps the conversational door open, or at least ajar.

The four chapters comprising Part I of the book establish a conceptual framework and explicate the authors' scholarly and ethical commitments. Following that, Part II of the book examines how distinguished thinkers have developed theories and moral precepts to confront commonsense issues of their particular moments. With a deep respect for others' work and the eras in which it emerged, they consider Carl Rogers's pragmatic optimism, Abraham Maslow's science/values project, Martin Buber's "the between," Carol Gilligan's moral voice, Paulo Freire's dignity and dialogue, Sissela Bok's ethical imagination and coherence, Viktor Frankl's pragmatic spiritualism, Nel Noddings's ethic of care, and Robert Bellah's community and broken covenants. Taken together, these thinkers provide compelling bases for a "public interpersonal model" that is grounded in historicality, respect for multiplicity, a commitment to dialogue, and a willingness to live with dialectical tension between hope and cynicism.

Unwilling to leave their inquiry at a purely theoretical level, the authors devote the final chapter of the book to sketching practical implications of their inquiry. Here they focus on praxis, or theoretically informed practice. They argue for praxis that is shaped by a theory of dialogic civility because this holds promise for effective communication based on respect for diverse voices, knowledges, narratives, and experiences.

The implications of this approach are multifold. Obviously, the model Ron and Pat propose has important implications for how we conduct conversation in an era marked by diversity and cynicism. Equally important, their model has implications for teaching in communication courses. Those who are persuaded by the arguments of this book will find themselves rethinking traditional approaches to interpersonal communication and the concepts and processes that are conventionally highlighted. As one who teaches in this area, I left the book feeling compelled to devote more attention to respect and civility as minimum conditions for communicative engagement and to listen more carefully, more openly to my students' cynicism while simultaneously asking them to listen more thoughtfully to my arguments for hope, now strengthened by this book.

This is an important book. Consistent with its insistence on a dialectic between cynicism and hope, the authors offer a model and a vision of communication that is both pragmatically useful and theoretically informed, both optimistic and realistic. In the pages that follow, readers will encounter thinkers in the dialogic tradition whose voices are clarified and extended by the authors' analysis. The result is a hopeful vision of communication in which we keep the conversation going by enacting civility to temper, but never disregard the cynicism of our era.

JULIA T. WOOD

A cknowledgments

This project began out of friendship and ended in significant enthusiasm for the communication project of the twenty-first century—revisiting the public domain as the communicative arena where diversity and difference can meet. We offer dialogic civility as an interpersonal guide in this new terrain of public interpersonal life where diversity might be met with interpersonal care, not unreflective cynicism.

Our thanks go to Julia Wood, Ken Cissna, and Barnett Pearce for their assistance with this project. We would also like to thank the editors and dedicated staff at SUNY Press.

Our thanks also go to St. Cloud State University and Duquesne University, "communities of memory" that made the conversation between the co-authors possible. We offer deep thanks to Duquesne University President Murray, Provost Weber, Father Hogan, and Dean Ramirez. They have labored long and effectively to bring dialogic civility to a campus home in the form of caring service that provides Education for the Mind, the Heart, and the Soul.

Finally, we thank our friends and loved ones for their support. Ron would like to thank Millie, Adam, Aimee, and colleagues at Duquesne University who provide a sense of community at home and work that makes the challenges of life worth the journey and the joys of life so much richer. This work is dedicated with thanks and respect to my Father (1919–1996) with deep appreciation. Pat would like to thank Ron Arnett for inviting me into the conversation, and Stan Deetz, David Descutner, Algis Mickunas, and my friends for their encouragement and support in keeping the conversation going.

Part I

Interpersonal Praxis: From Communicative Crisis to Narrative Action

Part I introduces dialogic civility in a twofold fashion. First, dialogic civility is recognized as a metaphor that addresses the historical problematics of this communicative era, including routine cynicism, collapse of metanarrative agreement, and the loss of narrative background. Second, dialogic civility is framed as a potential background narrative capable of reminding us how to address the other if we are to pragmatically accomplish the task of co-constituting meaning between persons in a postmodern age of virtue confusion and contention. If a commitment to a "web of metaphorical significance" constituting dialogic civility becomes central to the communicative life of many people, a narrative is invited that functions as an implicit background for guiding everyday interpersonal discourse.

Chapter One

Introduction

Beginning the Conversation

On Understanding —

Understanding, writes Hans-Georg Gadamer, is a fundamental endowment of humans, one that appears to distinguish us not only from domesticated pets but also from even our dolphin and primate cousins. Efforts to explain understanding almost universally rely on the construct "linguisticality" or "language." As Gadamer puts it, "above all, [understanding] takes place by way of language and the partnership of conversation [1989, 3]."

—John Stewart, *Language as Articulate Contact*

Roots as the Wellspring of Life —

To be rooted is perhaps the most important and least recognized need of the human soul. It is one of the hardest to define. A human being has roots by virtue of his [or her] real, active and natural participation in the life of a community which preserves in living shape certain particular treasures of the past and certain particular expectations for the future. This participation is a natural one, in the sense that it is automatically brought about by place, conditions of birth, profession and social surroundings. Every human being needs to have multiple roots. It is necessary for him [or her] to draw wellnigh the whole of his [or her] moral, intellectual and spiritual life by way of the environment of which he [or she] forms a natural part.

—Simone Weil, *The Need for Roots*

T he aim of this interpretive work, *Dialogic Civility in a Cynical Age: Community, Hope, and Interpersonal Relationships*, is to understand the contributions of a number of
authors who have written about dialogic approaches to interpersonal communication, linking some of their central ideas and
insights to our historical era. The writers we discuss have in common a dialogic voice. The concept of a dialogic voice suggests, for us,
the ability to meet life in this historical moment and seek to uplift
the human spirit, propelling us toward what Seyla Benhabib calls
more "respectful" interaction with the *other* (1992, 38), even in
painful circumstances. Our communicative task becomes increasingly complex in our attempt to respond with respect and sensitivity to multicultural perspectives. This work invites the reader into
an ongoing conversation about human dialogue in a changing historical era.

An Overview

Part I: "Interpersonal Praxis: From Communicative Crisis to Narrative Action" examines our contemporary moment. Part I outlines
the philosophical focus of this interpretive work, calling attention
to the problematic nature of unreflective cynicism in daily interpersonal communication. We suggest the wholesale use of cynicism
has contributed to interpersonal rootlessness; we offer "historicality" as an alternative to the therapeutic/relational perspective on
interpersonal communication. We assess our contemporary era, a
time we equate with the lack of a collective guiding moral story.
Disenchanted communicators make it difficult for dialogic voices to
be heard—such persons spend more time lamenting the lack of an
ideal than listening to and meeting the common sense questions of
the historical situation. We ask, *"How might dialogic voices invite
civil interpersonal exchange, not in quest of a theoretical ideal, but
in the historical moment of routine cynicism and lack of metanarrative direction?"* In summary, Part I includes chapter 1, *"Introduction: Beginning the Conversation"*; chapter 2, *"Voices of Cynicism
and Hope"*; chapter 3, *"Historicality and Presence"*; and chapter 4,
"Common Ground: Interpersonal Narrative."

Part II: "Interpersonal Voices" outlines the work of scholars
speaking in dialogic voices about human communication and discusses historical questions that may have prompted their dialogic

work. Section 1, "Narrative Decline: Interpersonal Dialogue and Self" (chapters 5 and 6), examines how Carl Rogers (1980) and Abraham Maslow (1971, 1954/1970a) responded to an era in which previously accepted narratives were questioned and critiqued. Their answer to that historical moment was the dialogic self. Rogers emphasizes trust in the organismic self, while Maslow places trust in the actualizing self as an alternative to narrative decline and confusion. Section 2, "Narrative Confrontation: Interpersonal Dialogue and Crisis" (chapters 7, 8, 9, 10, and 11), outlines how Martin Buber (1966b), Carol Gilligan (1982), Paulo Freire (1970/1974; Shor and Freire, 1987), Sissela Bok (1978/1979, 1989), and Viktor Frankl (1959/1974) demonstrate concrete ways in which dialogue is necessary in the midst of crisis-ridden environments. Their answer in the historical moment was dialogue in response to crisis. Buber writes in response to hatred propelled by ethnic and nationalistic impulses. Gilligan offers a response to the crisis of muted voices based on gender. Freire responds to literacy denied, resulting in oppressed voices. Bok issues a response to the ethical crisis of value disagreement in postmodern discourse. Frankl responds to narrative destruction resulting in lack of meaning. Their dialogic voices were heard over the chaos of crisis. Section 3, "Narrative Construction: Interpersonal Dialogue and Story" (chapters 12 and 13), describes the work of Robert Bellah (Bellah, Madsen, Sullivan, Swidler, and Tipton 1985, 1991) and Nel Noddings (1984), who point to the importance of hope in the midst of an unclear sense of moral direction. Their answer to our historical moment is dialogue and story. Bellah suggests a nonpsychological community-based story. Noddings points to the story connections of fragmented lives. In short, we explore dialogue propelled by three distinct metaphors—self, crisis, and story. None of the authors ignore self, crisis, or story, but each tends to punctuate one of the emphases with greater vigor in understanding human dialogue.

We associate each author with the historical commonsense question that seems to propel his or her writing. We ask, "what common sense questions did the author knowingly or unknowingly address in the given historical moment of theory construction?" We enter dialogue with the authors with a bias—we ask how each responds to the notion of metanarrative decline, either in implicit or explicit form. Clearly, one could see different questions that propelled the authors, if a different interpretive bias (other than the question of metanarrative decline) guided the inquiry.

In addition, a summary of some of the major concepts comprising the author's work is included. Finally, we respond to the question, "What elements of a given theory seem particularly important as we develop a view of interpersonal communication from a perspective of dialogic civility that meets our contemporary moment of routine cynicism and the decline and/or collapse of metanarrative agreement?"

Part III: "Dialogic Civility" addresses components of dialogic civility as an alternative to interpersonal communication issues of technique-driven cynicism and interpersonal rootlessness in our present historical moment. We offer components from the previous chapters that suggest the greatest potential for the interpretive task of understanding routine cynicism and interpersonal rootlessness driven by a lack of moral stories.

This final chapter keeps hope alive in a narrative of dialogic civility, concerned with the welfare of the common good—"us." Dialogue (interpersonal discussion focused on the "other," person, text, and historical moment) and civility (bringing respect for person, topic, and historical moment to the public domain) frame our view of dialogic civility. Diversity of persons, philosophies, races, religions, and ideas call us to celebrate difference. Impulses of dialogic civility encourage grace toward difference and move us to seek points of common ground within our present historical moment.

Horizon of Significance

A number of terms are central to this interpretive work. We point below to their horizon of significance or general use within the text. These terms provide commonplaces for discussion of dialogic civility as a needed narrative background for daily interpersonal interaction.

a. Practice is engaged in an unreflective manner and in routine action.

b. Praxis requires reflective integration of theory and action.

c. Metaphor is a term whose characteristics exemplify and point us poetically and indirectly to meaningful understanding beyond the symbol itself.

d. Narrative begins with a speech act that is tested by people and competing world views, then is fashioned into a story with main characters, a history, and a direction; a story becomes a narrative only when it is corporately agreed upon and no longer the product of an individual person.

e. Metanarrative is an implicitly and uniformly agreed-upon public virtue structure that functions as a universal standard.

f. Metanarrative decline is the gradual awareness of lack of agreement on virtue structures that many people no longer consider responsive to the historical moment.

h. Interpersonal communication, as we limit it to dialogic civility, is shaped by dialogue between persons, appropriately connected to the historical moment of interaction. Interpersonal communication includes both intimate and public discourse. The former is tied to agreement on communication in the private domain and the latter is key in an era of diversity and difference. While our use does not exclude private intimate discourse, we focus our discussion on the public domain of interpersonal communication.

Dialogic civility is used in a twofold fashion. First, as a metaphor that points to the importance of public respect in interpersonal interaction. And, second, when such a metaphor is agreed upon by a large number of communicative partners it begins to take on the character of an implicit background narrative for interpersonal communication.

The Conceptual Key

This book-length series of interpretive essays points to dialogic civility as one narrative background commitment that might offer guidance in an era of narrative confusion. Much work on interpersonal communication concentrates on the foreground issues of how we might communicate with one another. This book assumes a much different focus; exploring the why for beginning an interpersonal exchange with another person.

Dialogic Civility in a Cynical Age: Community, Hope, and Interpersonal Relationships is a story calling for a narrative background to undergird daily interpersonal action. Concepts of cynicism, historicality, praxis, and dialogic civility are the main characters in this story. These concepts act as main characters, appearing throughout the text, weaving continuity and meaning into our story that calls for a public narrative of dialogic civility in this historical moment of routine cynicism and narrative confusion.

This work deliberately brings together the hope of dialogic voices and the cries of cynicism. As suggested in *Dialogic Education: Conversation about Ideas and between Persons*, our task is to embrace contraries, offering a view of life that avoids undue optimism and is simultaneously guided by a realistic and enduring sense of hope:

> Hope and disappointment compose a sort of practical philosophy that calls for an education that can make a difference while offering a realistic warning that pain and disappointment will need to be met and dealt with creatively along the way. Caring is not just something that emerges spontaneously. It can and should be part of the practical education on a campus or department. When Aristotle detailed the importance of a practical philosophy, he was concerned about the education of virtues. The virtue of caring that embraces both hope and disappointment is fundamental to dialogic education. . . . Dialogic education works with a dialectic understanding of caring. Somewhere between the extremes of undue optimism and too much focus on difficulty and disappointment rests an education that prepares us for lifelong learning. (Arnett 1992/1997c, 113)

We invite you to enter into a conversation about what we consider to be a significantly needed task—providing hope for dialogic voices with the conviction that the cynics' singular world view must be met head on, not ignored. We are convinced Martin Buber (1966b) was correct: "According to the logical conception of truth only one of two contraries can be true, but in the reality of life as one lives it they are inseparable" (111). Life is best lived in the unity of contraries. We must temper unreflective cynicism with a sense of hope so a background commitment of dialogic civility can propel interpersonal communication and not be lost in our confused and disrupted historical moment.

We offer dialogic civility as a metaphor that reminds us of respect and possibly as a public narrative background that propels us toward the other in an action of respect. Perhaps our ability to work together interpersonally in an age of diversity may depend on dialogic civility becoming an agreed upon minimal background narrative structure that guides our communication together. From metaphor to narrative, we invite the reader into a story about dialogic civility.

*C*hapter *T*wo

Voices of Cynicism and Hope

Maintaining Cynicism—

[People maintain cynicism when they dispute] any meaningful change can take place in the nature and functioning of public life. Such cynicism comes packaged as sociological realism and its effect is always to make the suggestion of meaningful change sound idealistic, if not naive. As a sociologist, I am professionally inclined to accept such determinations, but as a citizen I see no choice but to hope against them. The obligation to hope becomes all the more poignant when one is reminded of all that is at stake.

—James D. Hunter, *Before the Shooting Begins*

The Routine of Disbelief—

Cynicism in our world is a form of legitimation through disbelief. There exists an odd but by now common practice. Leaders use rhetoric which neither they nor their constituents believe, but which both leaders and followers nonetheless use to justify their actions.

—Jeffrey C. Goldfarb, *The Cynical Society*

We recognize the emergence of routine cynicism in a world where style frequently triumphs over substance, immediacy is often more respected than reflective deliberation, and where what is publicly stated is privately ignored. Additionally, the rapid pace of contemporary life permits little time for public questions and inquiry to determine the eth-

11

ical dimensions of behavior; thoughtful reflection is a luxury unknown to many people. The terrorism in Oklahoma City on April 19, 1995 ("This Does Not Happen Here"), and the development of paramilitary groups within the United States point to intense cynicism that too quickly demonizes authority. Such action reveals cynicism in caricature form. We also meet cynicism in its lesser dimensions in daily communicative life. Routine or unreflective cynicism has become a normative part of our everyday culture, from the greed of athletes and team owners, to inappropriate behavior of sports fans, to student cheating, to faculty who have given up on the ideals of higher education. In some cases, cynical evaluations and actions are situationally appropriate. But overall, the cynical wave of looking out for one's own interests, adopting a "survival mentality" (Lasch 1984, 64) without a commitment to the common good, carves a pathway to social disaster. While routine cynical communication may offer ingredients for short term individual successes, it presents a long term hazard for a society and culture.

We do not reject the occasional use of cynicism; however, we deem the routine, banal, and unreflective use of cynical communication to be a significant problem for discourse between persons. A social problem emerges when routine cynicism is used as a communicative technique. Alternatively, we suggest that a dialectic of cynicism in companion with concern for the common good and a sense of hope can frame a realistically grounded interpersonal voice. An interpersonal concern for "us," not just "me," needs to be renewed among us once again. With all our technological advances—and more coming daily—we still are left with the question: "How do we invite good interpersonal relationships?" Getting along with others is a central question for living in the social diversity of the twenty-first century (Makau and Arnett 1997).

Routine Cynicism

One of the ways to determine appropriate commonsense questions in a given historical moment is to observe what has taken on a character of banality from overuse or overappearance. Cynicism has joined the ranks of banality. Unreflective cynicism is the basis for many television sitcoms and talk shows, and offers the communicative basis for lunch conversation in organizations from churches to construction firms. Cynicism, an unceasing attitude of negativity, has become an interpersonal epidemic that limits lives in organizations and families.

> There are three key ingredients in the development of the cynical outlook. One is the formulation of unrealistically high expectations, of oneself and/or of other people, which generalize to expectations of society, institutions, authorities, and the future. A second is the experience of disappointment, in oneself and in others, and consequent feelings of frustration and defeat. Finally, there is disillusion, the sense of being let down, deceived, betrayed, or used by others. Turning their disillusion inward, cynics fear they might be seen as naive or be taken for suckers. (Kanter and Mirvis 1989, 3)

Certainly no one word about communicative life can typify the contemporary historical moment. Routine cynicism, however, dominates much contemporary communication. Acknowledging some cynical reaction is warranted. However, the commonplace communicative practice of an unreflective cynical attitude/world view needs attention and response.

The *New Webster Encyclopedic Dictionary of the English Language* defined cynicism as "contempt for whatever is or might be proposed; it is a constant act of fault finding, a general rejection of the pleasures of life" (Thatcher 1965/1969, 213). Thoughtful "fault finding" as a reasoned act is healthy. However, when cynicism becomes routine—an automatic response before one studies a situation—a philosophical loss of trust in existence and in the possibility of goodness is made manifest.

The banality of cynicism is marked by a person's rejection, disbelief, or inability to distinguish the important, the vital, and in some cases the sacred from the profane and the trivial. A brief glance at television offerings reveals sitcoms that contain characters who are rude and insensitive to family or others, inviting an unthinking cynical response to important interpersonal relationships. Popular talk show formats quickly and openly discuss issues that require careful private deliberation, inviting the audience to become communication voyeurs of an individual's personal trauma—again inviting a cynical response to another's problems. Essentially, we must ask who receives a stranger look—a person offering a quick cynical response to a given action or idea, or a person interpreting an action or idea within a positive context? If cynicism is part of our everyday life then we need to acknowledge its power while seeking to move it to the occasional response rather than its being a routine basis for our communicative life together.

In *Democracy on Trial* (1933/1995), Jean Bethke Elshtain calls for a new covenant in which unreflective cynicism is replaced with a willingness to work together to solve problems, in spite of difficulties:

> Is there any way to break the spiral of mistrust and cynicism? Yes, but it will be difficult. Some, and I include myself in this number, embrace the ideas of a new social covenant. But unless Americans, or the citizens of any faltering democracy, can once again be shown that they are all in it together; unless democratic citizens remember that being a citizen is a *civic* identity, not primarily a private sinecure; unless government can find a way to respond to people's deepest concerns, a new democratic social covenant has precious little chance of taking hold. (30–31)

We must work together to create a democratic community by encouraging independent voices to work together as interdependent voices united in an effort to continually live out a commitment to the common good in a given historical moment. International and now national terrorism point to the practical need for a dialogic concern about one's communicative partner and the quality of communicative life together. Knowledge of diversity of persons, philosophies, races, religions, and ideas may evoke unreflective cynical calls for *our* or *my* power over *them*, or such knowledge can evoke respectful impulses toward difference. Meeting diversity calls us to choose between the narcissism of "my kind" or the tougher task of learning to work with one another in the task of co-constituting a "global community."

We recognize that routine cynicism is propelled by those who do *not* listen to the historical moment. Viewing a situation "out of context" by interpreting meaning through an inappropriate historical framework fuels the flames of routine cynicism by setting unattainable expectations in motion. We open the door to the myth of Don Quixote (Cervantes Saavedra 1909) by demanding of life something other than what is currently before us, desiring what is not historically possible.

Failure to listen to the historical moment can be seen in the interpersonal results of unrealistic optimism. To avoid such a utopian path, we address some of the serious problems that continue to make cynicism an option without suggesting the total rejection of all cynicism. Robert Bellah, Richard Madsen, William M. Swidler, Ann Sullivan, and Steven M. Tipton (1991), Stanley Hauerwas (1981), and Alasdair MacIntyre (1981/1984) suggest we live in a time of interpersonal rootlessness which contributes to a routine cynical mindset that frames many communicative styles around "me" and an unrealistic sense of hope that can too quickly degenerate to cynicism.

Too often interpersonal literature has been led astray by undue optimism. Yet we are simultaneously unwilling to give up hope on the interpersonal voices that need to work together in diversity and difference in the twenty-first century. Herman Cohen, in *The History of Speech Communication: The Emergence of a Discipline, 1914–1945,* sets the tone of this lament as he connects us to yet another moment of idealism in the discipline—pre–World War II attention to ethics, democracy, and social responsibility.

> As we look back at the writing on ethics and democracy, we are struck by how different they were from the material to be found in present day journals. One is struck by the high moral tone of the profession and the importance that was attached to the responsibility of insuring that the teaching of speech measured up to scrupulous standards. Perhaps those years were a more naive and less "scholarly" time. Nevertheless, one must admit to warm nostalgic feelings for the idealism of early writers. Some of us may even regret that not even in the pages of *Communication Education* are such issues raised today. (1994, 15)

The interpersonal writers we revisit set a similar moral tone of hope. Our task is to invite a dialogue between their voices and the best of contemporary scholarship, sensitive to the dangers of routine cynicism, but still hopeful of pointing to a story of dialogic civility in communication between persons.

Interpersonal Suspicion

Maurice Friedman suggested a need for "existential trust" (1972/1974, 318–331), while Martin Buber said that too much "existential mistrust" (1967c, 309) has dominated the latter part of the twentieth century. With a loss of trust, we lose the ability to distinguish genuine problems from manufactured problems, the genuine friend from a disingenuous salesperson, and genuine hope from a lost cause. "Existential mistrust" moves us to distrust all aspects of everyday life rather than engaging in the occasional and situational use of mistrust.

> The existential mistrust is indeed basically no longer, like the old kind, a mistrust of my fellow-man [or fellow-woman]. It is rather the destruction of confidence in existence in general. That we can no longer carry on a genuine dialogue from one camp to the other is the severest symptom of the sickness of present-day man [or woman]. Existential mistrust is this sickness itself. But the destruction of trust in human existence is the inner poisoning of the total human organism from which this sickness stems. (Buber 1967c, 309)

One of the authors explained existential mistrust as an "atmosphere of suspicion and judgment" (Arnett 1986/1997a, 49), which emerges from continually looking for hidden meanings in what others say and do. In the practice of everyday living, stress is generated by constantly questioning the other. This often results in diminishing genuine stress—paving the way for what Christopher Lasch called the "trivialization of crisis" (1984, 62).

The end result of unnecessary interpersonal surveillance is personal exhaustion, as we unwisely turn a series of unfortunate but not earth shattering events into misperceived experiences or manufactured crises. Unnecessary moments of manufactured crisis legitimate unthinking cynicism, as does the act of consistent mistrust. In such an environment, we no longer meet life on its own terms. We either manufacture a response that is beyond what is called for or we ignore what others say as we offer our attributed "real" answer of depth and insight. Manufactured crisis and mistrust that are moved to ontological and normative status lead to what Jean Paul Sartre called "bad faith" (1953, 86–116), in which we lie to ourselves—not knowing how much we are making up and fail to meet life on its terms. Persons are able to convince themselves about the reality of something that, in actuality, never happened. Lying to ourselves fuels an environment prone to unnecessary interpersonal struggles, each person fighting imaginary actions and cynically rejecting the other's perspective while unknowingly fabricating one's own position.

As unhealthy as the above material sounds, many of us can easily recognize a cycle of unthinking cynicism. Take, for instance, parents of students on a high school team caught up in a self-serving bias. They begin to make negative statements every time the coach speaks and are unable to recognize their own faults or those of their children. They make comments such as, "The administration doesn't care. They don't listen. No one's concerned." Yet when contrary facts are brought to the parents' attention, they are dismissed with statements like, "Don't lie to us. We know what's really going on here." Civil argument and discussion cannot occur when public facts are dismissed whenever they do not support one's own private argument. Richard Sennett explained, "The questioning of the motives of others similarly works to devalue their actions, because what matters is, not what they do, but fantasies one has of what they are feeling when they do it. Reality is thus rendered 'illegitimate,' and as a result, in perceiving others in terms of fantasied motives, one's actual relations with them become apathetic or colorless" (1974/1992, 325–326). Sennett reminds us that public discourse requires information to be available and discernable to all.

Unthinking cynicism is a form of blindness that leads us to fail to recognize the actions of a real friend, a genuine crisis, or ideas that demand our attention and response. Life is too often lived with the conviction that something or someone has already gone wrong or surely will go awry. Of course, cynicism must be used in some environments—where human speech points to a world in which the rhetoric is consistently at odds with the action. However, we must not permit cynicism to overtake those times, places, and people who *do* speak with a conviction that actions support. The difference we need to discern is when to be cynical, not just to what degree.

Language Disconnected From Action

Cynicism is not only an attitude; it is the logical result of the use of language no longer substantiated in action. Cynicism as a communication technique is the invitation to destroy human connection— we cease to trust what has been said without evaluating or testing the statement for its public truth value.

Hans Gadamer (1980), in *Dialogue and Dialectic: Eight Hermeneutical Studies on Plato*, discussed the problem of word and deed. He recognized the need for "the Doric harmony of *logos* [word] and *ergon* [deed]" (1). Socrates' discussion of what makes a complete friendship points out the inadequacy of friendship disconnected from word and deed; Socrates discussed two young boys' understanding of friendship to illustrate this point. The boys' understanding is based upon action alone, without the accompanying word or understanding of what actually constitutes friendship. There is a need for both the action of friendship and knowledge of it, if one's behavior is to be appropriate and assist in the growth of the friendship.

Granted, Socrates was correct in pointing out that it is problematic to be guided by a view of friendship based upon action without the accompanying words to support such a commitment. However, such a view of friendship is less likely to generate cynicism than the word of friendship without accompanying action. When the word is present and action rings hollow, we open the door to routine cynicism and to a distrust of language. This unfortunate disconnection of word from appropriate action fuels the legitimate use of a deconstructive hermeneutic, which like cynicism has a place in a quality communicative life, unless it becomes normative or another blind technique. In a time of disparity of word and deed, people are called to witness for the word; the word must be pulled from humiliation. Jacques Ellul, in *The Humiliation of the Word*, suggests a careful rejoining of word and action is needed: "The witness must commit himself [or herself] entirely to what he [or she] says, recovering the unity of the possible form of the word—the clearest and sharpest. He [or she] must dispel misunderstandings and steadfastly repeat, emphasize, and reproduce in all possible ways the truth revealed to him [or her]" (1985, 108). Ellul recommends that people should say no more than can be delivered and perhaps even a little less. We live in a time in which the harmony of word and deed needs to be rebalanced.

Of course, we dare not ignore the reality that has given rise to cynical responses between persons. For instance, an executive refers to employees as a "community" or "family." Days later numerous workers are dismissed in a decision to "right size" the organization, just as high quarterly earning reports are released. Language is used as an "aesthetic" vehicle to placate workers in the practical reality of lost employment. Indeed, disparity between language ("family") and action (release from employment) invites legitimate cynicism. Words lose their power each time the Doric harmony of word and deed is rejected by someone working on impression management without action to substantiate the personal advertisement.

Our era of fragmented and defrocked narratives in which many people feel existentially displaced and unable to agree on what constitutes guiding public virtues turns the soil and makes ready for planting routine cynicism. In essence, unreflective cynicism is an inevitable result of living in an era *After Virtue* (MacIntyre 1981/1984), without common narratives that can guide us. People find it easy to become cynical when the words stated no longer motivate people to action consistent with the narrative call. The narrative begins to look like a television commercial with actors mouthing compensated endorsements that do not really reflect the private positions of speakers/actors. In such an era, individuals who want change will be disappointed with the slowness of the pace—while those longing for a romantic view of yesteryear will be disappointed with any new actions or ideas. Ironically, both the person who calls for change and the person who resists change end up in a similar cynical destination. One says, "This company moves too slow. We have to keep up with change!"—while the other cries against change, "These decisions are simply crazy; these new ideas and practices won't work." Each style invites cynicism against another.

Christopher Lasch recognized that neither the political right nor the political left have initiated a sense of moral order and collective purpose. Many lives seem to lack "everyday virtues of honesty, loyalty, manners, work, and restraint" (1978/1979, 22). From this lack of moral victory—from either the left or the right—has emerged, not compromise, but instead a routine cynical appraisal of our modern social condition.

Unthinking cynicism about life and interpersonal communication is not only ultimately self-defeating, it is an ineffectual defense against the harsh realities we face in the twenty-first century. Such cynicism is the garb of watchers and critics—those unwilling to get their hands dirty in the ongoing and difficult process of seeking answers to complex communicative problems in everyday human interaction and decision making. The watchers of the "slowness" of change and the watchers of the "problems" of change have become all too common—each polarized by his or her smug position. Personal lament and constant criticism do not substitute for thinking, building, gardening, nurturing, and being of service in a troubled era.

Listening to Two Sides of Cynicism

The cynic may be nourished by two extremely different actions—maniacal optimism that leads to despair and overt hopelessness that leads to pessimism. These seemingly opposing actions are two sides of the same coin. In both cases, the reality of the historic moment is less important than the cynic's preconceived assumptions.

For the cynic, unpredictable experiences in life may be met with a psychological attitude of unwarranted good cheer or the contrary companion, despair. When we force ourselves to be extremely optimistic, we falsify reality. Once exhaustion from maintaining a false front sets in, inevitable disappointment leads us to miss genuine possibilities. Unfulfilled false optimism can unearth extreme depression, fertile soil for unreflective cynicism. Continual pessimism, likewise, nourishes the response of unthinking cynicism. The cynic ignores the experiences of life, content to live within the stability of receiving either all good news (which holds for the potential cynic the ground of unmet high expectations) or receiving no good news at all (a "mature" cynic).

Routine Cynicism as Debilitating

As stated above, cynicism becomes problematic when fault finding ceases to be a situationally appropriate act and becomes the common approach for addressing others. A friend of one of the authors accepted a director's job with a social agency. The association was in significant trouble, financially and organizationally, and seemed to be without a clear sense of mission or direction. She knew she had been given an important opportunity to assist others. However, members of the board that hired her were unwilling to make any of the changes she suggested. Board members seemed more willing to fail and let the agency collapse than to try new options and ideas. Each idea offered was considered inadequate. Members had become so cynical they could no longer weigh the positive and negative aspects of new proposals. "That won't work" was their consistent response.

The director wanted to offer a guiding voice to the agency that was in need of a new vision. At her most desperate moment, she called a friend to seek advice. "How do I defeat cynicism in this organization?" The answer was straightforward and simple. "Cynicism is defeated one person at a time, one project at a time. Promise only what you can deliver. Remember cynicism never appears in a vacuum; it has a reason, a history. Confidence and trust replace cynicism only when you consistently deliver on your promises." Many sporting contests are won or lost by a matter of mere inches. Perhaps meeting, addressing, and defeating cynicism can happen only when a similar philosophy is followed.

In variation on the old adage, "Hear no evil, see no evil, speak no evil," a routinely cynical approach to interpersonal communication might embody, "Hear no good, see no good, speak no good." Such an extreme position limits life to a single negative picture.

The impulse for wanting optimism and good to guide a life is noble, worthy, and often misused. Such an impulse defines the cliche, "The road to hell is paved with good intentions." This act of unrealistic optimism simply ignores what these two authors accept as ontological—good and evil walk hand in hand. Although we may not desire to deal with both good and evil, it is our fate if we are to avoid escaping into the realm of arrogant assurance that life is composed of either all good or all evil. The unthinking cynical communicator misses rich variations of good and evil, unable to sensitively work with the ambiguity of gradations between extremes.

This ontological linking of good and evil within a life has been described by many writers. Our task is to find guidance and insight in the midst of the diversity of experiences life sets before us and to forgo the temptation of a closed perspective, whether draped in the totality of optimism or pessimism. One of the most powerful portrayals of this dialectic reality of the human was penned by Victor Hugo in *Les Miserables* (1862/1961). James Robinson's introduction to *Les Miserables* captures this duality within which each of us must walk if we are to meet life in the reality of a given historical moment, rather than in the hopes and imaginations of illusion.

> Not until he is on his deathbed does Jean Valjean feel the unrestrained love of Cosette and Marius and release from his painful past.
> This . . . drama . . . is . . . about a man who triumphs over evil in himself and in others. . . . It is a great humanitarian novel which shows how a man can be redeemed by accepting suffering, by doing the duty his conscience directs him to, by sacrificing himself lovingly. (8)

Our contention is that a narrative background for interpersonal communication needs to take the notions of good and evil, hope and despair, optimism and cynicism equally to heart. We live in a human drama that requires us to recognize that life offers an invitation to dance—guided by dialectic, oxymoron, and contradiction. Dialogic civility is situated in such a contradictory but nevertheless realistic spirit.

The cynical limits to dialogue are led by a "doubting model" (Belenky et al. 1986, 228). Mary Belenky, Blythe Clinchy, Nancy Goldberger, and Jill Tarule contend a doubting model of education is problematic because it encourages doubt to become normative. If one works in a dialectical fashion, we can see that cynicism and doubting are helpful in our culture. However, if our cultural norm is cynicism and doubt, then we need to explore alternative communication styles in the educational system, just to offer options and choices sensitive to the communicative needs of the moment.

Mary Belenky, Blythe Clinchy, Nancy Goldberger, and Jill Tarule call for a connected model of education. The more the teacher is connected and concerned about the whole person, the more the teacher needs to be in the classroom with students. When a person teaches in such a way that he or she processes information with students, then ideas are comprehended rather than processed in a rote manner by students acting like computers. Not only does the realm of constant doubt limit education, it limits the connections needed for human dialogue to be present in any setting.

Cynicism as Survival Tool

There is a reason for the beginning of cynicism; it does not emerge out of a vacuum. This habit, which we call "rhetorical overreach," is a prime source of routine cynicism in contemporary life. Unduly high expectations diminish people's hopes and dreams for accomplishment. In *The Cynical Americans* (1989), Donald Kanter and Philip Mirvis outlined how cynicism has invaded the workplace: organizational leaders advertise more than they can furnish their employees and the public.

As a defense against this abuse of language and limited honest exchange, cynicism offers a response to a world of deceit. Revelations about J. Edgar Hoover reiterated the need to be ever vigilant about leaders in powerful positions capable of directing the future fortunes of so many people. The McCarthy era, Vietnam, Watergate, Iran-Contra, and the savings and loan scandals gave validity to the justification for cynicism. Jeffrey Goldfarb explained:

> Ordinary people rightly understand that things are not what they appear to be. If we are not part of the successful propertied few, free enterprise does not set us free but confines us to salaried labor. We know that leaders, from the realms of politics to religion, deceive. What they say is not what they do. The promise of education leads not to social mobility for most of us but to social stasis. Ideological critiques and sociologies of knowledge do, then, uncover important correlations: prevailing ideas do generally support the status quo; challenging ideas are often linked to dominated social groups and marginal social movements and institutions. Cynicism, therefore, can be understood as a kind of modern realism, especially given the realistic social conditions of a massified social structure. (1991, 152)

A history of deception has created a cynical social structure.

In spite of a clear rationale for cynicism, we need to walk between the extremes of ignoring the reality and power of cynicism in everyday life and languishing in its daily prevalence, attempting to avoid entrapment in routine cynicism by embracing contrasting sides of the human spirit. It is possible to embrace hope about what human beings can accomplish together and simultaneously not be blind to the significant evil humans have done and are capable of doing. Such blindness invites unthinking cynicism that becomes a dangerous unreflective technique for meeting the other.

The Wedding of Cynicism and Hope

As odd as the synergy of cynicism and hope may sound, it is an extension of commonsense wisdom that sees dangers in extremes, calling us to be as "innocent as a dove and as wise as a serpent," uniting *Power and Innocence* (May, 1972/1976). Viktor Frankl (1959/1974), well known for his work in logotherapy, outlined this orientation very well. The objective of logotherapy is to describe the process of meaning perception by way of phenomenological analysis, to discover how normal people arrive at meaning and consequently at a sense of fulfillment.

Pain and Joy

Viktor Frankl was a survivor of the German concentration camps of World War II. He wanted us to remember that humans were able to live with dignity under horrendous conditions constructed by fellow human beings—for human beings were the architects and implementors of the gas chambers. For Frankl and for us, any dialogic voice in interpersonal communication needs to take into account human suffering, pain, and evil as much as we take into account human joy. Frankl embraced the construct of a realistic background narrative aware of the potential of both human good and evil.

Viktor Frankl (1978) pointed to this realistic vision in the following:

> I have again and again been accused of over-estimating man [or woman], putting him [or her] on too high a pedestal. Let me here repeat an illustration that has often shown to be didactically helpful. In aviation there is a business called "crabbing." Say there is a crosswind from the north and the airport where I wish to land lies due east. If I fly east I will miss my destination because my plane will have drifted to the southeast. In order to reach my destination I must compensate for this drift by crabbing, in this case by heading my plane in a direction to the north of where I want to land. It is similar with man [or woman]: he [or she] too ends at a point lower than he [or she] might have unless he [or she] is seen on a higher level that includes his [or her] higher aspirations.
>
> If we are to bring out the human potential at its best, we must first believe in its existence and presence. Otherwise man [or woman] will "drift," he [or she] will deteriorate, for there is a human potential at its worst as well. We must not let our belief in the potential humanness of man [or woman] blind us to the fact that *humane* humans are and probably always will be a minority. Yet it is this very fact that challenges each of us to join the minority; things are bad, but unless we do our best to improve them, everything will become worse. (29–30)

A background narrative that recognizes the value of situationally appropriate cynicism offers a unity of contradictions—a view of what humans might become and a recognition that we often fall short of humane responses to one another. We must not let the narrative about the human become too positive nor can we let our mistakes result in giving up on what the human can become.

A dialogic voice in interpersonal communication, within the spirit of Viktor Frankl, does not conceptualize cynicism and hope as oppositional, but rather as self-correcting of one another. Each voice—cynicism and hope—is in its own way concerned with protecting the human being. An enduring dialogic communication style makes a place for appropriate cynicism and simultaneously works to provide a foundation in which cynicism as a survival tool is needed less, but not dismissed as an option.

Elie Wiesel, winner of the 1986 Nobel Prize for Literature and a witness to and writer on the Holocaust, laid the foundation for our approach when he described the importance of embracing the contraries of despair and joy. His words demonstrate the gravity of bringing together both cynical and hopeful voices:

> There is no lack of despair among Hasidic teachers. They know that it exists. You would have to be thick-headed or insensitive not to know it. The important question is: what do we do about despair? We cannot turn our backs on it, so we must confront it and go forward. But the great genius of the Hasidim was that they found a joy within despair. Indeed, this is the purest joy of all, and the most noble . . . in spite of and within despair, for this joy does not deny despair. It is too powerful to be denied. But despite despair, within despair itself, there is a sort of space in which joy is both possible and necessary. Possible because necessary! This is Hasidic joy. (Wiesel and de Saint-Cheron 1990, 87)

Wiesel reminds us to embrace the Hasidim's acceptance of contraries out of a pragmatic evaluation that this is how life is actually lived. An alternative to routine cynicism in interpersonal communication is needed, but this alternative must not be false optimism. A genuine alternative needs to acknowledge the roots of cynicism; routine cynicism stems from overt deception and rhetoric that exceeds what realistically can be accomplished.

Hope Within Limits

A wedding of hope and cynicism within a dialogic perspective is guided by a metaphor, not of unlimited potential, but of hope within limits. Such a metaphor is grounded within a sense of humility about the limits one must accept in the role of being human, no matter how badly one desires to be an omnipotent god figure. This oxymoronic tension of cynicism and hope framing a dialogic spirit places dueling forces in juxtaposition, carving a foundation for interpersonal dialogue based on the solid footing of tenacious human realism. The beginning of a realistic narrative revolves around the ontological nature of death and our awareness of its inevitability. We are creatures in search of richer and expanded experiences who can not escape our limits.

The wedding of cynicism and hope that constructs a dialogic vision is a reminder that interpersonal communication rooted in dialogue can not escape the commonsense questions of a given historical era. These commonsense questions articulate the limits that frame our attention. We cannot fly to some ideal location and wish for a better world. We must take the world on its own terms, with endurance, tenacity, and hope, aware of the ever potential face of tragedy. We must walk into the heart of everyday life surrounded not only by awareness of limits, but by the conviction that the "good life" is found not in the optimism of abundance, but within the limits of a given historical moment. As Christopher Lasch suggested, "we need to recover a more vigorous form of hope . . . without denying . . . [life's] tragic character" (1991, 530).

To maintain the tension between a hopeful human spirit and cynicism, we rely on what Christopher Lasch called the "forbidden topic" of modern scholarship, limits (1991, 22). The word *limits* reminds us of our humanness. We are flesh and blood creatures who must live within limits that provide the shoreline which boundaries our lives. We must meet limits and recognize the historical moment in dialogue. Such realism moves routine cynicism from our repertoire of daily communicative responses, permitting cynicism to emerge when genuinely appropriate.

Limits are difficult to accept without feeling that somehow we have capitulated to a version of life that is less than possible. However, accepting the reality of limits does not lessen the conviction that making the world a better place is an important human project. The acknowledgment of limits simply brings historical realism into dialectical interplay with hope. Limits is a key metaphor for a view of interpersonal communication propelled by historicality, not a priori judgments and pronouncements.

We acknowledge that in many settings cynics control enough of the organizational culture that constructive action is not even attempted by persons who want change. Cynics accumulate power by articulating the obvious: we cannot accomplish all that is necessary or seemingly needed at a given time in history. Contrary to some television commercials today that encourage us to acquire all life has to offer, the cynic reminds us of limits. The cynic reminds us of limits as we struggle with how to use our precious time wisely, aware that life has an end. The cynic plays an important role, keeping undue optimism in check.

In an era in which limits are ignored, we should not be surprised that the focus is on prolonging life, staying "young." To understand limits calls for an examination of how one's limited life is to be used, not how it is to be taken for granted or unrealistically extended forever.

Elie Wiesel and Philippe de Saint-Charon's discussion concerning the reality of evil that propelled the Holocaust reminds us of the danger that accompanies one's denial of limits and an unwillingness to look truth squarely in the eye: "When an individual represses certain things, they reassert themselves later with extreme violence. If humanity today tried to banish all this suffering, all this agony, all this death and all the dead, it would all come back someday, rising up against the entire world with destructive violence" (1990, 132). When we ignore the reality of limits—whatever our capacity for good, our dedication to one another, or our ability to care—we open the door to backlash in which such actions raise their ugly heads.

Limits are best understood as "horizons of significance" (Taylor 1991, 38–39). Horizons, philosophically, are what could be called fuzzy limits. We do not have a code or rule that tells us how and when to stay within a "horizon of significance." Nevertheless, we need to remain within the limits of a given horizon or its significance ceases.

Without joining the camp of routine cynicism, we affirm their important insight; yet we offer conviction about what humans can accomplish. We can expand our minds. We can discover new things. We begin with the limits of being born in a particular historical moment, and we end not knowing all the answers. But, if we are wise and admit our questions about what the "good life" might be in our own historical time, we may find answers that neither the cynic nor the unrealistic optimist will discern.

We can choose to overcome "existential mistrust" (Buber 1967c, 309) by tempering cynicism with a realistic sense of interpersonal hope, which will determine the character of any dialogic perspective. Without an awareness of limits, the horizon of significance for dialogic civility is eclipsed by our demands for life to fit our pre-scriptions. Only as we embrace cynicism and simultaneously point to a realistic sense of hope does a historical narrative offer an enduring background for interpersonal communication in the twenty-first century—leading us to hear a voice of both caution and possibility; cynicism and hope in this historical moment. The story of dialogic civility begins with limits, historicality, humility, and the dialectic of cynicism and hope. Dialogic civility begins in the dialec-tic of daily life, of hope and willingness to meet life in the historical moment of the demands that confront us.

Chapter Three

Historicality and Presence

Historical Consciousness —

The "Thou" is what we generally call historical consciousness. Historical consciousness knows about the otherness of the other, about the past in its otherness, just as well as the understanding of the "Thou" knows the "Thou" as a person. It seeks in the otherness of the past not the instantiation of a general law, but something historically unique.

—Hans Gadamer, *Truth and Method*

Historical Situatedness —

The claim that hermeneutics fosters practical reason or an increased capacity to discriminate may appear fantastic in light of existing social problems and global threats. We have seen that Gadamer himself points to the increase in social irrationality which accompanies the hegemony of technical reason over practical deliberation. But he also points to specific historical advances such as the recognition, if not realization, of the freedom of all and asks whether it is "so perverse to think that in reality the irrational cannot hold out in the long run." The ideas of dialogue, experience and *Bildung* are meant to show that it cannot and that we can progress in tact, taste and judgment in such a way as to move towards its eradication. Of course, our capacity for discrimination may itself be systematically undermined by ideological connections of which we are unaware and Gadamer's faith in practical reason may therefore be problematic. Still, if others have used the insight into historicity to jettison the idea of reason itself, Gadamer does not. Our historical

situatedness does not only limit what we can know with certainty; it can also teach us how to remember and integrate what
we must not forget.

—Georgia Warnke, *Hermeneutics, Tradition, and Reason*

A dialogic civility perspective on interpersonal discourse is
grounded in historicality, not therapeutic discourse. "Historicality," as understood by Gadamer (1960/1986), offers an
alternative to the therapeutic model (Rieff 1966/1987) of interpersonal communication. For persons to pursue a common cause, we
must understand our common problematic—we must live in this
historical moment, not in an imaginary ideal. Without a willingness
to meet the demands of the historical moment, we lose a pragmatic
common center where a diversity of persons can gather together to
pursue a communicative project. Interpersonal communication that
seeks to confirm the other in diversity and difference works to
understand and address the historicality of the communicators and
the conversational context. Interpersonal communication that
misses the commonsense direction of a given historical moment
may be more appropriate to the speaker than to the listener or the
communicative moment, resulting in a "confirmation of narcissism."

A Foundation for Communicative Change

This work is indebted to Hans Gadamer's (1960/1986) understanding of historicality and philosophical hermeneutics. For Gadamer,
interpretation lives between interpreter and a particular text—in
this case, a communicative event. The process of interpretation is
deeply dependent upon the historical horizons of the text and the
individual's interpretation of that historical situation.

Hans Gadamer, with philosophical sophistication, outlined
what early communication process writers understood—communication is an active, continually changing process. Although the
notion of communication as process now seems pedestrian, this perspective offers a significant theoretical contribution to the study of
human interaction—communication is not static. David Berlo's
(1960) insight, forty years old, freed us from an understanding of

communication as unchanging between persons. He conceptualized communication as an active process, flowing among persons, context, and topic.

Another early process scholar, Dean Barnlund (1970), identified six aspects of the communication process. First, communication is a dynamic process, rather than a static entity. Second, communication is an ecology that ebbs and flows with our ever changing environment. Third, communication is circular, a series of interdependent actions between speaker and receiver, not a linear exchange. Fourth, communication is unrepeatable, what happens is spontaneous to the moment and cannot be duplicated. Fifth, communication is irreversible, we cannot alter what transpires between communicative partners or how it is interpreted. Communication is a process of equilibrium and disequilibrium, never returning to its original state. Finally, communication is complex, comprised of cross-linking sociocultural and psychological influences—illuminating interaction with both manifest and latent meaning. In consideration of this manifold complexity, the process of communication is problematic due to its ever changing nature, requiring "appropriate" communication to be historically grounded.

Historicality

We revisit early communication process scholarship to remind ourselves not to reify communication in the abstract. Communication is a process guided by persons, text, and the historical moment. The communication process does not take place in isolation. Multiple variables influence how, why, where, and with whom we communicate. Persons, topic, environment, culture (social and psychological), communication medium, and a narrative background influence the communicative result. Because communication is an ever changing process, we cannot divorce our communicative understanding from the historical moment of interpretation. The authors accept the assumption that any interpersonal communication theory explicitly and/or implicitly addresses deeper structural questions about the particular historical moment present in its formation.

This interpretive effort brings to the foreground the important link between interpersonal approaches to communication and commonsense questions guiding the historical moment in which a communication theory originates. Our point is twofold. First, approaches to interpersonal communication that seek to assist human beings— to give voice to the person—must be tied to genuine human problems and questions that are present in a common sense analysis of a given period of time. Second, applying concepts from a historical era other than our own requires concepts from a given theory to meet the needs (answer commonsense questions) of the present historical moment or we invite an interpretation of communication that is static and dangerously anachronistic. Interpersonal dialogue is sensitive to the other's historical needs and addresses common sense questions of that historical moment, not just the situation in which we wished the other lived.

Dialogue is not meant for the ethereal, but for those willing to walk with others through the mud of everyday life. In the preface to Martin Buber's (1966) *The Way of Response*, Nahum Glatzer did not confine dialogue to mystics, but recognized that all human beings who are committed to everyday activities have the opportunity to enter the world of dialogue. Dialogue is invited as we address limits, flaws, and difficulties presented by the nitty-gritty reality of common life together in a situated historical moment. Dialogue begins when we act out of our situatedness, not when we respond from a position of unrealistic hope.

Missing the Historical Moment

One of the authors' first praxis encounters with historicality and interpersonal communication pedagogy came early in his career. Like many praxis discoveries, this insight came not with clarity but with a nagging sense of something being wrong—anachronistic, out of place and time. Ultimately, as the following story suggests, the author realized the historical context from which another instructor approached a course did not match the students' historical context.

Bill taught interpersonal communication and had been considered an "outstanding" teacher, using experiential learning strategies at a time in which common sense questions of that historical moment asked for insight that did not rely upon tradition-bound cognition. His approach was perfect in a time of a divisive war— Vietnam. Many people mistrusted the traditional rationality that authority figures used to override the images of death, suffering, and confusion that entered our living rooms on television each evening in the daily account of Vietnam. The students loved Bill's experiential interpersonal communication course at that time. As the Vietnam war ended, students became increasingly less enamored with the course. At first, the author assumed Bill was becoming stale, not staying up with literature. But he remained incredibly energetic and well read. Puzzlement followed. All the concepts taught in his class were well taught. Nothing conceptually inaccurate was offered to the students when his course content was examined from the therapeutic model of communication. Yet student reaction suggested that his interpersonal course was becoming increasingly anachronistic.

Slowly it dawned upon the author that Bill was attempting to teach interpersonal communication as if it were ahistorical, unaffected by prevailing questions of a new historical moment. The instructor was failing to teach to the historical movement of the students before him; instead, he unknowingly was focused on his own time and place of formation. He was not missing accuracy of concepts, but was ignoring the significance of concepts applied to a different historical moment composed of unique questions and needs.

The colleague, Bill, no longer addressed the historical moment of the students. He unknowingly taught to his own formation. Continuing to teach from one's own historical moment is easy to do. Yet in so doing we find ourselves asking, "Why don't they understand?" The answer lies in our teaching to our students' historical formation.

We use this story to make a point. The historical moment of our formation makes a difference in what we see and how we teach interpersonal communication. Our interpretive processes are shaped by the questions that guide us. In confirming the other, however, we need to attend to the historical moment of the other's formation, as well as our own. Consider commonsense questions appropriate for guiding a student today. Addressing their concern about a career, the business-like environment of the university in which students may feel more like numbers than individuals, and failed governmental economic and social policies might bring concepts alive within their historical moment. Our own concept formation came from a historical moment in which service to the community was a significant question. If teachers like us are not careful, we simply see greed and ambition in young students—and students see us as old people from the '70s with tenure and no need to worry about the demands of employment at a time when they are approaching a highly competitive job market. Teachers must engage in dialogue with students about their concerns. The praxis of interpersonal communication must be connected with the realities of everyday life. Interpersonal praxis is not ahistorical, but deeply tied to the historical situatedness of daily life.

Consider another example. In 1865, a man rode his horse into town and asked, "Where is the livery stable? I need to take care of my horse." No one thought his question was even slightly unusual. The existential demand of 1865 at that given moment made his question not only sensible, but necessary. The owner of the livery stable made a good living—until a contraption called the "horseless carriage" threatened his livelihood.

The family that owned the livery stable loved horses and valued the quality of life the income from the stable provided. Members of the family were divided on the need to adapt to a "horseless carriage" era. One member of the family orchestrated a campaign against the "horseless carriage." Another member of the family, however, eventually invested in a business selling horseless carriages called FORD; additionally, he developed a riding stable where people could keep their horses and ride for recreation. The disgruntled family member who campaigned against the "horseless carriage" was not only unsuccessful in his attempt to stop the use of automobiles, but lost his part of the family wealth and stable. The other family member found wealth in the FORD investment and continuing meaning as he started a recreational riding stable. Focusing only on how a previous historical situation shaped one's experience results in unnecessary unhappiness if one expects today to be the same as yesterday. Living in dialogue with a given era requires listening to the demands of the *current* historical moment. Ignoring the demands of the historical moment can invite cynicism as disappointment from misapplied actions is encountered.

Meeting the Historical Moment

Ideas, actions, and communication styles need to meet the needs of the historical moment. A given communication theory cannot be appropriately used as the singular means of communication when it is actually only one particular approach that may be used in a particular social situation. Appropriate use of communication as well as business investments need to be historically grounded in what is "appropriate" for a given era.

Existential demand requires us to ask, "What is appropriate for this historical moment?" We need to listen to the existential demand of a given historical moment in order to interpret situations within the present historical framework rather than one created by an earlier generation or by unrealistic optimism. We must reject the impulse to ask what was required of communicators twenty years ago or only what we want from life and focus on the realities of today. Granted, we may not always be in agreement with the content of the existential demand of our contemporary moment. But if we fail to listen and respond to that demand we sacrifice opportunities to shape the maturation of that same historical situation.

For instance, one of the authors is known for his work in dialogue and peace. A university faculty member concerned about an increase in societal violence asked him to outline what a Peace Communication major might look like. The author stated, "I am too interested in Peace Communication to offer suggestions in the abstract. What are *the* most important concerns of your students?" The answer was jobs and employability. The author then responded, "If you listen to the historical moment in which your students live and address their genuine concerns for employability, it is likely that they will listen to your concerns for peace. Some of us discovered peace as an issue in a previous historical moment of plentiful jobs and career opportunities (1960s and early 1970s). If we want others to understand peace in the twenty-first century, we must listen and respond to this particular situation. Our task is to live in today while finding a way to bring concerns for peace into genuine dialogue with this historical moment." We need not sacrifice our own past formation, but if we are to avoid narcissistic teaching we must connect our teaching with the contemporary historical moment of today's students. A curriculum, like any dialogue, must begin with the questions that respond to this historical situation—not issues we wish were present, but those that address us in this point in time.

Christopher Lasch's *The Culture of Narcissism* (1978/1979) was written as a reminder of the narcissistic failure to listen to the historical moment. Much of our communication is guided by our personal needs. Lasch, a historian, understood that what we feel is as much a product of our individual histories as it is a product of the current situation. What is appropriate, needed, or required in a given historical moment may or may not coincide with previous historical experiences that shaped an individual's interpretation of contemporary events.

The major interpretive question that guides interpersonal praxis is: "How can a dialogic approach to interpersonal communication offer historically relevant insights for us today?" In other words, is there an alternative to routine cynicism that does not lead us down a path of naivete, leading us to mimic the action of an ostrich in trouble—hiding our heads beneath the surface, refusing to face the reality of our time?

Failure to listen to the historical moment can put previously successful people and organizations at risk. James Belasco uses the phrase *Teaching the Elephant to Dance* (1990) to explain the danger of failed listening:

> Over the past decade I've consulted with, studied, and managed a wide range of organizations. My experience tells me that organizations are like elephants—they both learn though conditioning.
>
> Trainers shackle young elephant with heavy chains to deeply embedded stakes. In that way the elephant learns to stay in its place. Older elephants never try to leave even though they have the strength to pull the stake and move beyond. Their conditioning limits their movement with only a small metal bracelet around their foot—attached to nothing.
>
> Like powerful elephants, many companies are bound by earlier conditioned constraints. "We've always done it this way" is as limiting to an organization's progress as the unattached chain around the elephant's foot.
>
> Success ties you to the past. The very factors that produced today's success often create tomorrow's failure. Consider Xerox, for example. Xerox had a close call with disaster—and it was mostly because of its own success. In the early and middle 1970's Xerox could do no wrong—at least that's what they thought. They hired the best people, had the best marketing activities, and "owned" the market. Even to this day executives say, "Make me a Xerox," when they want a copy. But all the "right" activities led the company to the brink of disaster. (2–3)

Any of us can be led to the brink of disaster if we do not listen to what is demanded in the situation and continue to offer a familiar response—rather than what is needed—in the given moment. We can no longer view a horse as solely a means of transportation when it is now confined to recreational riding. We can no longer view computers as only word processing units when they enable worldwide communication. We can no longer take our natural resources for granted as global pollution contaminates our soil, water, and air. Failure to listen to a given historical moment paves the way for disaster.

Success in one moment can give birth to later failure if adaptation to a new historical moment does not occur. For instance, consider the "great" lecturer, who, unwilling to address his current students with a more limited attention span, loses his or her "greatness." Or take the parent unable to change communication styles as his or her children mature into adults in their own right. By living in the past, the parent loses a vital relationship with a loved one. If we do not listen to the demands of the existential moment—and instead rely on our own past formation—we can become deeply disappointed when the world does not coincide with our expectations.

One major point must be clarified about listening to the historical moment. We are not saying that one must like or approve of a given historical moment. We are suggesting, however, that any historical moment must be taken seriously and responded to, rather than ignored. The surest way for opportunities within a given moment to lose ground is for those who do not like the present to act as if they live in another time. Change comes from meeting reality, not from acts of denial. In short, no particular historical moment can be accepted forever as unchangeable and paradigmatic for communication. We note, however, that change most often comes from seeing what is, understanding why the current conditions and practices have emerged and beginning the demanding task of change by addressing what conditions are in place.

The process of listening to the historical moment requires us to discern commonsense questions voiced by a given situation. For example, the great Depression asked people to find meaning without financial security. The years of World War II required the sacrifice of time, careers, and even lives. The 1960s shouted questions about authority as children called for stories of meaning from their parents, raised in the shadow of World War II. The 1990s call for respect of social and cultural diversity. In each of these historical moments, dialogue is only possible when the historic moment is addressed. No one common sense question is available in the hermeneutic space of a given time, but each question when responded to in its own historical moment recognizes its rhetorical power. Just as the initial question that guides interpretation in philosophical hermeneutics changes the meaning of text, so does a historical question, which seeks an alternative to unreflective cynicism in this historical moment of the twenty-first century.

Listening to the historical moment differentiates a dialogic view of narrative from an ideology. An ideology is closed and attempts—appropriately or not—to impose a perspective upon a given moment. A dialogic view of narrative takes one's previous narrative formation and brings it into dialogue with a given historical moment. In such a conversation, both the narrative and the contemporary moment are enriched and potentially changed. When a person relies upon an ideology, he or she attempts to make life conform to his or her a priori interpretation. Persons operating from a narrative perspective work with the assumption that openness in interpretations and action, not predetermined dictates, are historical keys. An ideology substitutes one reality for another; dialogic narratives permit traditions to be altered and additively modified. A narrative that fails to address the contemporary moment and does not permit creative participation is no longer a narrative, but a dead tradition. Dead narratives no longer successfully guide contemporary action; they seek to confine reality.

Dialogic Limits

Try as we might to escape into metaphors of expansion, progress, and abundance, practical reality somehow permits unforeseen limits to emerge. Often our human task seems propelled by the impulse to find ways to extend our limits. We seek to prolong our lives through exercise and proper nutrition, extend our buying power through credit, and improve our productivity through technology. As we evade one limit, we discover another that replaces the earlier limit. Young adults, for example, often want independence and to escape parental limits—only to discover the limits of work and paying bills without the assistance of family members who for so long "held them back." Lack of technology limits us from having access to information, but information overload or access to less rigorously evaluated material can be problematic and limiting as well in a technological era.

Ontologically, limits are simply part of being human, and the concept of historicality seriously addresses the implications of this realization. As Hans Gadamer stated, "The finite nature of one's own understanding is the manner in which reality, resistance, the absurd, and the unintelligible assert themselves. If one takes the finiteness seriously, then one must also take the reality of history seriously" (1960/1986, xxiii).

We discuss four ways in which the notion of limits undergirds dialogic civility. First, limits are the cornerstone of being human. Dialogue without awareness of limits misses one of the defining characteristics of what makes us interpersonal communicators—in dialogue we do not have unlimited potential; we are limited by the interaction of self, other, text, and sociocultural perspective. Second, we prefer to limit how we understand interpersonal communication; we choose to "bracket" or hold in abeyance the temptation of a psychological paradigm. Third, historicality is defined by a humble sense of our situated limitedness. Finally, we connect the importance of limits and historical common sense.

A Dialogic Perspective

We begin with a self-confessed limitation that interpersonal communication from a dialogic perspective is both an informational and relational exchange (Ayres 1984). John Stewart defined a relational approach to interpersonal communication in *Bridges Not Walls: A Book About Interpersonal Communication:*

> Interpersonal communication maximizes the humanness of the persons involved. . . . Persons are different objects . . . in four special ways, and it's impossible to communicate with them as persons unless you keep those differences in mind. 1. Each person is a unique, noninterchangeable part of the communicative situation. 2. A person is more than just an amalgamation of observable, measurable elements; he or she is always experiencing feelings or emotions. 3. Persons are "unreliable" because they are choosers who are free to act, not just react to the condition therein. 4. Persons are addressable; they can be talked *to* not just *about* and they can respond in kind with mutuality. (1986, 20)

Stewart (1973, 1977, 1982, 1986, 1990, 1994, 1995a) and Julia Wood (1995) point interpersonal scholars in a constructive relational direction. Stewart's various editions of *Bridges Not Walls: A Book About Interpersonal Communication* offer a metaphor of openness to the other, as does Wood's (1995) understanding of relational communication.

John Stewart and Carole Logan discuss characteristics of interpersonal communication in *Together: Communicating Interpersonally*:

> When you treat others as interchangeable parts, ignore their feelings, their choices, and their questions, and talk at them, and when they treat you similarly, the communication between you will be more impersonal than interpersonal. On the other hand, when you treat others and are treated by them as unique, unmeasurable, choosing, reflective, and addressable, your communication will be . . . more interpersonal. (1993, 25)

Stewart and Logan remind us of a basic interpersonal assumption: how we treat another significantly influences the quality of our interpersonal communication with him or her. Treating the other as a person, not as an object, and affirming the significance and worth of the other might be considered the "golden rule" in interpersonal communication. To this "golden rule," we would add the importance of responding not to an abstract communicative ideal, but to the concrete communicative possibilities in a given historical situation.

This dialogic view of interpersonal communication is revealed by Maurice Friedman's book *The Confirmation of Otherness* (1983). This approach is guided by openness and is complemented by the notion of confirmation of otherness. Friedman, a leading interpreter of the work of Martin Buber, stated that confirmation cannot be manufactured or relied upon as a technique. Confirmation must fit the historical moment of the other or it does not ring authentic and can backfire.

> All the phoney attempts at confirmation that pervade so much of the healing and helping professions and the human potential movement, not to mention the "faith healers" and the downright quacks, have done a lot to promote existential mistrust in our culture today and with it the loss of faith in words. Often we cannot really accept the other's attempt to confirm

us because we think that he [she] is either selling us a line or is trying out on us the latest therapeutic technique. (Friedman 1983, 47)

An overly optimistic view of confirmation or an effort to make the act of confirmation into a technique can actually lessen the possibility of a dialogic interpersonal perspective. When one communicates with another out of one's own historical formation without reaching out to understand and address the historical formation of the other, a confirmation of narcissism, not "otherness," is invited.

We offer a pragmatic response to the personhood of the "other" in the act of confirmation through a lens of historicality. Listening to the commonsense questions of a given historical moment is essential if the concept of "confirmation of otherness" is central for understanding the move from therapeutic language to a focus on historicality. Confirmation cannot be forced. "Confirmation on demand" is a contradiction in terms. The historical moment must call for words and actions that can confirm and inspire others. To be human is to experience both confirmation and its lack. Phony attempts at confirmation serve to insult the other, encouraging suspicion that the effort is driven by ulterior motives.

Maurice Friedman encourages people to confirm the other as we see the *human*, not just in glory and victory, but in "mutual revelations of weakness, of humanness, of hope and doubt, of faith and despair, of the very ground in which each of us is rooted, and of the strengths and foibles of our unique stances, there can be no revelation of the hidden human image" (1984, 191). Confirming the other in strength and weakness is central to a dialogic impulse. However, the language we use to understand this confirmation needs to answer the needs of the historical context, not just the therapeutic setting.

A Practical Dialectic

Hans Gadamer (1960/1986) makes it clear that being human is a learned activity—one in which we must struggle with our personal limits and then attempt to go beyond them without ignoring historical limits. *Bildung* refers to educating or cultivating ourselves within a culture, and is both a task of expansion and a way to acknowledge practical limits. We call this simultaneous effort to retain a knowledge of limits and advance one's cultured potential the practical dialectic of dialogue. This practical dialectic guides our view of dialogic civility.

Hans Gadamer's (1987) work on philosophical hermeneutics points to one's knowledge base, question, and text as inherent limits in the interpretive process. Several authors have used Gadamer's work to inform their writing about interpersonal communication. John Stewart (1983) brought the philosophical hermeneutics of Gadamer (1981) and Paul Ricoeur (1983/1984) to the study of interpersonal listening. Dialogic openness, linguisticality, play, and "fusion of horizons" are key terms for Stewart. He revealed the importance of philosophical hermeneutics for studying interpersonal communication.

Kenneth White (1994) also connected the work of Hans Gadamer to the study of interpersonal communication. He added to the insight of John Stewart (1983) by stressing Gadamer's (1960/1986) emphasis on "historicality": "We always understand within a social tradition, rather than solely with individuals, and within a tradition that is embodied in language. We let tradition 'speak' to us, for we cannot understand ourselves or others apart from the prejudices and presuppositions tradition has supplied" (White 1994, 97). We live within a historical tradition that generates bias and prejudice, which inevitably guides what we see and the questions we ask of a given era or historical moment.

The concept of historicality begins with limits; limits in which we live between the tensions of what we hope to achieve and the reality in which we are rooted. The following offers a clear sense of Hans Gadamer's (1960/1986) understanding of historicality tied to relation:

> Mutual relationship . . . helps to constitute the reality of the "Thou" relationship in itself. The inner historicality of all the relations in the lives of men [or women] consists in the fact there is a constant struggle for mutual recognition. . . . A person who imagines that he [or she] is free of prejudices, basing his [or her] knowledge on the objectivity of his [or her] procedures and denying that he [or she] is himself [or herself] influenced by historical circumstances, experiences the power of the prejudices that unconsciously dominate him [or her]. . . . A person who does not accept that he [or she] is dominated by prejudices will fail to see what is shown by their light. It is like the relation between the "I" and the "Thou." A person who

reflects himself [or herself] out of the mutuality of such a relation changes this relationship and destroys its moral bond. A
person who reflects himself [or herself] out of a living relationship to tradition destroys the true meaning of this tradition in exactly the same way. Historical consciousness . . .
must, in fact, take account of its own historicality . . . to stand
within a tradition does not limit the freedom of knowledge but
makes it possible. (322–324)

For Gadamer, our historical bias is what makes knowledge possible, what makes change happen, and what makes the uniqueness
of life's events understandable. We, as human beings, are historically grounded in "conditionedness" and "limitedness" (1960/1986,
59).

The art of interpretation, the labor of the Greek god Hermes,
requires us to begin with the notion that finite limits govern the
acts of human beings. Gadamer sees evil in a fixed view of history:
"I think [Theodor] Litt is right when he sees the danger of a new
dogmatism in the philosophical opposition to history. The desire for
a fixed, constant criterion 'that points the way to those called to
action' always has particular force if failures in moral and political
judgment have led to evil consequences" (1960/1986, 490). Gadamer
uses the notion of historicality to discuss "situatedness" which cannot be escaped. For instance, both of the authors of this text have
earned advanced degrees and live middle- to upper-middle-class life
styles. The commonsense or everyday questioning of one's own era
is limited by the historical moment in which one asks any question.
None of us can escape this situation. A person can, however, admit
one's own historical limitations and ask questions available to him
or her at a given time. Such action allows us to see with humble
conviction what others from another historical moment may not
necessarily have witnessed. To understand historicality permits the
possibility of informed interpersonal praxis central to this work.

Interpersonal Praxis as Historical Common Sense

Hans Gadamer (1960/1986) quotes Giambattista Vico's notion of
sensus communis, connecting common sense to historicality. Common sense is the ability to bring the practical and theoretical
together, to be guided by what is possible in a given historical

moment. Aristotle referred to this practical intellectual effort as *phronesis* (1985, 1141a20–1142a). A person situated in a community makes decisions guided by knowledge of the "good life" gained from the *polis* and still shaped by the particular. This dialectic of community guidance and the particular shaped Giambatista Vico's (1993) understanding of *sensus communis*.

Commonsense knowledge is often not conscious; we know, tacitly, what we are unable to clearly recognize and state as one's point of view. Charles Horton Cooley makes this point well in *Social Process*: "Generally speaking, social organisms feel their way without explicit consciousness of where they want to go or how they are to get there, even though to the eye of an observer after the fact their proceedings may have an appearance of rational provision" (1918/1966, 21). "Common sense" guides us as "taken for granted assumptions" (Schultz 1990, 23). We are guided and directed by the prevailing questions of a given historical moment.

Historical common sense may help us understand a given ideal, but the ideal is driven by what is possible and appropriate in a given historical moment. Such an understanding of historical common sense is deeply tied to the notion of praxis. Interpersonal communication guided by historicality is not a philosophy of the ideal, but a dialectic of the theoretical and the practical into what is possible at any given historical moment.

Praxis is an appropriate guiding metaphor for our view of interpersonal communication. Understanding interpersonal communication responsive to the historical moment requires informed action, praxis. Praxis represents the move from concentration on theory in the abstract to the interpretation and application of theory tested in the action of a given historical moment (Schrag 1986).

This understanding of praxis is by no means anti-intellectual. For us to interpret something, we need to bring our own horizon of experiences and ideas to the event. In short, the more we know, the richer the potential possibilities available for interpretation. Praxis acts as the testing ground for interpretation and understanding. Aristotle (1985) would say intelligence guided by theory is limited. On the other hand, intelligence guided by knowledge and seasoned by the test of praxis points toward wisdom.

Theories can be practical, if connected to the historical moment by praxis. Julia Wood (1995) discussed the practical value of relational communication theories. She reminds us that theories describe, explain, and predict. Theories are practical because they guide what we see and how we respond interpersonally. We suggest that a theory is a practical effort to formulate a verbal picture that helps us understand a given historical problem. The theory ceases to be practical when the guidelines it offers continue to be used long after the question(s) that called for the theory cease to be historically relevant. Using a theory that no longer addresses common-sense questions within a given historical moment is not practical. The practical limits of a theory are reached and our interpersonal ability to confirm the other is forsaken when we ignore the historical context that requires historically appropriate application. Instead of keying the word *sensitivity* to a psychological world view, we connect sensitivity with a response to the praxis of the historical moment. The following examples of praxis in an educational setting highlight the importance of historicality for shared meaning.

Whether an interaction is between a supervisor and a subordinate, a teacher and a student, or close friends, both persons in an interpersonal interaction have an obligation to the other. However, Martin Buber asserted that the person who is sought out for insight and support has the greater obligation at that time in the relationship: "You have necessarily another attitude to the situation than he [or she] has. You are able to do something that he [or she] is not able. You are not equals and cannot be. You have the great task, self-imposed—a great self-imposed task to supplement this need of his [or hers] and to do rather more than in the normal situation" (1965b/1966a, 172). Each of us at different times bears the burden of greater obligation in a relationship. In the interpersonal communication classroom, the teacher as facilitator holds the burden for greater communicative competence and for guiding instructional practices.

Each person's life history is shaped by sociocultural limits and personal experiences. In the educational setting, the teacher and student come together to engage in dialogue between the historical moments represented in the learning environment. The subject matter must address similar commonsense questions, which traverse the historical moments that shaped each individual's perspective and which are mutually important in the contemporary historical situation. The interpretive center of the classroom experience must address significant aspects of the topic with respect to the historical and contemporary moment of the interactants.

Unknowingly, a teacher can languish in the confirmation of one's own formation, appropriate for what Christopher Lasch called *The Culture of Narcissism* (1978/1979), teaching from one's own historical moment, which bypasses the contemporary context of communication. We do not contend that the teacher gives up the task of shaping a perspective and being in dialogue with the student about that perspective. A phenomenological dialogue (Arnett 1981) is undergirded by the inevitability of the dialogue of horizons between teacher and student. Dialogue of horizons can be steered by practical wisdom, *phronesis*, given birth through examined praxis of the educational context and a willingness to address the contemporary questions of the moment.

Interpersonal Commonplaces

Dialogic Education: Conversation About Ideas and Between Persons (Arnett 1992/1997c) began with a question the author asked his favorite teacher more than a quarter of a century ago: "Professor, why did you choose this vocation? How did you decide to be a teacher? Did a vocational aptitude test point you in this direction? Did you want summers off to study and travel? Were your parents teachers?" (vii).

More than twenty-five years ago, the teacher's answer to why he entered the field of communication revealed the importance of making the world safe for democracy. The teacher discussed the connection between free speech and democracy. He wanted to make sure that the democratic story could and would counter the "bad" stories of World War II (e.g., Nazism, Stalinism, Fascism). We may ask, "What does such an answer have to do with the study of communication?" The uncomplicated answer lies within the historical era of that professor's window of professional decision making: he lived a life shadowed by World War II and, of course, the technological power of radio. The teacher went into public speaking to keep the world safe for democracy. His moment of vocational calling was couched within a commonsense knowledge of the power of public speech.

In an era in which we hovered as a family around the radio and listened carefully to powerful and dominant orators/leaders outlining steps toward hopeful victory, our common sense suggested the power of public speech. Great communication teachers were shaped by significant public conversations of so many powerful orators who emerged from this era. Is it a coincidence that we discover Karl Wallace (1944, 1950, 1955, 1963), Franklyn S. Haiman (1952, 1958), Paul Boase (1969, 1980), Marie Hochmuth Nichols (1977), and many others configuring the discipline around public discourse themes in hopes of countering stories inconsistent with democratic themes and keeping the world safe from an authoritarianism that almost captured the world spirit?

The rhetoric of Franklin Delano Roosevelt and Winston Churchill, as opposed to the rhetoric of Adolph Hitler and Joseph Stalin, offers a keen picture of the power of democratic versus auto-cratic public discourse. Many people considered becoming teachers at that time to make a practical difference and assist the persua-sive cause of "justice, right, hope, democracy"—emotionally laden terms that soldiers had so recently given their lives to protect. Occasionally, we still find a teacher of rhetoric who joined the study of communication for similar reasons. But clearly there are far fewer colleagues who have entered this discipline for those reasons. The historical moment in which few could escape the common ques-tions of World War II—"How can rhetoric lead people to good and evil?"—does not play as powerful a part of our commonsense ques-tioning of communication today.

In no way do we intend to suggest that such questions are not asked or that we should not ask them. We continue to encourage and applaud such efforts. Our point is more modest: communication scholars no longer ponder the power of public discourse as part of our everyday taken-for-granted life with the same intensity as did scholars around the time of World War II, although this focus is beginning to emerge once again. Witness the writings of Jurgen Habermas (1973/1975) and Seyla Benhabib (1992). While the com-monsense ground for asking questions about the power of democra-tic public speech is behind us, we suggest that concern for the pub-lic square is returning anew, in light of the many calls for connecting communication to background public narratives (Fisher 1984).

Just as the guiding metaphors for our teachers were public dis-course, democracy, and argument, which addressed the commonsense historical needs of keeping "bad" stories from overtaking global sanity again, when we, the authors, became teachers we saw a historical need for healing. The Vietnam war had not ended in joy and economic prosperity like the conclusion of World War II. Vietnam concluded with the alienation of people on both sides of the issue of American involvement and the advent of runaway economic inflation.

One of the authors confesses to his students that the middle-class generation of his era began to lose hope in the rhetorical "big picture." The deaths of John and Robert Kennedy and Martin Luther King Jr. plus the ongoing crisis of faith in leadership surrounding Vietnam led to a different path. Some people lost faith in public rhetorical calls; democratic words and actions seemed too large and remote. We settled for a smaller and, some of us thought, more private and manageable picture—the support and care of interpersonal relationships. Our hope was no longer in the power of rhetoric to save or to destroy us, but in the power of interpersonal relationships, reaching one person at a time.

The commonsense question at that time was, "How do we heal the rupture in the country and in the lives of so many?" We looked for healing and discovered the close relationship between communication and the healing professions. The impact of third-force psychology or humanistic psychology on the study of interpersonal communication should come as no surprise. Their psychological efforts tried to address a commonsense call for healing.

Extending this example, one of the authors has been touched by three quite different historical moments that have shaped the commonsense questions of communication professors. First, his teachers were shadowed by World War II—a war in which we learned to fight against "bad" stories of Nazism, Stalinism, and Fascism. Second, he was shaped by Vietnam. Many in that generation took the notion of questioning the "bad" stories to the point of questioning *all* stories that offer insight and guidance. Finally, in working with students today he is touched by a different generation of narrative questioners. These students are expected to meet life without the foundation of narratives that give a reason, a why, in the midst of disappointment and hard work. Should we be surprised when much of our "teaching" outside the classroom is often not content-related, but involves working with students to find a why, a direction for their lives?

We contend that interpersonal communication driven by commonsense historicality needs to address the concerns of today's students, not the questions of World War II or Vietnam. Students in today's colleges and universities are faced with pragmatic questions of employment and the use of technology. They are saddled with the burden of overcoming stereotypes perpetuated in the media about "Generation X." In addition, health issues such as the AIDS epidemic, alcoholism, and drug abuse confront students daily. Interpersonal communication must begin with the reality of everyday life. Students need a narrative foundation to use as a guide for their action, not just the routine cynicism of their teachers.

Interpersonal communication is deeply contextual, grounded not in abstract theory, but in the historical questions that drive a given era. We suggest that we live in a historical moment in which commonplaces are at risk and the everyday acceptance and use of emotivism has driven much interpersonal interaction to the level of private, not public, discourse. Commonplaces are simply the narratives or stories that we hold in common that provide for us a common base for interaction and argument (Bellah, Madsen, Sullivan, Swidler, and Tipton 1985; Fisher 1984; Hauerwas 1981). Private discourse does not demand commonplaces. Public discourse, on the other hand, requires commonplaces. We work from public commonplaces to test the praxis of each other's ideas. A narrative offers a baseline for public discussion. A narrative involves the public articulation of the story formation of a people, group, or organization. Narratives offer implicit guidelines for suggesting what is important and how we should act with respect to significant events and issues.

Interpersonal communication without commonplaces results in argument by feeling or complaining, and ultimately, argument by power. Emotivism draws us away from a common center:

> Buber's analysis on common center is similar to the more recent scholarship of Alasdair MacIntyre. In *After Virtue*, MacIntyre stated that what holds people together is agreement on the importance of particular moral stories. People in a community will argue over what the moral stories suggest or imply. The stories are not understood literally. Creativity comes from agreement on a common base and a willingness to permit competing interpretations. Thus, as people argue they use evidence that is publicly known by many in the community. They then must convince others of the viability of their interpretation on a particular issue.
>
> The stories act as a text or base from which agreement can occur. The loss of the common text paves the way for "emotivism," a decision by personal preference without reference to a moral story that another knows and might counter with a contrary interpretation. Emotivism propels us against the grain of one of the major contributions of the Enlightenment—movement of ideas into the public arena where they can be tested and debated. Argument by "I feel" leaves a common public center, in this case a known moral story, and leads to privatized feelings, or emotivism (MacIntyre [1981/1984]). (Arnett 1994, 232)

Richard Sennett, in *The Fall of Public Man* (1974/1992), additionally warns of the danger of the therapeutic orientation used substitutionally as a public domain commonplace.

Sennett offers a foundation for questioning the psychological perspective. He reminds us that multiple paradigms about how people can and should interact are possible, but when one paradigm begins to reign supreme a sense of tyranny is invited:

> One of the oldest usages of the "tyranny" in political thought is as a synonym for sovereignty. When all matters are referred to a common, sovereign principle or person, that principle or person tyrannizes the life of a society. This governing of a multitude of habits and actions by the sovereign authority of a single source need not arise by brute coercion; it can equally arise by a seduction. . . . Intimacy is a tyranny in ordinary life of this last sort. It is not the forcing, but the arousing of a belief in one standard of truth to measure the complexities of social reality. It is the measurement of society in psychological terms. (1974/1992, 337–338)

Sennett underscores the limits of a therapeutic "ideology of intimacy" (1974/1992, 259) without giving up hope on a dialogic view of interpersonal communication situated in public commonplace background narrative assumptions about the importance of dialogic civility—interpersonal discourse with respect in the public arena. If we are to meet the historically grounded questions of students today, we must teach to their formation, not our own. We must guide, but within a world that makes sense (common sense) to them and to us. We still need commonplaces to draw us together.

We do not offer a theory of interpersonal communication, but rather suggest a path that might lead us out of this "*therapeutic cul-de-sac*" (Arnett 1997d, 149) that some have confused with the relational view of interpersonal communication. The interpretive task is to once again link communication to historical content, narratives, and the humble limits of the time in which we live. By examining the tough content questions our era points us to address, we suggest an interpersonal communication framework that will enrich our connectedness to one another. We posit a dialogic view of interpersonal communication guided by public stories and questions that can bind us together in the midst of the diversity (Makau and Arnett 1997). We need to discover not only individual uniqueness, but interpersonal commonplaces that offer us text for conversation, questioning, and mutual learning. We offer dialogic civility as a philosophical commonplace that might bring us together as we attend to the unique and particular historical moment before us.

Chapter Four

Common Ground

Interpersonal Narrative

Value of Narrative Hope —

Even in the numerous scenarios of decline and fall . . . studies such
as [Max] Horkheimer and [Theodor] Adorno's *Dialectic of the
Enlightenment*, [Alasdair] MacIntyre's *After Virtue*, [Kenneth
Baynes, James Bohman, and Thomas] McCarthy's *After Philosophy*, [Jeffrey] Stout's *Ethics after Babel*, and [David] Tracy's *Plurality and Ambiguity*, assume some intelligible baseline of normalcy as a margin for their own schemata of decline. . . . It can be
said that the modality of potential is alive and well.

　　　　　　　　　　　—Thomas B. Farrell, *Norms of Rhetorical Culture*

Difference between Hope and Optimism —

If we distinguish hopefulness from the more conventional attitude
known today as optimism—if we think of it as a character trait, a
temperamental predisposition rather than an estimate of the
direction of historical change—we can see why it serves us better,
in steering troubled waters ahead, than a belief in progress. Not
that it prevents us from expecting the worst. The worst is always
what the hopeful are prepared for. Their trust in life would not be
worth much if it had not survived disappointments in the past,
while the knowledge that the future holds further disappointments demonstrates the continuing need for hope. Believers in
progress, on the other hand, though they like to think of themselves as the party of hope, actually have little need of hope, since
they have history on their side. But their lack of it incapacitates

them for intelligent action. Improvidence, a blind faith that things will some how work out for the best, furnishes a poor substitute for the disposition to see things through even when they don't.

—Christopher Lasch, *The True and Only Heaven*

The task of offering dialogic civility as a public narrative or common ground for interpersonal communication is not an effort without risk. Postmodernity does not look favorably upon narrative background structures. For many people the term *narrative*, as a call to gather people together in a similar conversation, has lost its power. Yet we contend that a minimal common ground is a necessary background narrative structure for guiding interpersonal discourse in an age of diversity and difference.

A public narrative is a means to invite common ground between communicators. Narrative serves as a background for communicative action. Our use of narrative is tied to "humble narrative" (Arnett 1997b, 44–45). A humble narrative does not dictate the way to approach a situation, but offers a background set of assumptions agreed upon by enough people to permit it to influence everyday perception and actions. Whenever narrative is used in this work, it implies a background, in gestalt terms. At times, we use the term *background narrative*, or *narrative background* in order to emphasize this key "background" component of narrative in relation to interpreting "foreground" communicative action.

Our understanding of narrative lies between metaphor and metanarrative, closer to the former. Metanarrative assumes a uniform virtue system, which the project of postmodernity has revealed as impossible. A communicative metaphor points beyond itself, in this case orienting the reader to a philosophical sense of place, which we term dialogic civility. If there is sufficient agreement about a narrative, it begins to function as a background for making sense of daily communicative action. Narrative is the background that illuminates the significance of foreground communicative action. In essence, dialogic civility serves both as a metaphor and a potential guiding public narrative for daily interpersonal praxis, reminding us of the importance of co-constitutional conversational respect. We invite discussion about the importance of "an agreed upon public narrative as a background for interpersonal communication that begins the conversation within a framework of public 'respect'" (Benhabib 1992, 30). In an era of social diversity and public discourse awareness, we move from the term *respect* to *civility* in hopes of further emphasizing the public nature of dialogue between persons in a time of increasing difference.

Opening Narrative Structures

In beginning this project, we struggled to find a "public" term that could offer common ground between persons and encourage social diversity. We began our search with a familiar term—*humanism*. Humanism, once associated with the public domain, is today too privatized—offering too limited a cultural perspective. Unlike the term *humanism*, dialogic civility points us to the more open and less defined public communicative terrain of the twenty-first century.

Humanism is now tied in daily discourse to a privatized world view, but originally it opened closed narrative structures, or what we call ideological structures, to interpretation. In interpersonal communication, humanism is generally associated with the Humanistic Psychological movement or what was called "third force" psychology. Humanism emerged as an alternative to psychoanalysis (first force psychology) and behaviorism (second force psychology). Historically, themes of freedom, naturalism, and the civil function or earthly commitment of religion and the emergence of science all contributed to a public humanistic narrative in which the individual human being made a difference. From the time of the sixteenth-century Italian Renaissance, the human mind was bursting forth, but not without some way to describe the emergence of a broader based story on how the human could pursue the "good life" within a dialectical tension of self and institutions (Abbagnano, 1967). Humanism was a counter to the power of overarching metanarratives, and a counter to rigid ideological structures.

Humanism takes the limits of human nature and the ideals of dignity of the person seriously, attempting to understand what it means to be human in a given historical moment in time. Humanism for some was the beginning of the end of treasured narratives of the authority of the church and state. On the contrary, humanism was initially offered, not as a means to destroy old narratives, but as part of an effort to place them in perspective. The Renaissance brought recognition of difference, creativity, and individual thought; it recognized some degree of diversity. Humanism sought to infuse institutions with a reminder of who they were to serve—not themselves, but the people. A narrative that calls us to be concerned about others and remember to serve them is the foundation of the Western Renaissance philosophy of humanism.

Without the humanist movement, philosophical hermeneutics had a minimal chance of having an impact on society, the church, and intellectual thought. Previously, knowledge was gathered in collective memory and through dogma; the humanist impulse for interpretation broke open the doors of dogma. Hans Gadamer opened *Truth and Method* with a discussion of "The Significance of the Humanist Tradition." Gadamer referred to the German classical tradition *Bildung*—the shaping or the cultivating of oneself.

> When in our language we say Bildung, we mean something both higher and more inward, namely the attitude of mind which, from the knowledge and the feeling of the total intellectual and moral endeavor, flows harmoniously into sensibility and character. . . . Bildung calls . . . on the ancient mystical tradition, according to which man carries in his soul the image of God after whom he is fashioned and must cultivate it in himself. (1960/1986, 11–12)

Thus, the first major key to the humanism of which Gadamer speaks is the cultivation of the human, to make ourselves better, to shape who we might become. A second major element comes from Gadamer's discussion of the Jesuit educator, Giambatista Vico, and his understanding of *sensus communis*, common sense. Common sense is founded within a human community—we learn what we practice. However, unlike us, "Vico lived in an unbroken tradition of rhetorical and humanistic culture and had only to reassert anew its ageless claim" (Gadamer 1960/1986, 23). We live in a time of metanarrative disruption in which common sense is more rare simply because we have fewer common experiences. One cannot have common sense, nor appreciate it in another, when it is tied to experience so alien to one's own. Unlike Giambatista Vico and Aristotle before him, we live in a contested time of conflicting narratives. There is no one humanistic tradition from which to draw ideas, examples, and models of human behavior that all will understand.

Dialogic civility is a minimal set of background ethical commitments designed to keep a conversation going in an era of postmodern disagreement about virtues. Respect for persons, topic, and historical moment need to guide the dialogue, permitting the public nature of interpersonal conversation to encourage examination of common ground that will keep the communicative participants in the communicative arena together.

A foundation for our understanding of dialogic civility is historicality, limits, ethical bias, text or conversation, the other, and narrative. We describe an interpersonal approach to communication that does not rest solely on the metaphor of "self" and the emotive needs of "me." Dialogue suggests that "we" more than "me" must guide the discourse of self, other, text, and historical moment. There is necessarily a productive tension between "we" and "me"— "we" includes "me." However, in this historical moment we downplay the impulse toward self to highlight the connection between interactants present in the "we" of dialogue. Civility calls us to reexamine the public domain as the arena where common ground in an age of diversity will need to be located.

Diversity, change, and variety are central to any person in dialogue with the historical moment, permitting development of the human within one's own historical situation. The grounding of dialogic civility in historicality recognizes "an inexhaustible productivity of historical life" (Gadamer 1960/1986, 178). The moment in which we live is our interpretive text that sets the stage for dialogic civility. As this work asserts, communicative interaction is shaped by dialogue between the present historical moment and the person. The person cannot solely define what is the right communication in a given historical moment, nor can the historical situation solely limit the vision of a communicator to the confines of the moment. In dialogue, person and historical situation offer glimpses of appropriate communicative action. In an effort to combat the routine of unreflective cynicism, we offer a vision of dialogic civility as a metaphor calling for concern beyond "me" which is sensitive to the historical moment.

We offer dialogic civility as a metaphor that offers a minimal basis for a public narrative. Our assumption is that diversity and particularity are woven together in a linen of commonality, which offers the best chance for interpersonal communication to prosper. Other forms of communication can take place without this common narrative commitment, but we cannot presuppose that interpersonal concerns for the "other" will happen without a story base telling us why we should be concerned about the "other," a diverse "other" that we meet in the public space of the twenty-first century.

Dialogic civility, as a public narrative, has a baseline of respect for others as human beings. In the public domain, such a narrative background offers common ground from which diversity of persons and cultures can begin conversation. Like any approach, this one begins with a bias, an ethical assumption: a pragmatic concern and respect for the other needs to undergird our interpersonal communication, in order to keep the conversation going. This assumption is no small request. We live in an era in which many people are quick to judge another's communication style toward them, yet lax in evaluating their own communication assumptions and actions.

The key that distinguishes *dialogic* civility from other approaches to interpersonal communication is dialogic civility as public narrative background. Dialogic civility, as a public narrative, begins prior to conversation between two people. A narrative provides a context for communication to be resumed or explored. In the Bible, John 1:1 begins, "In the Beginning was the Word." We suggest in secular terms, "In the beginning was a Narrative." A narrative operates as a background set of assumptions, a story line that opens (or closes) the path for interaction between people (Kurtz 1933/1973). Dialogic civility is offered as a background bias that exists prior to communication between people.

We suggest a public narrative that will guide, not dictate responses in particular situations. Our view of a public narrative, dialogic civility, is tested not in the abstract, but in the lives of people in particular relationships with others. Seyla Benhabib works to connect narrative and the particular, as we do in this work:

> Because women's sphere of activity has traditionally been and still today is so concentrated in the private sphere in which children are raised, human relationships maintained and traditions handed down and continued, the female experience has been more attuned to the "narrative structure of action" and the "standpoint of the concrete other." Since they have had to deal with concrete individuals, with their needs, endowments, wants and abilities, dreams as well as failures, women in their capacities as primary caregivers have had to exercise insight into the claims of the particular. In a sense the art of the particular has been their domain, as has the "web of stories" which in Hannah Arendt's words constitutes the who and the what of our shared world. (1992, 14)

We reject ideological positions that offer answers a priori to the event; such a view is to be held in contrast with the narrative requirements of participation, *phronesis*, and genuine listening to the particular historical moment and offering a unique response to the other.

Narrative Background

In an interpretive essay, "Existential Homelessness: A Contemporary Case for Dialogue," one of the authors outlined the problematic consequences of life without clear narrative structures to guide the communicators. Using gestalt language of *foreground* and *background*, the connection between narrative and interpersonal communication was expressed in the following manner: narrative provides a background set of tacit assumptions and knowledge about communication that guide and offer meaning to the foreground event of a given conversation (Arnett 1994).

When a person goes to a foreign country there is always room for misinterpretation, even if one is bilingual. Meaning is not only carried by oral symbols, but also by people's nonverbal customs. A given nonverbal act that catches one's interest is a foreground point of attention. However, the background narrative of the culture permits one to understand what a given nonverbal act might suggest or imply. A favorite story from Gregory Bateson includes a conversation with his daughter. She asks why Frenchmen wave their hands when they talk.

> **D:** Daddy, when they teach us French at school, why don't they teach us to wave our hands?
>
> **F:** I don't know. I'm sure I don't know. That is probably one of the reasons why people find learning languages so difficult. (1972, 19)

After a number of exchanges, the daughter begins to understand that a Frenchman who waves his hands and arms while speaking actually communicates something of significance not only in the conversation, but about the French culture itself.

Perhaps we misunderstand the significance of waving hands in French speech because we are without narrative knowledge that offers background insight and understanding of a given exchange. Strangers are often ignorant of the everyday narrative background common to native people. Geographic, socioeconomic, and cultural differences do alter the way in which a narrative structure must be appropriately implemented. A narrative of a people is learned through both study and praxis within a specific culture or subculture. Receiving rewards for certain behaviors and experiencing consequences from errors socializes us to particular narratives. A cultural native learns through practice, requiring little awareness of the learning. However, the outsider must consciously work to understand culturally appropriate implementation of a narrative; such knowing action is often tacit to natives who comprise what Robert Bellah et al. called *Habits of the Heart* (1985). The outsider will only be able to appropriately implement the learning through praxis, theory informed action.

A narrative is often implicit, discovered not by following rules, but through everyday practice. The power of a narrative is often noticed when a particular narrative no longer commands respect or when it is violated. Narratives as tacit background structures are counted on much like gravity. Only when people of practice wake to find that they no longer can assume a background narrative or when another violates the narrative that guides them, do they recognize the power of a given narrative to offer order and structure to a people.

The vibrant power of a narrative is revealed by the intensity of a convert's commitment to the narrative. Those who practice a narrative on a daily basis often ignore the significance of a given narrative—taking it for granted. The power of a given narrative can grow weak at the hands of those who unknowingly take it for granted. The life of a person who takes narratives for granted is driven more by practice or rote implementation within a narrative framework than by understanding *why* (praxis) that narrative offers meaningful action. Perhaps this taken-for-granted nature of narratives is why a convert to most narratives often comes to understand the narrative more explicitly and is able to articulate its content better than some natives. Clearly, the convert cannot take a narrative for granted; the narrative must be learned. The convert will engage in narrative violation as he or she learns through praxis of the narrative.

Perhaps use of a more common example will assist in understanding the vital nature of narrative in everyday events. Let us turn to what used to be called "America's national pastime," baseball. With the advent of the 1994 baseball strike, we were unable to witness a World Series and missed the march on Roger Maris's sixty-one home run record. The owners' and players' general assumption was that the game could simply pick up and begin again the next year, if the strike could be resolved. The strike was stopped; the players returned; however, one-third of the fans stayed at home. Why? Many baseball fans come to the park, not just to see the game, but to be part of the narrative of a larger game—one attached to "Ty," "Shoeless," "Satchel," "Lou," "the Babe," and "Jackie." When the umpire calls "Play ball!" the play begins, but the narrative of the game is what makes many of us interested in watching the sport.

The players on the field and the management confused themselves with being sufficient unto themselves. They are necessary, but not sufficient for the GAME (narrative) of baseball to prosper; they are only sufficient unto themselves for play to take place on a given day or night at the park. What the owners and players put at risk was the necessary connection between the public narrative of the GAME and willingness of fans to watch their play after the management and players concluded their struggle over financial demands. When a batter steps to the plate, a background narrative permits us to see significance in a person holding a hunk of wood and swinging at a ball thrown by another person who does not seem to have a job and has enough time to take the afternoon off to play catch. Particularly in a sport such as baseball, which has such a leisurely component to its pace, the narrative is essential to understanding the importance—the "Why?"—of the game. It took until the 1998 season for the sport to fully recover, as home runs kept the names of Maris and Ruth before the public, along with McGwire, Sosa, and Griffey Jr.

The narrative *why* or reason to communicate with another in a manner that responds to his or her sense of humanness and worth is central to our discussion. We, like the baseball fans, have much to do. Why should we take the time to address one another in a special fashion? Perhaps if we recognize that we do not just begin with ourselves, but we pick up conversation in the midst of a narrative of persons who have come long before us, we might keep our own significance in perspective and work within historical limits that our era offers. We suggest that a public narrative provides minimal "common ground, common standards, a common frame of reference without which society dissolves into nothing more than contending factions" (Lasch 1995, 49).

The above may sound like a small point, but it is crucial to a narrative of dialogic civility for interpersonal communication. We suggest that a public narrative of dialogic civility can offer a guide for interaction between persons. We need not rely solely upon the private disposition or moods of the communicators, but rather ground communication in public action of respect for persons, topic, and sociocultural perspectives in dialogue within a given historical moment. Narrative points to a *why* prior to engaging in communication together. Other works focus on the *how* of communication; we are propelled by the narrative call to keep the conversation going with public respect for persons, topic, and historical moment.

We live in a time in which the background narrative that gives meaning to our action cannot be taken for granted. When some baseball announcers lament how little is known about the history of baseball by current players, announcers are not simply engaging in romantic nostalgia. They instinctively understand that something much larger than individual memory is at stake. They understand that without what Robert Bellah et al. call a "community of memory" (1985, 152–156), the game itself is at risk. It has been suggested that Cal Ripken Jr.'s September 6, 1995, breaking of Lou Gehrig's consecutive game record permitted the game to begin to reestablish its narrative ties.

Viktor Frankl (1959/1974), a survivor of the concentration camps and author of logotherapy ("meaning therapy"), was fond of quoting Friedrich Nietzsche's "He who has a *why* to live can bear with almost any *how*" (Allport 1959/1974, xi). There are many private reasons that motivate one to talk with another—from affection and liking to religious calling. Our task, however, is to suggest that in a time of significant diversity, public narratives that are held in common are still necessary for discovering the *why* for action—particularly when communicative action is recognized to be co-constitutive and intersubjective. We suggest that our task is to build new public narratives that can bind us together.

Alasdair MacIntyre, in *After Virtue* (1981/1984), described how one could tacitly live off the power and direction of a given narrative while failing to teach the background narrative that gives direction to action. Teaching is often focused upon implementation strategies wherein students are deprived of an overt connection to the background narrative that the teacher tacitly assumes. MacIntyre's point could be called a generational story about *how* and *why*. The first generation connects *how* (implementation) and *why* (narrative reason for action). The second generation tacitly assumes the *why* and works on the *how* of implementation. Because the second generation wants to spare the third generation from the boredom of old stories that they so often heard, the third generation is only taught implementation. The second generation sees little value in inviting the learner (third generation) to investigate the *why* (narrative background) of action. Again, like the taken-for-granted nature of gravity, the second generation cannot image life without such a narrative background. However, from the lack of instruction comes a third generation who wonders *why* he or she should work so hard to implement what is of clear value to the second generation, but of ambiguous significance, at best, to the third generation.

The error does not belong to the third generation, but to the second. The second generation acted unknowingly in a narcissistic fashion. Unable to bear hearing any more of the stories detailing why they should act a particular way, their teaching addressed their own needs, not the knowledge requirements of the third generation. MacIntyre's philosophical discussion is consistent with an old adage about family businesses; they are often put at risk and then sold by the third or fourth generation—the love for the work is simply not present. Obviously, we consider it historically appropriate to discuss the notion of *why*; such narrative knowledge cannot be assumed in our contemporary communicative existence.

One of the authors was invited to a junior high school to assist with low morale of the faculty. The students were disrespectful, the teachers angry, and the administration was a revolving door—just as soon as enough experience warranted some form of promotion they moved to another school. Finally, after two days of observation one faculty member at the junior high with thirty years experience asked, "How did this school become such a bad place for students and faculty?" He then answered his own question: "We used to talk about why we were teachers. Then society got confused and in our effort to help students we no longer had the time to discuss *why* we were teachers. We simply attempted to survive. There seemed little time for any conversation, any action, except survival. We were busy trying to make a difference [implementation]. Now most of us are too tired to make a difference. As we merely tried to survive we lost our sense of why we became teachers." The teachers, like most of us preoccupied with survival and implementation, had no time to talk about why. Implementation became the essential focus. Plans failed and the *why*, as a background companion was able to offer reasons for continuing to care in demanding circumstances. Perhaps we live in a time in which we should warn ourselves and others that moving too fast can put at risk the narrative *why*, which offers a way to sustain us and place life in perspective in the midst of both successful implementation and the pain of trial and failed strategies.

From Metanarrative to Therapeutic Culture

A narrative is teleological; it is a story that guides a people while propelling them with energy toward a project worthy of doing. In common terms, a narrative provides a reason, a *why*, for doing a project that keeps us going when we are tired and discouraged. Additionally, a narrative consists of main characters and works within the dialectic of tradition and change. From a narrative perspective, change is best put forth by someone such as Martin Buber's "Great Character"—the person who knows a narrative well enough that he or she has earned the right to violate that tradition (1947/1965a, 113–114). A similar point was made by William Barrett in his quoting of T. S. Eliot: "the genuinely original creation is that which draws most deeply upon tradition even when it shakes up and transforms this tradition" (1986, 5). A metanarrative is a universal, expected background that directs actions and outlines restraint.

As metanarrative agreement was collapsing, a new method of decision making vied for acceptance—the therapeutic culture, undergirded by what Alasdair MacIntyre calls "emotivism." He suggests that emotivism has generated a major danger to the life of public narrative. Simply defined, emotivism is decision making by personal preference, guided by the self rather than a narrative of knowledge understood by a larger public (1981/1984, 23–35). Emotivism rests at the center of a therapeutic culture. If one accepts the premise that the human being is innately good and invulnerable to any evil process, then making decisions by personal preference and visceral impulses can be justified. If one does not accept this premise, we need to discover another grounding for interpersonal communication. The emotive variations are powerful and many of our former teachers adhered to the philosophy of "emotivism" so firmly that it is necessary for us to offer an explanation of their enthusiasm for an approach that has caused so much mischief in interpersonal and organizational life.

One young child, after being called to account for an inappropriate action, asked, "Now is it my turn to state my feelings?" The child did not disagree with the fact that what he had done was wrong, but he wanted others to know that he felt his punishment was inappropriate; it did not make him feel good. When asked where he had learned such feeling-oriented language, the youngster stated, "In Sunday School." Putting aside the issue of religion in a theological sense and limiting discussion to narrative, the following was learned in conversation with the young child. "What do you talk about in Sunday School?" The answer came back, "We are encouraged to state whatever we feel and then we discuss it together." Interested in the process of education, the adult asked, "Do you study scripture, moral lessons, or Biblical stories?" The child replied, "No. We talk about our feelings from the past week and then eat doughnuts." For this young child, the narrative of the church goes unexplored as his 1960s styled teacher continues to rebel against the narrative of the church, focusing instead upon individual feelings. The major difference between the teacher and her students is that she has a narrative from which to respond or rebel; these young people have no such narrative background from which to understand and put in context their own feelings, let alone to act against in rebellion.

The above exemplifies how the "therapeutic culture" has permeated many of our institutions that previously were understood through a narrative structure. Whether one likes religion or not is beside the point. Public institutions need to address their own particular public narratives or their narrative significance eventually dies and followers will not know why they should come or stay. We could make the same case for telling the narrative of democracy, if we want voting to be seen as part of a contribution to the common good, not just an effort to win "my" agenda.

Robert Bellah, Richard Madsen, William Sullivan, Anne Swidler, and Steven Tipton, in *The Good Society* (1991), lamented a lack of commitment to institutions. We should not be surprised that people's commitment to institutions is minimal in a time of "emotivism." "Emotivism" cannot replace narratives that tell us what the "good life" should look like and why and how institutions should be supported. If "emotivism" accomplished all we wanted it to do, there would be little reason for education. Learning narratives is part of an education, even if it does not happen within a traditional classroom structure.

> We described a language of individualistic achievement and self-fulfillment that often seems to make it difficult for people to sustain their commitment to others, either in intimate relationships or in the public sphere. . . . We called for a deeper understanding of the moral ecology that sustains the lives of all of us, even when we think we are making it on our own. "Moral ecology" is only another way of speaking of healthy institutions, yet the culture of individualism makes the very idea of institutions inaccessible to many of us. (Bellah et al. 1991, 6)

The "moral ecology" of which Bellah et al. speak is tied to the organizational narrative that guides institutional life. We must hear good stories to know how to frame good actions.

Historical Mismatch—The Therapeutic Metaphor

A co-constituted invitation to dialogue in interpersonal communication is an alternative to the failed project that has been called *The Triumph of the Therapeutic* (Rieff 1966/1987), "emotivism" (MacIntyre 1981/1984, 11–14), and that suggests meaning is in the person (Korzybski 1933/1948). We suggest that philosophical hermeneutics, and the notion of historicality in particular, offers a ground from which dialogue can be invited as an alternative to a psychological world view centered on meaning within the metaphor of "self." Historicality is situated in limits, particularity, and sociocultural influence. Historicality grounds communication in reality that is shared with others, not centered on one's self.

It is possible to affirm interpersonal concern for the other while rejecting the therapeutic metaphor, not as inaccurate, but as historically inappropriate. We define a therapeutic model of interpersonal communication as embracing three general characteristics: an overgeneralization of therapeutic language into everyday discourse, the blurring of private and public discourse, which encourages unreflective expression, and "emotivist" (MacIntyre 1981/1984, 11–14) language, which privatizes truth and minimizes the public domain.

Overgeneralization of therapeutic language into everyday discourse is pointed to by Bellah et al. (1991). Therapeutic language is contextually driven; it emerged from the private practice of the therapist/client relationship. Such a communicative language, if effective, should continue within the realm of therapeutic practice. However, we advocate praxis, theory informed action, when a communicative practice is thoughtfully moved from one context to another. We contrast praxis with practice—unreflective habitual action or use. One cannot determine responsible communication behaviors without considerable reflection on appropriateness in a given historical moment—moving from practice to praxis. However, one can unknowingly misapply a practice that is propelled by action without theoretical reflection. Such is the difference between an engineer (praxis) and a technician (practice).

Problems emerge when one overgeneralizes therapeutic language and moves it from the private communicative arena of therapy into the general public communicative domain. Such unreflective practice does not consider the historical dimension of the language context, thereby violating contextual appropriateness of language use. In moving therapeutic language inappropriately from the private realm to the public realm, therapeutic language is often used as unreflective practice, ceasing to be appropriate in this historical moment. The use of therapeutic language in a public setting is fueled by good-willed optimism that the public arena can easily absorb therapeutic exchange within a different context, plowing ground for the seeds of cynicism rooted in unmet high expectations.

Before proceeding further, we want to stress that our position is in no way hostile toward the private act of therapy. Therapy is a private act that encourages expression of unreflective thoughts and feelings in hopes of inviting undeveloped ideas into the open in a controlled environment for hearing and consideration. Our concern is that therapeutic language developed within a private context and a private practice between counselor and client can be misused if brought unreflectively to public contexts. When therapeutic language is moved into the public domain it is no longer grounded in its original place of practice. This transfer inappropriately extrapolates from the private arena of counseling to the everyday public domain of interpersonal communication. This action blurs the distinction between public and private discourse—generating confusion in communicative life and lessening options beyond the realm of therapeutic discourse.

Philip Rieff (1966/1987) and Richard Sennett (1974/1992) both discuss the blurring of public and private roles. Rieff's insights are central to this discussion and the fact that he wrote them thirty years ago only confirms the power of therapeutic language on everyday life. An expressive "therapeutic" communicative style has historically been part of a private, not a public, communicative domain. Rochelle Gurstein's (1996) *The Repeal of Reticence* outlines the problem of unreflective expressivism in the public domain. Moving therapeutic language into the public domain melded the desire for communicative comfort and the technique of expressive nonjudgment. Counseling as a private social good that enables clarity of identity and direction can become a public liability when a similar form of interpersonal discourse is used in public situations.

All one has to do is watch television talk shows for one day to discover communication that earlier in our history would have been limited to private therapeutic conversation inappropriately infused into the public arena of communication. Indeed, a conversational style that blurs private and public discourse is much different than Aristotle's (1991) public requirements for the accumulation of evidence, organization of materials, and careful deliberation before speaking.

Therapeutic conversation is guided by "emotivism" (MacIntyre 1981/1984, 11–14)—or how one feels—not a commonly held narrative or story that permits divergent opinions and discussion within a community. A background narrative does not ensure agreement, but offers a commonplace from which difference can be centered. A number of authors have tried to call people back to the importance of a content-driven narrative rather than feeling-oriented discourse as a guideline for discussion and argument (Bellah et al. 1991; Fisher 1984; Hauerwas 1981). Therapy provides a context for expressing and understanding one's feelings. However, when one enters the public domain, argument by feeling does not permit public testing and verification of content. Emotivism privatizes truth within the individual self; evidence becomes private feelings, not public statements that can be examined and verified by others.

When personal preference dominates interpersonal communication in public settings, confirmation of the other is likely to occur only if the other's needs coincide with one's own. The public domain of everyday conversation cannot be left to personal preferences of emotivism, unless we assume that human beings are innately intelligent (via emotions alone), are driven by innately good emotions, are willing to be empathic in all settings, and are able to respond with respect to each other at all times. If we reject any of the above assumptions, we must locate interpersonal communication in a framework other than emotivism to guide us in public discourse settings.

We need a framework for communicative discourse that emphasizes public content and knowledge over the private emotive conviction of the knower. Diversity of persons requires us to move to the public domain, where testing ideas must occur between persons of difference. We are suggesting that interpersonal communication is larger than intimate/private discourse. As one of the author's friends states, cliches are commonplaces that frequently point us to practical truth. In this case the bath water, not the baby, needs to be rejected. In fact, the offspring (new approaches to dialogic communication) now need nurturing in different philosophical homes; this work offers one perspective, situating dialogue in historicality.

Philip Rieff identified the evolution of two major philosophical approaches that have guided human interaction—first the religious approach and now the therapeutic: "Religious man was born to be saved; psychological man is born to be pleased. The difference was established long ago, when 'I believe,' the cry of the ascetic, lost precedence to 'one feels,' the caveat of the therapeutic. And if the therapeutic is to win out, then surely the psychotherapist will be his secular spiritual guide" (1966/1987, 25). The task before us is to find yet another way, another path, another philosophical home for guiding a dialogic view of interpersonal communication. If we contend that the metanarratives of religion have failed us, we can also make a case that the overextension of a therapeutic language into everyday discourse has failed us, and perhaps even more fully.

An Overextended Metaphor

The key to therapy is "self-understanding," calling for legitimate expression of feelings that might not get a hearing in another context. The key to business is profit. The key to education is accumulation and wise use of information. The key to a sport is mastery of the game. The key to religion is an understanding of the faith. When all the above are placed as secondary to emotional expression, the "therapeutic culture" begins to absorb contexts that are inappropriate for the language of the private exchange between therapist and client. Therapy is a needed activity in a confused time of public narrative, but therapy belongs in the private domain of interaction between therapist and client. The realm of private therapy makes sense when one's request is to say whatever pops into one's mind while expecting nonjudgmental listening from the other. In therapy, the client is trying to generate order out of a life and needs to talk in order to work through issues and find a direction. However, a much different social result emerges when one expects to say whatever comes to mind and also expects to receive nonjudgmental affirmation in a public setting of work or education.

Philip Rieff, one of the first major critics of the therapeutic culture, powerfully calls attention to the mistaken path of the "therapeutic culture" (1966/1987, 71–74). His words add a practical and concrete face to Alasdair MacIntyre's philosophical lament against "emotivism" (1981/1984, 6–22). Rieff (1990) comments on his earlier writing:

The Triumph of the Therapeutic first appeared twenty years ago. Then years later, titling the book "prophetic," the editor of *The American Scholar* referred to the American "state of unconditional surrender" to the type. The surrender is now no longer American. As Western culture continues to be Americanized, the therapeutic, in his triumph, has spread beyond these borders and even beyond Europe. (351)

So long as we do not question the established dogma of the therapeutic; that there is no sacred order, now, if ever there were any, to which anyone can belong. I suspect Hamlet asked that question long before we see him on stage. The rest, for him, was bound to be tragedy and silence. (364)

Better call it, as my old rabbi did, the "evil impulse." Because the instinctual unconscious contains no either-or, it is worse than immoral: amoral, positively transgressive. Therapeutic neutrality in this matter is more than mistaken: It has been a tragedy for our, or any other, culture and for anyone alive to its deadly condition. (364)

Here I am brought back, in an older . . . language of despair and hope, to the uses and abuses of the faith that was and is the question, asked, ironically as I know how, of these present and permanent culture class wars. To that generation born during the triumph of the therapeutic, I would repeat Kafka's great exordium on the first thing he, and not he alone, thought necessary for recognizing faith in our received sacred order: *"For the last time psychology!"* [as a corrective to therapeutic language of comfort and self-actualization]. (364–365)

Rieff understood, before many others, that the domain of psychology was misplaced when transferred inappropriately to the public domain.

Philip Rieff has functioned as a commonsense prophet calling us to examine what people who work with their hands and without much power and status understand in any culture. We offer the following suggestions in the spirit of Rieff's insights. First, be careful when something is offered without a request for something in return. Second, tragedy waits behind a corner for us; beware of managed smiles that attempt to deny this unpleasant reality. Third, remember evil is not a fiction and those who see no evil may inadvertently do much of it as they walk through life blinded to this reality. Fourth, despair and hope are companions; hope without an understanding of despair is a recipe for disaster. Fifth, patience and tenacity are needed to endure; life is not just comfort; sometimes our only hope is to hang on and look for light and new paths in the midst of darkness, fatigue, and pain. Finally, beware of a psychological language that does not take seriously the roller coaster ride through the evil and good, despair and hope, that each of us must take on our way to death. Rieff does not write for the fainthearted; he writes for those who work with a world of adults who are willing to see the world as it is, and then work to make it better, not more blind! The "therapeutic culture," when watered down in the public arena, is a fast food meal for a culture dying of cholesterol and lack of exercise—in this case a society placing undue emphasis on self-absorption and comfort.

When one begins to talk about listening to emotions, any background narrative, no matter how powerful, goes undiscussed; a narrative sense of *why* is simply assumed. A number of our teachers needed to find a way to break free from limits their narratives set before them. However, as our teachers were breaking free from one narrative, they were failing to provide an alternative background narrative for their students. Their emphasis was on emotive implementation, not the narrative background out of which emotions emerged and were evaluated. Our teachers' energy was spent calling attention to the importance of the individual self; they tacitly assumed the power of the public narrative of responsibility and service. These teachers offered an emphasis on self to counter "bad stories." They wanted to make sure that no narrative (such as that of Nazism, in particular) was ever again taken so seriously. They saw "bad stories" leading to the atrocities of two World Wars. They were not ignoring public narratives; they wanted to place any narrative within the dialectical tension of the individual questioning the narrative and his or her historical situation. To do so would maintain a perspective less likely to lead to destruction. Little did our teachers know what would be born within twenty-five years of education focused on countering public narratives. Without the tacit commitment to a background narrative of responsibility and service to others outlined by major public narratives of civic commitments, our teachers unleashed "expressivism," "emotivism," and a "therapeutic culture" into the public domain.

Christopher Lasch, in his final work, *The Revolt of the Elites and the Betrayal of Democracy*, discussed the danger of equating what we are calling narrative with constant referrals to "the extreme pathologies of ideological thought—Nazism, Bolshevism, or whatever . . . personal depravity" (1995, p. 189). Some work in the humanities has been dialectically extreme, questioning not some, but all narratives. The task has been to unmask "bad stories" and permit the preferences of individuals to lead us to a "better" and "brighter" future. In reality, however, just as there are people with good and bad preferences, there are good and bad stories.

Unless we assume that a human being is solely a biological creature, stories are needed to shape the preferences we select. People need to debate what narratives should guide us, but debate that paints all stories as "bad" and attempts to cast our lot with personal preferences is misdirected. We learn our personal preferences from stories. This simple fact was taken for granted when our former teachers directed our attention to the importance of the individual and the danger of narratives that bind people together.

Both a critical life and emotive sensitivity have places in the effort to live life well. However, any technique that assumes banality of application, that offers an a priori answer to a "particular" situation, misses the historical moment. Such an orientation makes a leader evil before he or she acts or makes a narrative oppressive before it is understood. This orientation permits one to offer an emotive response with conviction toward an issue not yet studied. Ironically, the technique takes on the practice of a "Universal." Just as no one can claim to have discovered *the* narrative, no technique for understanding life guided by critique or emotion can illuminate the complexity of the journey that a sensitive human being needs to follow in working to assist the common good of "us"—especially in an era when the narrative suggestions for how such an effort is to be invited are unclear at best.

Our era may be defined as one of dialectical overreaction without an awareness of consequences. As one of the authors shared with a colleague, "We have all witnessed what autocratic and totalitarian governments and groups can do with bad stories that can mislead a people. We are only beginning to sense what the opposing alternative of personal preference over responsibilities for the group might do to the implicit set of assumptions held by so many of our teachers. Much of life is a calling to responsibility and service to others."

The notion of "emotivism" moved us into private decision making. Argument based on individual feeling and an atomistic view of truth became commonplace. How often have we argued for an idea without any public evidence to back our position other than our own feelings? Once we move into a greater world of diversity, public statements are needed that can be reviewed and examined. Otherwise, we are left with decisions based upon private power resources rather than decisions rooted in agreement that a particular position does or does not have merit and value according to some public standard.

Walter Lippmann's Warning

Walter Lippmann (1955) warned us about the loss of a public philosophy. Lippmann described the need to work dialectically within the limits of the ideal and historical reality, honestly facing the given moment. The ideal of total freedom and ignoring of public interest are too often isomorphic companions. Lippmann, writing after the practical results of World War II were etched on the hearts and minds of survivors, recognized that totalitarian environments are made possible when freedom without responsibility for the public good goes unchecked. In situations where people do not take responsibility for their actions, a practical dialectic emerges wherein a swing from one extreme to another guides policy. For example, it is not unusual for a dictator to move from the extreme of individual rejection of authority to an autocratic keeper of order. Lippmann conceptualized the rise of a dictator as a misplaced effort to compensate for the anarchy invited by individual chaos and refusal of corporate responsibility.

Walter Lippmann warned against two extremes: on the one hand, totalitarianism, and on the other hand, too much power assumed by the individual without concern for the public good. He reminded us of the practical need for a public philosophy that calls us to "civility," suggesting concern for the public good while being wary of building a country on the "private" beliefs of the people. A significant and interesting insight from Lippmann that needs to be underscored is his connection between "private" and "mass." A "mass" of people can be guided by "private" thoughts that simply tend to be in momentary agreement. Lippmann's concern is that "mass" often equates to large numbers of people being emotively led to follow "self interest," rather than public interest (1955, 32–38). Private emotion can be carried out collectively without any commitment to a public narrative that binds a people together.

The theme of *To Kill a Mockingbird* (Lee 1960) makes this point vividly when the lynch crowd forms. The "mass" of men are held together by visceral impulses of hate. What appears or poses as "public" action is actually only a collection of individuals gathered in a "mass" and held in union by the convenient junction of "private" emotions held by multiple people. In this case, the "mass" is a collection of private emotions held in common. A public narrative—or, using Walter Lippmann's (1955) language, a "public philosophy"—requires reflective and deliberative skills, not merely the coincidence of multiple and similar emotional outbursts. One must ask not only "What is right for 'me'?," but "What is right for this historical moment?," "What is right for 'us'?," and "What is best for the 'common good?'" The answer to each of these questions may not be the same, but the overall theme needs to be consistent: good public policy has a tradition of concern for the "common good," requiring that personal restraint and conviction are not held captive to emotions called forth in a given moment of action.

To explain Walter Lippmann's (1955) position, one of the authors uses the following example in a course centered around "Ethics and Responsibility in Communication." Upon approaching the voting booth to cast a ballot, this author proceeds as a citizen holding various positions and roles: father, husband, teacher, male, middle-class, Christian, and American. This author often votes for candidates whose positions differ from his own private view but are historically needed public positions. In a democracy based upon the support of diversity, one votes not for a single issue—rather, one should attempt to vote in a manner capable of assisting the public good, not just oneself. Of course, we can and should debate what may assist the common good or the public good. Discussing specifics may place us in opposition, however we can still be held together by a commitment to discover the "common good" at any given historical moment. If Lippmann is right, voting needs to be done not out of one's private role or value, but out of a public view of what is needed for the common good—one's private value and the public good do not always equate. Argument over what is good for us—the common good—is important; rejection of a common concern undercuts a democratic community.

This combination of potential private opposition on specific instances and general commitment to a public narrative of the common good is not a mere contradiction; this is a vibrant and alive democracy in action. We are called to vote for public, not private concerns. Such a philosophy reminds us that voting is not for "me," but for "us." There is no guarantee that agreement over what constitutes the common good will be easy to determine. A concern for the common good, however, is a practical way to remind oneself of the responsibilities of being a citizen within a public philosophy that attempts to make a place for many people, not just for "me" or "people like me."

Walter Lippmann's own words, written shortly after World War II, may be even more applicable for us today than when he first penned them:

> In this pluralized and fragmenting society a public philosophy with common and binding principles was more necessary than it had ever been. The proof of the need is in the impulse to escape from freedom, which Erich Fromm has described so well. It has been growing stronger as the emancipation of the masses of the people from authority has brought the dissolution of the public, general, objective criteria of the true and the false, the right and the wrong. . . . But until the historic disasters of our own time, the loneliness and anxiety of modern men had been private, without public and overt political effect. As long as the public order still provided external security. . . . Observing the public disorder in which he himself had always lived, and knowing how the inner disorder provoked the impulse to escape it, Hitler conceived his doctrine . . . *Mein Kampf.* (1955, 85–86)

If one reads the above as a longing for some universal posture, a major point has been missed in applying Lippmann's work to dialogic civility. We are working dialectically and trying to walk the "narrow ridge" (Buber 1947/1965a, 168) between the two extremes of a single universal public position and an infinite number of private positions being pushed upon the public as the position to follow. Our goal is not to magically arrive at the public position to undergird interpersonal communication, but to admit that we are in significant need of conversation about the need for public narratives, no matter how seemingly impossible such a task appears to be.

Emotivism and forgotten narratives have invited a world of interpersonal talk centering around "meism" and "rights" that misses the call for concern about "us" and the common good. No matter how elusive concerns for the "common good" may seem, they are at least pointed to by narrative guidelines. As Mary Ann Glendon stated so well in *Rights Talk: The Impoverishment of Political Discourse*:

The strident rights rhetoric that currently dominates American political discourse poorly serves the strong tradition of protection for individual freedom for which the United States is justly renowned. Our stark, simple rights dialect puts a damper on the processes of public justification, communication, and deliberation upon which the continuing vitality of a democratic regime depends. It contributes to the erosion of the habits, practices, and attitudes of respect for others that are the ultimate and surest guarantors of human rights. It impedes creative long-range thinking about our most pressing social problems. Our rights-laden public discourse easily accommodates the economic, the immediate, and the personal dimensions of a problem, while it regularly neglects the moral, the long-term, and the social implications. (1991, 171)

To live life without a narrative base is a failed experiment. Our teachers did not make a narrativeless journey; they walked with implicit narratives and then talked an emotive game. Now, however, is the historical time to once again co-constitute narrative structures, time once again to open background narrative conversation about why, not just how to implement interpersonal concepts.

A Narrative Ethic for Interpersonal Discourse

In this historical moment of diversity in the workplace, school, and neighborhood, interpersonal communication cannot be limited to the private domain. Connecting the terms *public, narrative,* and *interpersonal communication* can be accomplished without destroying private, intimate discourse between long-term friends. Dialogic civility is not offered as private, but as a public interpersonal model in an era of diversity.

Charles Taylor, in *The Ethics of Authenticity* (1991), made a similar point that some language that can be taken as self-centered may actually have a moral base. Taylor stated that we cannot simply lament that many people are nourished by the language of self-actualization and authenticity. He does not see this language or world view quickly leaving the contemporary scene. Yet he simultaneously recognizes that such an approach will generate social fragmentation and division unless we can find a way to place this notion of authenticity within a context that provides a narrative context for understanding the other.

Charles Taylor further rejects the extremes of the authenticity movement and the extremes of technology. He questions those who choose one side in opposition to the other. He points to an authenticity of self that can use technology without becoming lost in the process. Our vision of dialogic civility is similar. We call for a dialogue that lives within today's historical world of technology and information accumulation, while understanding that human wisdom asks how, when, why, and for whom such information will be used for potentially bettering the human community. Our public view of dialogue for our historical era cannot turn to a Romantic past. We must carve a human future in an era of technology and activities of today's world—a future in which public respect for person, text, and historical moment can still be a guide.

A communicative emphasis on dialogic civility as a public background for interpersonal discourse is driven not by undue optimism, but by the interaction of theory, action, and experience converging upon a similar road calling for an alternative to untamed individualist impulses in a postmodern age. Our perspective on interpersonal communication presupposes a willingness to accept a public level of concern for the welfare of the other. One of the authors was called by an associate superintendent of an upper-middle-class school system and asked to provide a workshop on communication skills to students. The author, instead, wanted to discuss the notions of background and foreground, why and how, reason to act and implementation, but considered another act instead. He asked the associate superintendent to meet with the wealthy students and ask them to define empathy, caring, and active listening.

After a number of focus group sessions, the associate superintendent stated that he was amazed how clear students were about the definitions. At that point the author stated, "They know how; they just do not know *why* they should care for another." After a long pause, the associate superintendent stated, "We have a bigger problem than can be addressed in a workshop, don't we?" The answer was, "Yes, but remember it is *our* problem—not just the students' problem. *Why* is the agenda for twenty-first century communication, even as much as a technological *how*."

We assert that in this historical moment one person cannot take for granted that another person would want to take the time and energy to address him or her as a human being in the midst of an interpersonal exchange. Seyla Benhabib and Fred Dallmayr, in *The Communicative Ethics Controversy*, center their work around a phrase that has metaphorical and practical import for this project, "a fragmented universe of value" (1990, 365). In such a diverse historical moment we simply cannot assume people's agreement on virtue structures. If such a virtue is of importance, as we contend, then we must open the conversation, present views, and air the call for some form of public narrative background for interpersonal communication to take place.

Granted, any public narrative effort will be historical, limited, and open to constant reassessment. But in the spirit of David Tracy's *Plurality and Ambiguity: Hermeneutics, Religion, Hope*, we accept:

> There is no release for any of us from the conflict of interpretations. . . . The alternative is not an escape into the transient pleasures of irony or a flight into despair and cynicism. The alternative is not a new kind of innocence or passivity masking apathy. Whoever fights for hope, fights on behalf of us all. Whoever acts on that hope, acts in a manner worthy of a human being. (1987, 114)

Our point is that this difficult task is made impossible, if we persist on trying to locate common ground at the private level of discourse. Working on the public background set of assumptions we may find common ground that can transcend many of our private value positions. Previously assumed conclusions are in dispute, but we still need to reach out to one another using behaviors that are civil and that keep conversation going in the midst of difference.

We point to the need for a narrative ethic that reminds us of the importance of the other and moves us from a *cul de sac* of narcissism (Arnett 1997d). Such an ethic lies at the heart of an author such as Emmanuel Levinas's work. In *Time and the Other*, Levinas pointed to the importance of three themes central to this work: historicality, intersubjectivity, and relationship between humans in time. "The situation of the face-to-face would be the very accomplishment of time; the encroachment of the present on the future is not the feat of the subject alone, but the intersubjective relationship. The condition of time lies in the relationship between humans, or in history" (1947/1987, 79). We posit an ethical stance of dialogic civility, which takes seriously the notion of the other and the historical moment in which the exchange occurs. However, such a position does not in any way assume affirmation of another's ideas or actions. Our effort is to offer a dialogic view of communication in the public domain with full awareness that such a backdrop for communication will not always be possible. When dialogic civility as a narrative guides interaction it only keeps the conversation going; it does not assure compliance and agreement.

We call for a public dialogue that seeks minimal common ground between interpersonal communicators. The chance of discovering that common ground is less likely as we further advance into a postmodern culture of individuation and atomization of interests and connections, but no less needed. This project walks within the spirit of Charles Taylor's effort to counter "the danger [of] . . . fragmentation—that is, a people increasingly less capable of forming a common purpose and carrying it out" (1991, 112). We offer dialogic civility as an intentional background for understanding and meeting the other in conversation, interpersonally.

Following the insight of Muzafer Sherif (1958), we seek a superordinate goal of a public background of information that can guide our interpersonal communication in a world of difference with a base of minimal agreement. We offer dialogic civility in the spirit of a common-ground requirement calling for an appreciation of diversity. We want to embrace two ends of the dialectic of diversity simultaneously: the need for diversity, and a public bias that works to find a human connection in the center of significant ideological, racial, ethnic, gender, and socioeconomic diversity.

We accept that we are in a moral crisis in which little public agreement exists on what constitutes public virtues that will guide us in interaction with one another. However, our response is not despair. A tough-minded hope described by Christopher Lasch— hope that lives in company with disappointment; hope that knows that further disappointment will eventually meet us, yet endures— is now needed. Lasch called us to reject a "frail optimism" for a sturdier and more realistic sense of hope (1991, 80–81).

As we frame a narrative of dialogic civility for undergirding interpersonal communication, Lasch's understanding of hope assists in two ways. First, a hopeful dialogic civility must reject the impulse for frailness and unrecognized limitations of the aesthetic. Second, hope in this task is not so much that we might be right, but that the effort is worthy of doing. In this historical moment, we need to find ways to both affirm and link our diversity. Realistic hope capable of walking with disappointment keeps alive the conversation—about "us," not just "me." Dialogic civility vies for acceptance as a public narrative that can guide our interpersonal inter-action in dialogue encouraging public civil respect for one another. Part II of this work examines how a number of writers addressed decline of a metanarrative. The final part of *Dialogic Civility in a Cynical Age: Community, Hope, and Interpersonal Relationships* outlines a temporal narrative for interpersonal discourse, dialogic civility.

Part II

Interpersonal Voices

Part II examines the work of interpersonal writers under the lens of the historically based question of declining metanarrative. We explore three dialogic approaches that, in part, contribute to our story of dialogic civility. "Narrative Decline: Interpersonal Dialogue and Self" offers a dialectical alternative to blind institutional support in a time of declining metanarrative. "Narrative Confrontation: Interpersonal Dialogue and Crisis" points to how genuine oppression and social change can meet through a courageous spirit of dialogue. "Narrative Construction: Interpersonal Dialogue and Story" suggests why narrative is still needed as a guide in interpersonal discourse.

Section 1

Narrative Decline:
Interpersonal Dialogue and Self

*C*hapter *F*ive

Carl Rogers

A Voice of Pragmatic Optimism

Experiential Knowing—

Knowledge *about* is not the most important thing in the behavioral sciences today. There is a decided surge of experiential knowing, of knowing at the gut level, which has to do with the human being. . . . I would like, rather than talking to you *about* communication, to communicate with you at a feeling level.

—Carl Rogers, *A Way of Being*

Interpersonal Communication—

I trust that you will see in these experiences some of the elements of growth-promoting interpersonal communication that have had meaning for me. A sensitive ability to hear, a deep satisfaction in being heard; an ability to be more real, which in turn brings forth more realness from others; and consequently a greater freedom to give and receive love—these, in my experience, are the elements that make interpersonal communication enriching and enhancing.

—Carl Rogers, *A Way of Being*

Howard Kirschenbaum (1979) on Carl Rogers—

With some emotional distance and some historical perspective, we can perceive things that Rogers could not—just as Rogers perceived things thirty years ago that many of us are only beginning to understand and assimilate today. We can love someone and still see him or her objectively, the good and the bad, separate from our own projections. This is what I have attempted to do—neither hide my affection for the man and his ideas, nor gloss over the occasions when he was not at his best, as a scientist, as a practitioner, or as a person. If I have failed to maintain this balanced perspective throughout, my error is surely on the side of affection. (xvii)

—*On Becoming Carl Rogers*

C arl Rogers is an essential figure in any interpretive study on a dialogic view of interpersonal communication (see for example Anderson and Cissna 1997; Anderson, Cissna, and Arnett 1994). Rogers's life and work provided the foundational base from which his twentieth-century humanistic psychological understanding of interpersonal communication was encouraged and shaped. Rogers's remarkable career withstood attacks from psychotherapists, behaviorists, and even rhetoricians. Rogers was a model of what Buber (1947/1965a) called a "great character"; he understood his psychological tradition well enough to challenge it where and when necessary. In many ways Rogers's biographer is correct; Rogers's orientation is "as American as apple pie" (Kirschenbaum 1979, 138). He was optimistic, willing to explore new territory, and a genuine supporter of individuals against systems that curtail personal growth. Rogers's "nonjudgmental" orientation toward the person was both philosophical and political. He offered interpersonal grace to the person; however, his understanding of institutions and corporate life was much less generous.

This chapter addresses Rogers's contribution to interpersonal communication, centered on the importance of self and the innate wisdom of individuals. Rogers's work holds continuing insight for our historical moment today with his call for confidence in the self at the initial stages of metanarrative decline. The dialogic self is an important element of dialogic civility when narrative-rich persons become aware of institutional corruption and narrative decline and must rely upon their own resources.

Introduction

Carl Rogers's work revolved around trust—trust in the person, rather than in institutions or philosophical systems. Rogers affirmed the innate goodness of the person while simultaneously cautioning against an unknowing introjection of institutional and philosophical value systems into one's life. His person-centered message contributed to a communication revolution that was equally anti-institutional and deeply supportive of the constructive nature of human potential.

The keynote of Carl Rogers's practical and scholarly projects was trust in the person and suspicion of philosophical systems and institutions that in a previous historical moment had outlined the notion of the "good life." He no longer trusted philosophical systems or institutions as capable of providing a helpful background for shaping communicative interaction patterns with others. Rogers sensed what postmodern scholarship now details—narrative meaning structures, philosophically and institutionally, were in substantive decline (Benhabib 1992, Lasch 1984, MacIntyre 1981/1984).

Racism, sexism, deep divisions over an unpopular war (Vietnam), and the resignation of President Richard Nixon prior to inevitable impeachment laced the daily landscape of conversation in the lives of Carl Rogers's patients. However, more correctly, Rogers's work became conceptual at the conclusion of the Nuremberg trials, where individual conscience was called as the alternative to blind institutional commitment. Working in a historical moment of increasing distrust toward institutions, it is not surprising that Carl Rogers's practice would lead him to look for alternative ways to support and guide lives. He discovered what he called an innate sense of wisdom that guided the people with whom he worked. Rogers believed if people would only follow this innate sense of self-wisdom, many would find themselves on the road to health. Questioning narrative guidelines of institutions, culture, and religion led him to trust in the self.

Carl Rogers did not elicit his insights from the writings of Michel Foucault (1980), Jacques Derrida (1987), or Jean-Francois Lyotard (1988). Rogers discovered what we term "narrative decline" in the practice of therapy with his clients. Commonsense questions and concerns of patients moved him intuitively to conclusions about the loss of metanarratives. Rogers's faith in the person emerged from the practice of therapy, as he observed people making good decisions, putting their lives together, and changing their reactions to circumstances as they listened constructively to themselves. His clients were unable to find insight, aid, and assistance from a declining metanarrative structure that previously offered guidance. The healthy nature of his patients' personal values emerged when the self, not metanarratives became the focus.

Instead of universal values "out there," or a universal value system imposed by some group—philosophers, rulers, or priests—we have the possibility of universal human value directions emerging from the experiencing of the human organism. Evidence from therapy indicates that both personal and social values emerge as natural, and experienced, when the individual is close to his [or her] own organismic valuing process. (Rogers and Stevens 1967/1972, 20)

Rogers was certain he had discovered a positive alternative to a fading virtue structure, no longer capable of offering a moral story suitable for the continuing development of the human person. He uncovered the value of the self as a constructive guiding force for not only communication between persons, but for directing a personal "good life."

The Rogerian approach to the person contributed to a revolution in interpersonal discourse. An unprecedented change emerged in communication theory; the person took center stage. Attention to script and drama of the play (narrative guidance) faded before the power, talent, and innate wisdom of the impromptu actor—the human self. Carl Rogers functioned as a communicative prophet proclaiming the innate wisdom of the human agent. He may not have proposed *the* solution to declining confidence in metanarrative structures, but he understood that the pulse of change was calling for different ways to guide lives in constructive directions. From this historical standpoint of awareness of metanarrative decline and perhaps collapse, we ask the following question about Rogers's work: "How can the dialogic self be a constructive guide in light of institutional disruption and metanarrative decline?"

Significance of Carl Rogers's Life and Practice

The significance of Carl Rogers's life and practice is far-reaching. Rogers's work can be understood in terms of his historical contribution to the field of humanistic psychology as well as religious institutions, families, and educational settings. Rogers's emphasis on the self was offered as an alternative to confidence in institutions and revealed pragmatic optimism of the self in a confused institutional era of metanarrative decline.

A Founding Voice

Carl Rogers was one of the founders of the Association of Humanistic Psychology, formed in 1961 (Kirschenbaum 1979). He was one of the major figures in the development of "third force psychology." First force psychology was based upon the work of psychoanalysis— Sigmund Freud (1900/1914, 1910, 1933), Carl Jung (1916, 1922), and Alfred Adler (1929/1964). In one form or another, the concept of the unconscious was central to each of the above approaches. Second force psychology, based upon the work of John B. Watson (1919) and later B. F. Skinner (1971), stated that the person was moved to action by "environmental contingencies" (18). The common thread of the above two approaches (psychoanalysis and behaviorism) was that the person was propelled by an unchosen force. In the case of psychoanalysis, the person was driven by the unconscious. In the case of behaviorism, the person was motivated by the environment. Rogers and others, such as Abraham Maslow (1954/1970a), offered a uniquely American alternative in which the image of the human was founded upon choice, growth, and a constructive assumption about the human's potential for good. The concept of "third force" implies psychology with a human face, where choice and development of human possibilities guide interaction with the other.

Richard Farson (1975), in an essay "Carl Rogers, Quiet Revolutionary," provided a thoughtful summary of the life contribution of this major interpersonal voice who almost singlehandedly changed the picture of American communication:

> [Rogers] has changed the way we all think about human relationship, the expectations we have about intimate personal contact, the nature of interpersonal and organizational behavior. Without realizing it he has revolutionized our ideas about human affairs. It is in the process that he has changed individuals by the millions. . . . As we become aware of the social and political consequences of the authoritarian movement, I believe they will be replaced by a new insistence on the dignity and worth of the individual and the right to self-determination. [Rogers's ideas] . . . dignify us as persons. We recognize that Rogers cares most about the quality and integrity of relationships and the protection of human rights. When all the varied approaches are weighed, we will see that his protects people best because it protects them against those of us who think we know what's good for them. (xxxix, xliii)

Rogers provided an image of humans with dignity, ability to choose, and innate impulses toward the healthy, noble, and good. In Rogers's (1989) own words, "it is not surprising that I object to the process of depersonalization and dehumanization of the individual which I see in this culture" (266). Rogers wanted not only interpersonal communication to be humane, but for a world to take on a human face, not a corporate image.

Scope of Carl Rogers's Influence

Carl Rogers's voice was heard well beyond the realm of therapy. In many ways, he was an icon of early interpersonal approaches to communication. He spoke to people who wanted to alter a society that focused primarily on institutions and was seemingly uninterested in the individual person. The longing for a voice like Rogers's came after World War II and was further nurtured by the Vietnam war, Watergate, and people's loss of trust in public discourse. Rogers attempted to answer a question that grew louder with each decade, "Where does one look for answers in an era in which authority figures and institutions are no longer trustworthy?"

The extent of Carl Rogers's influence was driven greatly by audience perception that institutions were genuinely in trouble. The following passage outlines the tone of Rogers's (1969) concerns, demonstrating just how unique his perspective was and in some cases still is:

> Teaching, in my estimating, is a vastly over-rated function. . . . Teaching means to "instruct." Personally I am not much interested in instructing another in what he [or she] should know or think. "To impart knowledge or skill." My reaction is, why not be more efficient, using a book or programmed learning? "To make to know." Here my hackles rise. I have no wish to *make* anyone know something. "To show, guide, direct." As I see it, too many people have been shown, guided, directed. So I come to the conclusion that I *do* mean what I said. Teaching is, for me, a relatively unimportant and vastly overvalued activity. (103)

Some people may remember such a perspective being introduced into education. Others now witness the results of an educational system much more interested in promoting students' self-esteem than in delivering a content driven education (Sykes 1995). Educators offered the student survival skills in a time of narrative decline, trust in the self. Such a message is of significant value when a narrative remnant is known and understood: the self is still story-informed by the narrative remnant. When the remnant ceases to inform, the focus on the self becomes an opportunity for self-absorption or confusion.

Our work guided by narrative suggests that Carl Rogers was in conversation with people (clients) who had earlier been given clear narrative guidelines about various versions of the "good life." People who came to Rogers needed someone to support them by listening to what they had already absorbed and to assist them in discerning what to keep and what to reject. As institutions became more confused, the stories of the past no longer guided many people toward a safer haven. However, a remnant of past narrative education from family, friends, and church provided guidance for the "self"; the self picked and chose from the remnant remains of narrative life to compose a structure that could direct one's life.

Through practice, Carl Rogers (1961) began to sense the following:

> Another trend which is evident in this process of becoming a person is related to the source or locus of choices and decision or evaluative judgments. The individual increasingly comes to feel that this locus of evaluation lies within himself [or herself]. Less and less does he [or she] look to others for approval or disapproval; for standards to live by; for decision and choices. He [or she] recognizes that it rests with himself [or herself] to choose; that the only question which matters is, "Am I living in a way which is deeply satisfying to me, and which truly expresses me?" This I think is perhaps *the* most important question for the creative individual. (119)

In a time of metanarrative decline Rogers brought the person to a self focus away from the unhealthy introjection of institutional values. Such a task was needed and at times is still warranted in places of institutional corruption.

The Quiet Revolutionary

Carl Rogers wrote in an interesting time in the development of modernity. His historical moment pointed both to how much the human could accomplish and to the evil that unrestrained institutional systems could inflict upon the world. With a sensitive ear, Rogers became aware of an era coming to an end. The status quo could not be trusted and the only place to look for answers was within the self. The self could be flexible and change when needed, relieved of having to follow orders that no longer made sense in a changing world. The self could be responsive to unique situations that arose:

> He [or she] senses, he [or she] feels that it is satisfying and enhancing. Or when he [or she] acts in a defensive fashion, it is his [or her] own organism that feels the immediate and short-term satisfaction of being protected and that also senses the longer-range dissatisfaction of having to remain on guard. He [or she] makes a choice between two courses of action, fearfully and hesitantly, not knowing whether or not he [or she] has weighed their values accurately. But then he [or she] discovers that he [or she] may let the evidence of his [or her] own experience indicate whether he [or she] has chosen satisfyingly. He [or she] discovers that he [or she] does not need to know whose are the correct values; through the data supplied by his [or her] own organism, he [or she] can experience what is satisfying and enhancing. He [or she] can put his [or her] confidence in a valuing *process*, rather than in some rigid, introjected *system* of values. (Rogers 1951/1965, 522)

Rogers's revolution is summarized in the movement from introjected values of the establishment to a deep confidence in the individual self.

Carl Rogers's insight and optimism was clearly part of his deeply American character and the historical moment of his contribution. Rogers's voice, at times, sounded like a therapeutic pioneer living in a log cabin of hope and optimism—willing to go to town to work, but knowing that life is ultimately made good by solitary integrity and knowledge on the farm—guided by trust in the self. Just as many pioneers moved from narratives of religious persecution and aristocratic power that no longer worked for them, Rogers was trying to locate a voice that made sense of a changing and problematic historical moment. Such a voice was a lonely cry guided by instincts and the awareness of interpersonal chaos resulting from declining narrative structures.

Early in his career, one of the authors outlined the differences between the works of Carl Rogers and Martin Buber. Rob Anderson disagreed with that portrayal of Rogers. A scholarly dialogue ensued. Anderson (1982) and Arnett (1982) were encouraged to meet by John Stewart (1995a, 1995b, 1996). Arnett and Anderson each held different views regarding the nature of Rogers's and Buber's work. After multiple panel presentations and collaboration on an edited book entitled *The Reach of Dialogue* (Anderson, Cissna, and Arnett 1994), the central theme of this project emerged: dialogic insight needs to be guided by commonsense questions about how a theory or an author's body of work attempts to answer questions significant to a given historical moment. What was learned from the praxis of that ongoing scholarly conversation was that interest in dialogue requires responding to a theory itself in dialogue—being respectful of the historical moment of its birth and the questions it sought to answer. A particular dialogic theory seeks to answer questions grounded in the historical moment—not to provide ahistorical universal wisdom. Rogers functioned practically with this same assumption. Rogers's confidence was in what we call a "story-filled" self that was required to pick and choose insights from previously unchallenged narrative structures.

Communicative Focus

Whether one agrees with or contests the work of Carl Rogers, his contribution to interpersonal communication is irrefutable. Rogers was a major force in the communication shift of focus from institutional narratives to the individual person—to listening to the self. One of the initial books on interpersonal communication in the area of communication studies was Charles T. Brown and Paul W. Keller's (1973) *Monologue to Dialogue: An Exploration of Interpersonal Communication*. Their work announced much of Rogers's influence in shifting the image of communication from a focus on the message to an emphasis on listening, which includes being heard by the other and listening to the other. Self-listening and listening to the other, "person listening" (Brown and Keller 1973, 204), was introduced as a major focus in the initial stages of interpersonal communication. The implications of Brown and Keller's work was that the message began to take a back seat to the human subject.

Carl Rogers brought the concept of the person into daily popular conversation. He proclaimed, at times like a polite secular evangelist, that the central focus of interpersonal relationships must be concern for human feelings, human relationships, and the human potential of the communicator. Rogers's interpersonal voice announced the importance of treating another like a "person," bringing the value of listening to national popular attention, moving the locus of communicative attention from institutional narratives and philosophical systems outside the person to the individual self.

Carl Rogers, perhaps more than any other writer in the humanistic psychological movement, shifted our communicative focus of attention not only to the self but away from a restricted religious narrative. Rogers (1980) began by deeply questioning the religious narrative of his youth. "Let me begin with my childhood. In a narrowly fundamentalist religious home, I introjected the value attitude toward others that were held by my parents" (27). He intuitively understood that a narrative shift from a religious metanarrative was in process.

One additional component that enlightened Carl Rogers to the decline of narrative structures was the abuse of authority. Anyone who has been unfairly treated by an employer, parent, teacher, or institution begins to think of "me." Trust in the other and in ideals are put at risk each time an additional accumulation of negative experiences are unfairly added to life encounters with authority figures. To abused people, and the number was not small then and is not decreasing today, Rogers offered a sense of hope. Even if everything is going wrong, this creation, called a "person," the "I," the "self," is capable of providing good direction.

Historical Grounding

Our admiration for Carl Rogers does not only rest upon his "penultimate" (Bonhoeffer 1949/1955, 120–187) trust in the self after the lessons of World War II. Our contemporary appreciation of Rogers is nourished by his intuitive insight into an era of communicative change and the importance of listening for what was an appropriate response at that time in history. Rogers was a sensitive practitioner who did what was needed for his given historical moment. Danger emerges when the historical moment is past and a theory that no longer appropriately addresses the current historical situation continues to be applied in everyday life.

In the following quotation Howard Kirschenbaum (1979) questions the lack of historical grounding of Carl Rogers's ideas:

> R. S. Peters of the University of London's Institute of Education wrote . . . "one begins to understand the free-floating character of the book [*Freedom to Learn*], its lack of any proper historical, social, or philosophical dimensions. It is not really an attempt to think systematically about the actual problems of teaching and learning in a concrete historical context. It is Carl Rogers 'doing his thing' in the context of education." (379)

We do not concur with Kirschenbaum's assessment. Rogers did his job and did it well. He called attention to a narrative decline. He offered a practical solution that worked for that historical moment. However, if we are to use Rogers's material today, we must make sure the historical moment calls for the natural application of his answers to particular commonsense questions. People coming from a strong narrative upbringing in which that narrative is now in dispute can still benefit from Rogers's insights.

In the practice of therapy, Carl Rogers listened and offered an alternative to declining narrative structures. In our words, he took people who knew stories of the good life from a time when the narrative structures were strong and asked them to adapt those stories to the needs of a new historical moment. Rogers asked the person to listen to the self, because the self was story-laden. Others that later assumed a Rogerian posture were caught off guard in historical situations where the self was no longer story-laden. When the self is no longer informed by rich narrative structures of the past it becomes an abstract text and something strange emerges—what Christopher Lasch (1978/1979) called *The Culture of Narcissism*. As time passed, focus on self turned from a solution into a problem. Rogers's work did not invite narcissism. However, the use of a self-focused terminology when the dialectic of a story-filled past was no longer in place permitted an understanding of narcissism, giving birth to what Lasch called a *Minimal Self* (1984).

An Optimistic Listener

A major key to Carl Rogers's work was his reputation as an outstanding listener, revealed in the following quotation from Howard Kirschenbaum and Valerie Land Henderson (1989):

Almost everyone who knew him, personally or professionally, from Ohio State onward, regarded him as the best listener they had ever met. Rogers not only popularized the term *empathy*, but more than anyone else demonstrated its potency in therapy, education, and all human relationships. . . .

As Rogers developed a reputation as the generation's leading proponent of good listening and clear communication, it was not surprising that participating in or witnessing a conversation with Carl Rogers became a memorable and sought-after experience. He was often invited to participate in panel discussions and dialogues with leading members of the helping professions, and eventually he was asked to participate in dialogues with some of the leading intellectual figures of the twentieth century. (5–6)

Rogers did what few males were able to do well in the immediate post–World War II America. He listened. Instead of wanting to be a conversational "boss," Rogers brought understanding to communicative life. He moved the focus from communicative domination to partners in conversation as he listened and learned from the ill, the needy, and the confused.

Carl Rogers's work revolved not only around the notion of listening, but an optimistic view of listening. He was not moved by existential *angst*. A genuine confidence in the other's finding his or her own way guided his research, counseling, indeed his life. The authentic depth of his spirit of optimism was an "event" in itself; people wanted to rub shoulders with an optimist that did not tell, but listened.

The optimism that propelled Carl Rogers's world view connects with the narrative of the American Dream and confidence in the notion of progress, which loomed large in the historical moment of Rogers's early contribution. His confidence in listening to the self might have been guided by a narrative background of optimism that one is hard pressed to discover in today's world of corporate downsizing and ethnic disputes. Rogers's early work emerged out of the immediate post–World War II era of prosperity and confidence in the future that was previously unknown by the United States. His popular work during the 1960s, 1970s, and 1980s was generated by optimism of a historical period that survived a great Depression and witnessed a country enter a great war as underdogs and emerge victors.

Our contention is that Carl Rogers was deeply moved by the optimistic narrative of the American Dream, at least as outlined by Alexis de Tocqueville (1889):

Americans love their towns for much the same reasons that highlanders love their mountains. In both cases the native land has emphatic and peculiar features; it has a more pronounced physiognomy than is found elsewhere.

In general, New England townships lead a happy life. Their government is to their taste as well as of their choice. With profound peace and material prosperity prevailing in America, there are few storms in municipal life. The township's interests are easy to manage. Moreover, the people's political education has been completed long ago, or rather they were already educated when they settled there. In New England there is not even a memory of distinctions in rank, so there is no part of the community tempted to oppress the rest, and injustices which affect only isolated individuals are forgotten in the general contentment. (Tocqueville 1835/1969, 69–70)

Although Tocqueville provided a romanticized view of America, Rogers recognized the image as one that recognized human potential amidst the reality of everyday life.

Ernest Bormann (1985), in *The Force of Fantasy: Restoring the American Dream*, discussed a particular form of communication that seems to be uniquely American and committed to offering a better world when a perceived evil becomes too powerful: "The tradition is Protestant, popular, pragmatic, and romantic. Practitioners of the tradition of romantic pragmatism tended to be reformers whose persuasion was largely cast into religious, recurring rhetorical forms whose basic vision was a conservative one of the restoration of an existentially good society to its former glory" (25). Carl Rogers was, in some ways, a Protestant preacher offering a pragmatic, popular, and romantic answer to narrative change—listen to the self and answers will emerge. Such a message fell on fertile emotional American soil.

Central Concepts in Carl Rogers's Work

The core of Carl Rogers's work revolves around three major themes: self, innate wisdom of the organism, and relationship. Rogers focused on self as fundamentally constructive, if one listens to the organism. This results in the invitation to positive relationships.

Self

Self is the center of Carl Rogers's work. In hermeneutics, there needs to be a text that commands one's attention and response. Rogers's text was the notion of the self. Rogers invited a patient to interpret his or her own life, making sense of oneself. Rogers (1980) used "nonjudgmental reflection" to let another hear his or her own words in order to begin to make sense of events for himself or herself (138–139). For Rogers, the interpretive focus of life is centered around the entity called the self and the final interpreter of life is the individual.

> Rogers' theory was also a "self theory," the *self* being one very important part of a person's phenomenal field. Here he followed a recent tradition in psychology, a relatively new school of thought, which regarded the *self* as the "organizing and creative and adaptive cope of personality" which was most influential in determining a person's behavior. For Rogers the self was "the organized, consistent conceptual gestalt" [i.e., overall picture] composed of perceptions of the characteristics of the "I" or "me" and the perceptions of the relations of the "I" or "me" to others and to various aspects of life, together with the values attached to their perceptions. (Kirschenbaum 1979, 238)

The notion of the self is somewhat amorphous. What is clear is that the self is both the organizing and the evaluative center for the person. Rogers placed his trust here, not in institutional and philosophical narrative structures.

The self permitted a foundation for change. The personal memory of the self, released from institutional and philosophical narratives, was short and trustworthy—making the call of change and freedom more attractive than introjected values (Rogers 1951/1965). The following quotation, from *Becoming Partners*, points to romantic love, trust of freedom, and what Rogers (1961) called "fully functioning selves" (183–198):

> Change and freedom, especially when they are meant "for real," are terms which make the American public shiver in its boots. We seem to hate to remember that this was a nation molded by revolutionaries, both nonviolent and violent. So perhaps we will be too frightened to say to members of part-

nerships of various kinds; "You *are* free; we accept the inevitability, and the conceivably great advantages, of *change*." (Rogers 1972, 214)

Rogers viewed the organizing and evaluating quality of the self to be more than sufficient to permit a person to be a risk taker—one who enjoys the journey of change more than the stability of tradition.

A major goal of Carl Rogers was shredding notions and ideas that clouded the vision of the self. First, he wanted the person to move away from facades and to be who he or she really is at the core. Second, Rogers (1961) encouraged a movement from "oughts" (168). The self, not a set of a priori values, needs to inform a person's behavior. Third, Rogers called for movement away from being *The Organization Man* (Whyte 1956/1957), who met the expectations of others and attempted to please others, to an organism confident of self-direction and willing to follow an uncertain process of change. "To be what he [or she] truly is, this is the path of life which he [or she] appears to value most highly, when he [or she] is free to move in any direction. It is not simply an intellectual value choice, but seems to be the best description of the griping, tentative, uncertain behaviors by which he [or she] moves exploringly toward what he [or she] wants to be" (Rogers 1961, 176). Rogers wanted persons to shed confidence in introjected answers from failing institutions, listening instead to the self.

Innate Wisdom of the Human Organism

Carl Rogers suggested that the human is innately able to determine the right course of action. If one can get in touch with the deepest sense of self, a constructive action, idea, or direction will emerge.

> *This person would find his [or her] organism a trustworthy means of arriving at the most satisfying behavior in each existential situation.* He [or she] would do what "felt right" in this immediate moment and he [or she] would find this in general to be a competent and trustworthy guide to his [or her] behavior. . . . [A] person would find his [or her] organism a trustworthy means of viscerally arriving at the most satisfying behavior in each situation. (Rogers 1969, 286)

Rogers could trust the self, because of his conviction that the self had self-directed positive tendencies.

> I have little sympathy with the rather prevalent concept that man [or woman] is basically irrational, and thus his [or her] impulses, if not controlled, would lead to destruction of others and self. Man's [or woman's] behavior is exquisitely rational, moving with subtle and ordered complexity toward the goals his [or her] organism is endeavoring to achieve. The tragedy for most of us is that our defenses keep us from being aware of this rationality, so that consciously we are moving in one direction, while organismatically we are moving in another. (Rogers 1969, 291)

Rogers's confidence came from the conviction that the self is guided by an innate sense of positive direction, the self can be trusted. Confidence in the direction of the human organism permitted Rogers to reach out in relationship to another person. His theory is based upon relational patience. If one can be patient enough and work with another long enough, one will assist the other in getting in touch with the constructive self.

Relationship

Carl Rogers invited quality relationships; he placed the importance of relationship over the informative content of a message. "It is simply that in a wide variety of professional work involving relationships with people—whether as a psychotherapist, teacher, religious worker, guidance counselor, social worker, clinical psychologist—it is the *quality* of the interpersonal encounter with the client which is the most significant element in determining effectiveness" (Rogers and Stevens 1967/1972, 85). To invite a relational focus with another requires empathy (understanding the other's inner world), congruence (connection between how one feels and how one acts), unconditional positive regard (genuine concern for the other), and finally the other's perception of the first three.

Carl Rogers (1980) offered two descriptions of empathy. Rogers's discussion of empathy in his later writing resembled Martin Buber's understanding of "inclusion" (1947/1965a, 96) and "turning to the other" (1947/1965a, 22). Rogers's earlier definition of empathy approximated a more individualistic version of empathy.

In his essay, "Empathic: An Unappreciated Way of Being," Rogers quotes his own 1959 definition of empathy as sensing the other's inner feelings as if they were his own without losing sight of the "as if" and falling into identification [similar to Buber's inclusion]. In this same essay, however, he updates his views on empathy in a way that sometimes resembles "inclusion" and sometimes empathy in the narrower sense: "An empathic way of being with another person . . . means *entering the private perceptual world of the other* and becoming thoroughly at home in it. It involves being sensitive, moment by moment, to the changing felt meanings which flow in this other person, to the fear or rage or tenderness or confusion or whatever that he or she is experiencing. . . . It means frequently checking with the person as to the accuracy of your sensings, and being guided by the responses. (Friedman 1984, 199–200)

Rogers's view of empathy, associated with "inclusion," is sensitive to limits that must be placed on one's interaction with another.

Carl Rogers was best known for his limiting, "as if" (1980, 140) qualification on empathy. This view makes a useful contribution for understanding interpersonal relationships. As Rogers wrote of I-Thou, the center of his philosophy still remained the self, but a self placed within limits, sensitive to the other. Indeed Rogers pointed to a dialogic self, concerned about the other.

Carl Rogers's limits on the individual self is a natural consequence of his philosophical assertion that the human is innately good, propelled by the "wisdom of the organism" (1969, 25). A good self seeks connection, relationship—not domination of another. Rogers contended that if one can get a patient to reach down into his or her depths, he or she will discover a nature that is social, constructive, and "unqualifiedly good" (Friedman 1984, 213). At the base of Rogers's system was the conviction that an interpersonal good life could be found and passed on to others through relationship-centered communication.

Before going to the next section, we want to bring attention to Carl Rogers and Barry Stevens's (1967/1972) statement about the "client's perception" of the acts of caring: empathy, unconditional positive regard, and congruence (85–101). The final ingredient that makes acts of caring possible is the "client's perception." If a person is grateful that caring action is directed toward him or her, the relationship is likely to be enriched. However, if a person does not recognize actions of care or concern for whatever reason, it is unlikely Rogers's approach would work. As we moved into an era of entitlement, not gratitude, the use of Rogers's approach is fenced with a caution: Rogers noted that ultimately the other's perception still determines the significance of a communicative exchange. The narrative background that we bring into a communicative encounter does make a difference—whether we are propelled by the possibility of gratitude or the expectation of entitlement makes all the difference. If a client does not hold an attitude of gratitude, Rogers's system is unlikely to work. Different background assumptions dramatically color our understanding and effectiveness of Rogers's communication style.

Historicality and Dialogic Civility

When is the insight of Carl Rogers appropriate today? Rogers's theory works when the narrative structure is partially known, but requires questioning. The story-laden self can draw upon insights without being locked into ideological blindness. However, Rogers's work can be turned into a closed ideology as well, if one does not apply his ideas with sensitivity to appropriate historically grounded situations.

Carl Rogers's (1980) emphasis on the inner goodness of the person, in conjunction with his reluctance to place "as if" limits on the individual self, point to a dialogic model in which a caring and listening self invites relationship with another. Carl Rogers's overall theory assists people that know the stories of a culture and are too constrained and limited by them. Persons who live in a narrative that has become too unyielding and inflexible may need to open the door of freedom by listening to themselves while they pick and choose elements from the narrative structure that they seek to escape. Parts of the story can continue to guide and assist—however, at that historical moment, the story as a whole has become oppressive.

Once the conversation ceases and the doors of oppression are opened, we suggest that a person needs to question a given story. At this juncture an emphasis on the notion of self is of value. Clarity needs to be given to the person, not to oppressive institutional systems. The person can lay claim to helpful parts of the story and reject other components. The narrative that is questioned can become a suggestion box from which the self can select given ideas or *Habits of the Heart* (Bellah, Madsen, Sullivan, Swidler, and Tipton 1985). However, life is more demanding when the suggestion box of old narrative structures is no longer available.

Many people in revolutionary movements go through such maturation. During revolutionary moments one rebels against the ongoing story—sometimes deliberately, but more often intuitively—relying upon the story-filled wisdom of the self. However, we would suggest that the self needs to contribute to a new narrative view of the world out of the positive remnants of the past and appropriate response to the present. If such an action of narrative development does not happen, we are likely to invite the next generation to walk into the grasp of narcissism without understanding how the previous generation lived in the positive remnants of an old narrative structure. Such a communicative action would misuse Rogers's insights.

The work of Nel Noddings (1984) is of significant value in that she is working with women who in a sexist culture needed to be called out as selves. She does so with the metaphor of "ethical self" that places individuality firmly within a commitment to relation (Noddings 1984, 51). We devote a later chapter to Noddings's works; however, it is important to see the connection between voices and it is, for us as authors, a conceptual joy to see ideas that build upon other ideas and do so in increasingly careful and sophisticated fashion—without losing the call to narrative praxis of dialogic civility. In essence, Noddings is doing what Carl Rogers did earlier—calling out to selves in the midst of broken narrative structures and working to lessen the chance for narcissism and a singular focus on "me" to emerge:

> The suggestion is that though modern man [or woman] no longer trusts religion or science or philosophy nor any system of beliefs to *give* him [or her] . . . values, he [or she] may find an organismic valuing base within himself [or herself] which, if he [or she] can learn again to be in touch with it, will prove to be an organized, adaptive and social approach to the perplexing value issues which face all of us. (Rogers and Stevens 1967/1972, 20)

As teachers, parents, and friends, we need to remember a clear message of Carl Rogers—communication needs a human face. We do not just process information, we impact and we shape human beings with our action and speech. Rogers's contribution to dialogic civility is a call to break the confines of oppressive narrative systems that do not reach out to the other. He wants a dialogic self, a responder and contributor to life, not a "yes" person blindly following institutional dictates. As institutions and philosophical systems misguide in a time of metanarrative decline, individuals can still make a relational difference.

Chapter *Six*

Abraham Maslow

Science, Values, and Additive Change

Human Values—

The state of being without a system of values is psychopathogenic. . . . The human being needs a framework of values, a philosophy of life, a religion or religion-surrogate to live by and be understood by, in about the same sense that he [or she] needs sunlight, calcium or love. This I have called the "cognitive need to understand." The value-illnesses which result from valuelessness are called variously anhedonia, anomie, apathy, amorality, hopelessness, cynicism, etc., and can become somatic illness as well. Historically, we are in a value interregnum in which all externally given value systems have proven to be failures (political, economic, religious, etc.), e.g., nothing is worth dying for. What man [or woman] needs but doesn't have, he [or she] seeks for unceasingly, and he [or she] becomes dangerously ready to jump at *any* hope, good or bad. . . . We need a validated, usable system of human values that we can believe in and devote ourselves to (be willing to die for), because they are true rather than because we are exhorted to "believe and have faith."

—Abraham Maslow, *Toward a Psychology of Being*

Additive Change—

I have been disturbed not only by the more "anal" scientists and the dangers of their denials of human values in science, along with the consequent amoral technologizing of all science. Just as dangerous are some of the critics of orthodox science who find it too skeptical, too cool and nonhuman, and then reject it altogether as

103

a danger to human values. They become "antiscientific" and even anti-intellectual. This is a real danger among some psychotherapists and clinical psychologists, among artists, among some seriously religious people, among some of the people who are interested in Zen, in Taoism, in existentialism, "experientialism," and the like. Their alternative to science is often sheer freakishness and cultishness, uncritical and selfish exaltation of mere personal experiencing, over-reliance on impulsivity and emotionality, unskeptical enthusiasm, and finally navel-watching and solipsism. This is a real danger. In the political realm, antiscience could wipe out mankind [or womankind] just as easily as could value-free, amoral, technologized science. . . . I certainly wish to be understood as trying to *enlarge* science, not destroy it.

—*The Psychology of Science*

Abraham Maslow's work pointed to yet another humanistic alternative to metanarrative collapse. Unlike Carl Rogers (1961), who turned primarily to clinical observations about the importance of the self, Maslow turned to science, a science of the self. Both men did research, but Rogers's ideas emerged first from clinical praxis and Maslow's ideas emerged from theory development and scientific research. Both Rogers and Maslow used the term *self-actualization*, which was originally coined by Kurt Goldstein (1939), to guide their inquiry.

Abraham Maslow's actions suggested that the human needs value-laden stories to live well; such stories are necessary guides for the direction of human action and life decisions. In a time of narrative decay, Maslow saw the importance of connecting value-laden stories to the vibrant narrative of his era—science. Maslow's humanistic impulses did not drive him to try and replace science, but to use science for good of the person and society. Maslow sought a foundation upon which to ground values; he was confident that ideals of social good would be nurtured, not destroyed, by a connection to a scientific narrative. "People can struggle on hopefully, and even happily, for false panaceas so long as these are not attained. Once attained, however, they are soon discovered to be false hopes. Collapse and hopelessness ensue and continue until new hopes become possible" (Maslow 1959/1970b, vii). Maslow's vision of an interpersonal "good life" is grounded in science used as a foundation for human values.

This chapter reviews the historical context of Abraham Maslow's work, in which a scientific narrative reigned. We articulate his project of defining a value-laden science and discuss central concepts that ground his ideas—including a science of health, the human as a valuing creature, the connection of a valuing framework to motivation and self-actualization, and the contribution of peak-experiences to the notion of the good life. Maslow offers a scientifically supported view of the dialogic self. Finally, we examine the relevance of his insights for our contemporary historical moment and dialogic civility.

Introduction

With the decline of a traditional metanarrative, Maslow began his work with three basic assumptions. First, the human needs value stories to guide an understanding of the "good life." Second, stories that previously provided guidance were no longer as useful. Third, it is possible to ground the reality of human values in the story of science, a value-laden science interested in growth, actualization, and development of the human being.

Abraham Maslow understood the value of a narrative-shaped life. He looked to what seemed to be the healthiest and most vibrant narrative available in the middle of the twentieth century—science—to support his work. Maslow's earliest work, *Motivation and Personality,* was first published in 1954. The Russians launched Sputnik in 1957 and John F. Kennedy rode the hope of science into the White House. Campaign rhetoric of competition with the Soviet Union was laced with a story about the possibilities of science. The country had great confidence in the scientific narrative. Talk about science increased as competitive impulses were interwoven with science as a way of knowing; we began the global race to be the first country to place a person on the moon. Within this competitive context, which required looking more and more to science for answers, Maslow wrote and studied about values that both could and should (as defined within his scientific description of appropriateness) guide an interpersonal good life.

Abraham Maslow found the work of Ludwig von Bertalanffy (1933), Michael Polanyi (1958, 1959), Jacob Bronowski (1956), Floyd Matson (1964), and Thomas Kuhn (1962) helpful in framing his view of a human science. In such a context, Maslow was able to write the following in the preface to *The Psychology of Science*: "I consider that my effort to rehumanize science and knowledge for myself (but most particularly the field of psychology) is part of this larger social and intellectual development" (1966/1969, 3).

As metanarratives were in seemingly problematic disarray, Abraham Maslow took as his project building a new approach to psychology based upon his value-laden science.

> We can no longer rely on tradition, on consensus, on cultural habit, on unanimity of belief to give us our values. These agreed-upon traditions are all gone. Of course, we never *should* have rested on tradition—as its failure must have proven to everyone by now—it never was a firm foundation. It was destroyed too easily by truth, by honesty, by the facts, by science, by simple, pragmatic, historical failure. Only truth itself can be our foundation, our base for building. (1964/1970c, 10)

Maslow's task was a building effort, an additive enterprise, an effort to place human values on sure footing—scientific ground.

Abraham Maslow accepted the narrative importance of science and simultaneously worked to expand the domain of science by asking significant value questions. He saw science as a narrative in ascension, while traditional narratives such as religion and family were in decline. He did not want the techniques of science to ignore value-laden questions. A value-laden science works to use the tools of science to explore both empirical and value-centered questions. Maslow noted that too often a problem-solving focus is

> discouraged by the philosophy that makes the scientist into a technician and an expert rather than a venturesome truth seeker, into one who *knows* rather than one who is *puzzled*. If scientists looked on themselves as question askers and problem solvers rather than specialized technicians, there would now be something of a rush to the newest scientific frontier, to the psychological and social problems about which we know least and should know most. (Maslow 1954/1970a, 14)

For Maslow, science was capable of exploring questions of the "good life." A value-laden science is used to enhance the quality of people's lives, not just for the sake of science alone. Maslow understood and accepted the power of the science narrative, while rejecting the value-neutral image of a Nazi scientist engaged in research, unconcerned about the impact of scientific inquiry on human beings.

Abraham Maslow was determined to connect science and values. He, like many others on the heels of World War II, had witnessed the failed effort of science as neutral, detached, and unconcerned about human values. Anatol Rapoport (1967) outlined this danger:

> [T]he "detachment" of the [scientific] strategist resembles not so much that of the surgeon as that of a butcher or still more that of all the other organizers of mass exterminations. Those technicians too were for the most part "detached" in the sense that their work was not charged with affect. German chemists were detached when they prepared the poison gas; German engineers were detached when they built the gas chambers; German transportation experts were detached and efficient as they kept the trains moving, carrying people to the slaughter sites; German bookkeepers were detached while keeping tallies of the dispatched, etc. Doubtless many of those responsible for this activity took a certain pride in having overcome any inhibitions they might have had in this matter. They might have been sincerely convinced that the "Jewish question" was a problem to be solved in a detached and definitive manner, possibly for the good of humanity. In other words, the charge of depravity, sadism, etc., can be made convincingly only against certain isolated individuals. It cannot be made against the entire corps of specialists who planned, designed, and carried out the exterminations of the 1940's. These people did not go berserk. They were carrying out their duties methodically and systematically. They were "normally functioning" human beings. (92–93)

Just as some were amazed with the "normalcy" of the value-free Nazi researchers, Maslow suggested another "normalcy," in which he connected science with values.

From this historical standpoint of awareness of metanarrative decline and perhaps collapse, we ask the following question about Maslow's work: "How can the dialogic self be shaped by a value-laden science, providing an additive story contribution to science and the human person?"

Significance of Abraham Maslow's
Science/Values Project

Abraham Maslow's work attempted to prove that values could be publicly verified by scientific investigation and description. His project sought to ground values in science. The following quotation from Maslow's (1959/1970b) *New Knowledge in Human Values* outlines his task:

> I think I have shown that the concepts of psychological health and of self-actualization need *not* be based on implicit value judgments. When properly defended, they *are* derived from scientifically observed facts. They are descriptive concepts in about the same sense that physical health is a descriptive concept. I agree that we urgently need more knowledge of what "humanness" and "human capacities" are before we can be unequivocal or avoid the appearance of circular reasoning when we define self-actualization as the fuller use of human capacities, or as being more fully human. As the defining and differentiating characteristics of humanness become better known, it will be easier and easier to select out people who are "more fully human" and to describe *their* values. . . . These must then be considered to be the ultimate values for all mankind [and womankind] (since all men [and women] press toward being more fully human). . . . In principle, we human beings may one day be faced with the task of discovering the values of some other kind of nonhuman species on some other planet. This too we shall be able to do. (246)

Maslow viewed the human as a valuing creature and conceptualized psychology as *the* discipline that could both describe and unleash the creative and constructive potential of the "healthy person."

Additive Approach to Science

A major point of significance in Abraham Maslow's project was his additive approach to science. Maslow was unwilling to permit a limited view of science to guide inquiry. Likewise, he ignored the impulse of some scholars who wanted to reject scientific inquiry altogether when human value issues propelled inquiry. Maslow was wary of substitutional strategies that replaced values with scientific inquiry and vice versa. Instead, he worked with traditional science in an additive fashion. He accepted the importance of science and combined it with a humanitarian concern—exploring questions such as, "What makes the human more healthy and positively directed?" Maslow built upon the narrative of science; he added the value of a humanitarian world view, attempting to humanize the narrative of science. Maslow did not attempt to destroy in order to create or change; he took what existed and built upon the foundation available in a given historical moment. Instead of attacking the narrative of science, he worked to enlarge its conceptual range.

Abraham Maslow's additive efforts at creation and change point to pragmatic interpersonal wisdom for those wanting to maintain relationships over time—often building upon what is already in place permits new life to emerge without putting relationships at risk. In the act of additive contribution, change can actually occur. Change need not be limited to substitutional acts of imperialism—wherein one idea is advanced over another.

We often face events we cannot change; these occurrences are powerful features in our lives—such as, who are our parents, where were we born, into which heritage were we born, with what potential were we born, and, of course, the fact that some decisions do have consequences and change a life forever. Some persons battle with the unchangeable for a lifetime, instead of taking what is available and building upon its significance. Perhaps we are afraid that if we accept "the given," change will cease to be possible. Yet often in the act of acceptance combined with taking the time and effort to build upon an older foundation, structures are frequently changed.

An additive approach to life does not mean that one is forever caught in the status quo. Take, for instance, a barn that is turned into a beautiful house or a belabored student who becomes a teacher with great compassion and dedication. In both cases the new is built upon the foundation of what is given. The structure of the barn lends itself to a home with a feeling of openness. The student, as a teacher, realizes that learning comes from dedication and providing appropriate tools of support for others. Maslow recognized a person can contribute "new" insights (altered paradigms) to the world, built upon the "old" (previously existing narratives).

The act of "building upon" intrigues the authors. Metaphors of change such as "additive" and "building" are pragmatically necessary for people with less power and for those who want to maintain relationships with others. When maintaining a relationship is of less value, change by substitution is a more viable option. A form of imperialism is often present in substitutional change. Substitution as a form of imposition should be used with care. Such action should only occur when the problem is so severe that little alternative is available. Substitutional change is often an interpersonal mistake when it is chosen as one's first course of action. For us, the pragmatic interpersonal genius of Maslow was to "add to" and "build upon" in the process of change.

Additive Education

Abraham Maslow, like Carl Rogers, is considered a central figure in the development of humanistic psychology. He and Rogers called for an alternative perspective to psychoanalysis and behaviorism. Maslow's dedication to the concept of additive change enabled a new school of psychology to emerge. Had his primary contribution been to critique the other schools, one wonders if a school of humanistic psychology would now exist.

Differences between Carl Rogers and Abraham Maslow were tied to how they informed the self about the ingredients of a relational good life. They both agreed with the need for an alternative view of psychology, however, and thought that the dialogic self offered a historically based answer to declining narrative power. Rogers and Maslow stressed different informational places for the self to be nourished. But to push this difference too far misses their commonality related to the importance of the other person getting in touch with his or her organismic valuing system. Maslow (1971) had a similar trust in the biology of the human:

> What if the organism is seen as having "biological wisdom?" If we learn to give it greater trust as autonomous, self-governing, and self-choosing, then clearly we as scientists, not to mention physicians, teachers, or even parents, must shift our image over to a more Taoistic one. This is the one word that I can think of that summarizes succinctly the many elements of the image of the more humanistic scientist. (15)

Maslow's work, however, was an oxymoron. He trusted the direction of biology, but science and education were needed for providing a narrative that offered clear and helpful direction. He simply wanted the trusted self to be fed good information from a value-laden science.

This additive educational theme prevails throughout Abraham Maslow's writing. Maslow understood how one might consider the human to be evil. He did not reject such a possibility; he simply said that with good science and education the more natural positive direction of the person is possible. Maslow did not romanticize the person; he worked to build on the natural behavior toward health and away from illness and danger.

> There is no neglect of weakness, badness, or what used to be called "evil," in Maslow's work. It was natural for him to reach a Socratic position—the view that most if not all the evil in human life is due to ignorance. His principle of explanation— developed from the "givens" of self-actualization and peak experience—were useful for understanding weakness, failure, and meanness, and he had no inclination to ignore these realities. He was not a sentimental man. (Geiger 1971/1973, xvii)

Maslow's commitment to education and learning was central in implementing his project and informing the self.

Self in Service to the Other

Throughout his work, Abraham Maslow related an awareness of human values with scientific support; he called the person to service with a scientific rationale.

> This volume springs from the belief, first, that the ultimate disease of our time is valuelessness; second, that this state is more crucially dangerous than ever before in history; and finally, that something can be done about it by man's own rational efforts. . . . We hope the conference will make an impressive demonstration of (a) the general concern of thoughtful people with this problem; (b) the convergence of conclusions by people working independently in different fields; and (c) the increasing hope that a "science" of values is possible, and that we need no longer be content only with exhortation, with authoritarian statements, or with "*a priori*" thinking. (Maslow 1959/1970b, ix)

Previously, only religious narratives pointed the human in a service direction. Maslow thought it was time, however, for a value-laden science to outline the why and the how of a life of personal growth through education and service to others.

Maslow (1954/1970a), using the term *self-actualization*, pointed to the healthy person living for something beyond himself or herself—in service to others as a natural act. Maslow considered love and acts of altruism and at times, patriotism, as moments when the individual self was transcended beyond ego limits. Maslow considered it essential for the self-actualizing person to be of service to another, to go beyond the self. Maslow's view of health called for action beyond the self that would simultaneously contribute to the health of the other and oneself.

Reaching out to others is not only good for the community; it is good for the biological organism. This understanding of "building/adding upon what is" in order to assist oneself and the other to grow is central to Henri Nouwen's (1972/1979) work, *The Wounded Healer*:

> To some, the concept of the wounded healer might sound morbid and unhealthy. They might feel that the ideal of self-fulfillment is replaced by an ideal of self-castigation, and that pain is romanticized instead of criticized. I would like to show how the idea of the wounded healer does not contradict the concept of self-realization, or self-fulfillment, but deepens and broadens it. (88)

In our current era of routine cynicism, which insistently calls for new to replace the old, Abraham Maslow's theme of additive change and call to service are still welcome ideas.

Central Concepts in Abraham Maslow's Work

Abraham Maslow outlined a value-laden science around the following related sets of concepts: a science of health, the human as a valuing creature, the connection of this valuing framework to motivation and self-actualization, and finally a description of "peak-experiences" and their contribution to the notion of the good life. In each of the above themes Maslow asked, "How could a value-laden science contribute to psychological health?"

Abraham Maslow's concepts may seem grounded in an overly positive view of science and/or the human. However, in a historical moment that virtually deified the science narrative, the most viable option was to build a value-laden view of the human on a scientific foundation. A key element in his science narrative—which was a direct product of the Enlightenment—is the importance of public verification of ideas. Maslow's desire to retain the scientific narrative kept alive the notion of public in the discourse area of psychological health, traditionally viewed as a private domain. We are not suggesting that this was the intent of Maslow; we are suggesting that this is one of the narrative consequences of his emphasis on science.

Richard Bernstein (1983), in quoting Hannah Arendt, reminds us that the Enlightenment project was an effort to bring ideas into the public arena; it is this impulse more than any other that made the narrative of science possible.

> Referring to the *philosophies* of the Enlightenment, whose importance, she says, lies in their shrewd insight into the *public* character of freedom, Arendt [1963] tells us: "Their public freedom was not an inner realm into which men might escape at will from the pressures of the world, nor was it the *liberum arbitrium* which makes the will choose between alternatives. Freedom for them could exist only in public; it was a tangible, worldly reality, something created by men to be enjoyed by men rather than a gift or a capacity, it was the manmade public space or market-place which antiquity had known as the area where freedom appears and becomes visible to all." (Bernstein 1983, 209)

Arendt (1963) romanticized the Athenian *polis*—particularly in light of the exclusion of woman and slaves from democratic participation. But she was also good at pulling a thread in the story through time without revealing the entire story—she did additive work. She saw participation in the public as a social good that the Enlightenment once again brought to awareness from the house of Athens. The public nature of verification was kept alive by her story.

Hannah Arendt understood that ideas can be flawed and still provide important assistance if they are not absorbed like a *True Believer* (Hoffer 1951). If we bracket the notion of science and examine Abraham Maslow's desire to place values in the public domain—

remembering that public verification of ideas was one of the original goals of science—admiration for his project is further enhanced. Maslow sensed that in a time of metanarrative decline, the role of the public domain was still necessary, even in the discussion of interpersonal issues.

Maslow's version of a value-laden science was to open up the experiential and unclear stages of learning, without rejecting the scientific hope that many of these ideas would be put to public test at a later time. Public statements of confusion, mystery, and admission of what he did not know was part of his commitment to a value-laden science. Maslow's public admissions indicated a willingness to be clear about the dual nature of science: "simplicity and condensation" and "comprehensiveness and inclusiveness" (Maslow 1966/1969, 72). "Science, then, has two directions or tasks, not just one. It moves toward abstractness (unity, parsimony, economy, simplicity, integration, lawfulness, 'graspability.') But it also moves toward comprehensiveness, toward experiencing everything, toward describing all these experiences, toward accepting all that exists" (Maslow 1966/1969, 76). Maslow added the notions of comprehensiveness and experiential knowledge to a more traditional understanding of science. Humility and curiosity accompanied Maslow's value-laden science; he wanted to study all of the concrete and the unfolding nuances of life.

A Science of Interpersonal Health

The overarching motivation for Abraham Maslow's project was to outline a science of psychological health; this motivation provides a background for understanding the direction of his work, *Toward a Psychology of Being*. "There is now emerging over the horizon a new conception of human sickness and of human health, a psychology that I find so thrilling and so full of wonderful possibilities that I yield to the temptation to present it publicly even before it is checked and confirmed, and before it can be called reliable scientific knowledge" (Maslow 1962/1968, 3). Maslow outlined a public view of his understanding of the dynamics of a "good life" that contribute to communicative health. With this public confession, Maslow (1962/1968) summarized the biases that guided his work and inquiry:

1. Each person has a biological inner nature.

2. This inner nature is both individually unique and a reflection of our kinship to others.

3. One can discover, not invent, this inner human nature with scientific inquiry.

4. The inner nature of the person is either neutral or generally good.

5. Since this inner nature is generally good or neutral, it is best to encourage following it as a guide.

6. If this essential core (inner nature) of the person is denied, sickness is invited.

7. The inner nature of a human being is not strong and can easily be damaged or suppressed by wrong habits or cultural pressures. (This is a key to the rationale for a value-laden science capable of informing the self.)

8. Even in a weak state this inner nature, however, is hard to kill; it can be encouraged in the weakest of persons. One's inner nature can re-emerge after years of being dormant.

9. The inner nature of the human is often found through challenge—not comfort.

[T]hese conclusions must all be articulated with the necessity of discipline, deprivation, frustration, pain, and tragedy. To the extent that these experiences reveal and foster and fulfill our inner nature, to that extent they are desirable experiences. . . . [T]hese experiences have something to do with a sense of achievement and ego strength and confidence. The person who hasn't conquered, withstood and overcome continues to feel doubtful that he [or she] *could*. This is true not only for external dangers; it holds also for the ability to control and to delay one's own impulses, and therefore to be unafraid of them. (3–4)

Maslow's work was guided by the above assumptions about interpersonal health, all of which could be taught and learned.

Human Values

One's inner nature is built on experiences that life offers. The task of a therapist is much like that of a mentor. Every problem, every difficulty, and every pain presents another opportunity to discover what Maslow would call one's unique inner nature—what we would simply call character. Difficulty is not ignored or walked around; it is used as a lesson and walked through to gain knowledge useful for future experiences.

Abraham Maslow was convinced that the human could find his or her inner nature and actualize the valuing part of one's being through the demanding process of increasing self-knowledge. Maslow's assumption was similar to Socrates' teachings—self-knowledge does make a difference (Sauvage 1961). Maslow's role of the therapist was to perform a role similar to a Socratic teacher— pulling knowledge from the other that could be used for guidance.

Abraham Maslow (1959/1970b) contended that self-knowledge from therapy assisted the person in the following ways:

1. Self-knowledge is a necessary part of self-improvement.

2. Such knowledge requires courage, a willingness to be part of a long-term journey of learning.

3. A skilled therapist assists with self-knowledge, taking life experiences, reflecting upon them with the intent of learning, not just remembering. One's life is interpreted as a text of richness and depth, not remembered as a mere collection of memories.

4. The study of psychopathology encourages us to respect the "forces of fear, of regression, of defense, of safety." (135)

5. "We can never fully understand or help human strength without also understanding human weakness. Otherwise we fall into the errors of over optimistic reliance on rationality alone" (135).

Maslow's process of therapy enabled persons to develop self-knowledge, permitting a constructive life direction to be pursued.

The first step of finding values in a life is self-knowledge or self-honesty. Jean-Paul Sartre would agree. Sartre believed the most dangerous act in life is "bad faith"—lying to oneself (1953, 86–116). Maslow encouraged an honesty of self-knowledge central to the process of a talk therapy. The key, for Maslow, was to understand oneself as the primary guide for a life. To ensure a successful life requires an honest appraisal of events and reactions to one's own life. Such an honesty permits one to ask, "What is needed in this historical moment and how might that communicative requirement for this situation be different from what I want to do based upon my own formation?"

The authors are convinced that if Abraham Maslow were to write today he would address the needs of this historical moment with a theory for this moment. The values of self-honesty and evaluation that supported Maslow's work are akin to those any good scientist needs to embrace.

Abraham Maslow's self-honesty functioned differently than Isidor F. Stone's (1988) version of Socrates' call for honesty. Socrates brought an honesty to the Athenian *polis* that displayed the inner limitations of Athenian democracy. "Socrates would have found it repugnant to plead a principle in which he did not believe; free speech for him was the privilege of the enlightened few, not of the benighted many. He would not have wanted the democracy he rejected to win a moral victory by setting him free" (Stone 1988, 230). Maslow never set out to embarrass or reject, but to enhance, to enlarge, and to enrich the scientific world with multiple levels and stages of knowledge.

Abraham Maslow would not have played the role of Stone's (1988) Socrates by calling attention to the limitations and the ignorance of the other. Instead, Maslow would have met in dialogue and offered an additive change to what is historically given. Maslow's greatest value was not a Socratic honesty, but a humble honesty that simultaneously sought inclusion without rejection.

Self-Actualization and Earned Self-Esteem

The notion of self-actualization is the final stage of human motivation, according to Abraham Maslow. Maslow stated that one must first take care of basic needs. The basic needs Maslow considered central to health are as follows. First, physiological needs must be met. These include the basic needs of hunger, sex, and thirst. Second, safety needs are met when physiological needs are fairly well satisfied. These include issues of security and freedom from fear as motivating influences. Third, belonging and love needs refer to a sense of relational connection with others. These are addressed when physiological and safety needs are generally satisfied. Finally, esteem needs become important when one's other needs are satisfied. Esteem needs refer to one's search for personal significance.

> We have been learning more and more about the dangers of basing self-esteem on the opinions of others rather than on real capacity, competence, and adequacy to the task. The most stable and therefore most healthy self-esteem is based on *deserved* respect from others rather than on external fame or celebration and unwarranted adulation. (Maslow 1954/1970a, 46)

To reach self-actualization, one must attend to all the above needs.

Before examining self-actualization, two points need to be made about the above discussion. First, Abraham Maslow was not tied to a rigid hierarchy of development. He understood the general development of needs in a direction of health from basic physical needs to more complex social needs. Second, the way in which he described self-esteem is interesting. He connected self-esteem to genuine capacity, not wants, imagination, or hopes. Self-esteem cannot be given to another person; the opportunity to build self-esteem through genuine tasks and development of ability can, however, be provided for another person. Maslow conceptualized self-esteem as an interaction between what life presents and how one learns to deal with life's turns and twists via self-reflection or assistance from a mentor. The result of meeting life, understanding, learning, and not being conquered by the inevitable difficulties that each person must face is the development of self-esteem based upon genuine capacity and accomplishment.

The reason we draw attention to Abraham Maslow's view of self-esteem is that it is based upon genuine productivity and ability. When self-esteem is discussed in an everyday sense, people often refer unknowingly to an aristocratic form of self-esteem based upon blood line, wealth, or in some situations a fictional account about one's worth and ability, not productivity. This aristocratic form of self-esteem is based upon who one is, not one's genuine capability and productivity. Lewis Lapham (1993) described such a form of self-esteem as the root of inappropriate self-promotion. Many of us have met someone like the following king of self-promotion:

[Prior to appointment in the Bush administration as the director of the Office of Management and Budget, Richard] Darman performed various services for the Reagan administration, and in 1985, when he moved from the White House staff to the Treasury Department, he took with him a letter of praise signed by President Reagan. Handsomely framed and prominently displayed on the wall of his new office, the letter awarded to Darman all the credit for all the great works of Reagan's first term. Here at last was the indispensable man. . . . [The truth, however, was] Darman composed the letter himself. (Lapham 1993, 68)

We will not quote from Darman's letter, but it reads as a form of self-esteem that Maslow would surely question! Accolades coming from others, as a genuine byproduct of our service are important. Something is wrong, however, when we feel so entitled to feeling good about ourselves that self-production of applause may be hung on one's own office wall.

The final stage of Abraham Maslow's theory of motivation of human personality development is self-actualization:

[Self-actualization] may be loosely described as the full use and exploitation of talents, capacities, potentialities, etc. Such people seem to be fulfilling themselves and to be doing the best that they are capable of doing, reminding us of [Friedrich] Nietzsche's exhortation, "Become what thou art!" They are people who have developed or are developing to the full stature of which they are capable. These potentialities may be either idiosyncratic or species-wide. (1954/1970a, 150)

The above quotation provides a classic description of self-actualization, gleaned from Maslow's work. Note there is *action* implied in self-actualization; action requires doing what one is "meant" to do with one's given talent and capacity.

Abraham Maslow (1954/1970a) chose a small number of people, including public and historical figures for his study on self-actualization. The rigors of and response to his study are not as important to us at this stage as the following. First, Maslow focused upon the public. He used public figures; he wanted a common sense evaluation of his choices. Second, he contended that self-actualization requires education and maturity.

The following list identifies Abraham Maslow's (1954/1970a) characteristics of the self-actualizing person:

1. Able to evaluate reality well and to be comfortable with an honest evaluation.

2. Able to accept the actual reality of self and others.

3. Ability to live life with spontaneity and naturalness.

4. Problem-centered, forgoes too much unproductive time on introspection.

5. Uses time in reflection and solitude.

6. Ability to function with some autonomy from the culture and not simply follow the crowd.

7. Able to see novelty in routine.

8. Open to peak-experiences.

9. Manifests an affection for and connection with humankind— specifically and in general.

10. Has a small circle of friends, but deep interpersonal relationships.

11. Displays a democratic character; the person not the rank makes the difference.

12. Possesses a clear sense of right and wrong without being rigid or ignoring the needs of a given moment.

13. Offers a philosophical sense of humor that does not elicit fun at another's expense.

14. Lives with a creative impulse.

15. Manifests a resistance to enculturation; culturally transcending to a degree.

16. Demonstrates an ability to live with imperfection in self and others.

17. Recognizes that values are central to self-actualization. "A firm foundation for a value system is automatically furnished to the self-actualizing person by his [or her] philosophic acceptance of the nature of his [or her] self, of human nature, of much of social life, and of nature and physical reality" (176).

18. Displays an ability to unify dichotomies.

Maslow ends this description of the self-actualizing person in the following fashion:

> Healthy people are so different from average ones, not only in degree but in kind as well, that they generate two very different kinds of psychology. It becomes more and more clear that the study of crippled, stunted, immature, and unhealthy specimens can yield only a crippled psychology and a crippled philosophy. The study of self-actualizing people must be the basis for a more universal science of psychology. (1954/1970a, 180)

In essence, self-actualization is the teleological goal of Maslow's value-laden scientific narrative of self-guidance.

Taken from the language of psychology and placed within a narrative framework, Abraham Maslow's use of the self-actualizing person became central to many discussions of popular moral and value-laden narratives. For such a narrative to have rhetorical power it must be embodied in a number of people. Maslow pointed to a "standard" of the "excellent person" outlined in Aristotle's *Nicomachean Ethics* (1985, 1113a25), in which a person lives such a value system. Each moral story needs to have a standard bearer of excellence that points the way for others to follow. The self-actualizing person is the standard bearer of Maslow's value-laden science.

The human is motivated by basic needs and in the final stages of value development affirms the characteristics of the self-actualizing person. Abraham Maslow grounds this person in science and provides the narrative elements of a story worthy of being lived (a value-laden science) and a main character (self-actualizing person) that points the way toward implementation. The final area of significance in Maslow's work reflects his fascination with "peak-experiences," which are connected to his understanding of the self-actualizing personality.

Peak-Experiences

Abraham Maslow, in his book *Religions, Values, and Peak-Experiences* (1964/1970c), connects the notion of peak-experience to self-actualization. He made it clear that a person does not have to have peak-experiences to be self-actualized. However, the more creative and the more artistic a self-actualizing person is, the more likely he or she will participate in peak-experiences.

Maslow (1964/1970c) listed twenty-five elements associated with peak-experiences. The primary characteristic, however, is a connection with the whole—a sense of insight and clarity beyond the norm, situated in a feeling of peace and calm. Such peak-experiences evoke being-values that inform us what is and is not of great importance in life. Perhaps the feeling one has upon seeing the birth of a child or watching a person you have cared for and nurtured mature and make a significant contribution in a given area permits life to seem right and in place.

The importance of the mystical illumination for Abraham Maslow is to remind us that life is more than cognitive processing. Maslow (1964/1970c) is aware that one of the primary teachings from the Third Reich is to beware of using only cognition. One's life must include action appropriate for the historical moment and it must be open to peak-experiences that tell the story of what is right and good in human life. Maslow offered a scientific story with values, a main character, and a moral message—life has sacred moments, do not defile them by failing to see and hear the messages of the peak-experiences of a life.

Historicality and Dialogic Civility

Abraham Maslow's work points to the importance of the following: for many people who have a desire to re-tool, additive change is a welcome metaphor. We learn more when our energy is directed toward possibilities, rather than grieving about what has been lost. Building on narrative structures that have some currency left is a worthy task. The metaphor of the broken covenant (Bellah 1975) is important here. Narratives are not perfect; they require maintenance, repair, support, and additive change. Societal health requires valuing life and others while calling attention to standard bearers of health. A respect for self, others, and ideas permeates Maslow's work. We need to identify healthy mentors/role models in society with the guidance and support of others. Cognition, emotion, and hallowed moments of life's peak-experiences point to what is of vital importance in an interpersonal "good life." Special moments mark a life and frame the story of one's interaction with others.

As Abraham Maslow stated, "education must be seen as at least partially an effort to produce the good human being [dialogic self], to foster the good life and the good society" (1964/1970c, 58). Maslow pointed to a value-laden science to inform the self who could then contribute and be of service. In both cases, he assumed a dialogic stance: learning from science and reaching out to the other. He pointed to a dialogic self by calling us to build good metaphors for growth and for change, recognizing that houses are built with foundations first and only then can additional floors be constructed. Adding to a powerful narrative that is unlikely to be overcome is important for the dialogic self. One must choose one's battles with care, and often change happens without complete rejection. As we add to a story, we realize violent substitutional change is not always needed.

Abraham Maslow's value-laden science informed the self, permitting a dialogic self to make relational contact with the other. His calls for additive change and verification in the public arena provide important elements for dialogic civility in interpersonal discourse. He had a firm but patient hand that did not have to destroy the "old" to build the new, the unique, the innovative. He began with the historical situation and ended with genuine insight.

Section 2

Narrative Confrontation:
Interpersonal Dialogue and Crisis

Chapter Seven

Martin Buber

Attending and Response Between Persons

Power and Focus of Attention —

So long as man's [or woman's] power, that is, his [or her] capacity to realize what he [or she] has in mind, is bound to the goal, to the work, to the calling, it is, considered in itself, neither good nor evil, it is only suitable or an unsuitable instrument. But as soon as this bond with the goal is broken off or loosened, and the man [or woman] ceases to think of power as the capacity to do something, but thinks of it as a possession, that is thinks of power in itself, then his [or her] power, being cut off and self-satisfied, is evil; it is power withdrawn from responsibility.

—Martin Buber, *Between Man and Man*

Care and Focus of Attention —

When I was eleven years of age, spending the summer on my grand-parents' estate, I used, as often as I could do it unobserved, to steal into the stable and gently stroke the neck of my darling, a broad dapple-gray horse. . . . The horse, even when I had not begun by pouring oats for him into the manger, very gently raised his massive head, ears flicking, then snorted quietly, as a conspirator gives a signal meant to be recognizable only by his fellow-conspirator; and I was approved. But once—I do not know what came over the child, at any rate it was childlike enough—it struck me about the stroking, what fun it gave me, and suddenly I became conscious of my hand. The game went on as before, but something had changed, it was no longer the same thing. And the next day, after giving him a rich feed, when I stroked my friend's head he did not raise his head.

—"Autobiographical Fragments"

127

Martin Buber's dialogic voice reminds us of the importance of attending to the other—even in an era of narrative destruction from a genuinely evil presence. Dialogue, for Buber, suggested that life is lived in the *between*—between persons, between person and event, between person and idea, even in crisis. Life is not captured in the other or in me, but between us. Buber's understanding of communication points to the interdependent nature of life. He provided a communication alternative to extreme polar choices, i.e., self or other, individualism or collectivism. Buber consistently reminded us that the metaphor that sustains dialogic life is the between. The person, the other, the event, the idea—none are sufficient unto themselves—necessary, but not sufficient for dialogue to occur. Dialogic life is lived *Between Man and Man* (Buber 1947/1965a). In this chapter, we examine Buber's dialogic world view. We explore the principle of between, as expressed in Buber's poetic narrative, and discuss basic concepts that comprise his view of interpersonal communication. The significance of his work for contemporary society is also addressed. Out of dialogue and crisis, Buber affirmed that the quality of life still rests between us.

Introduction

In an age of quick readings, the dialogic voice of Martin Buber can be misheard and ignored due to its poetic complexity. Some consider Buber to be a mystic, while others too quickly group his understanding of dialogue with work akin to those in the Humanistic Psychological Association. Buber's insights into interpersonal communication make his dialogic voice unique. First, Buber was interested in lived reality, not the otherworldly. His interest in the mystical centered around its impact on one's attitude in daily living; he did not use mysticism as a route to escape human interaction. Buber's concern was existential, grounded in everyday life. Second, Buber did not begin dialogue with an emphasis on the psychology of the communicators; the between is an ontological reality for Buber, not a psychological concept of self.

Martin Buber understood dialogue as rooted in a common center of conversation between persons. The common center of discourse is what brings people together in conversation; the common center, not the psyche of the partners in conversation, is fundamental. The notion of a common center is a metaphor that points to a world view distinct from an emphasis on individualism, collectivism, or psychologism.

Martin Buber illuminated the face of the human—in trial and tragedy, hope and joy—with the metaphor of the between. Additionally, he pointed to the narrative grounding of such a view of human life. Ontological alternatives are carried in the story of a people and can go unused, be ignored, or lost when a culture is no longer guided by metanarratives. Buber not only contended that answers did not exist in the individualism of "meism" or the collectivism of group tyranny, he considered such extremes a foundation for the demonic, the human destruction of society.

> The name Satan means in Hebrew the hinderer. That is the correct designation for the anti-human in individuals and in the human race. Let us not allow this Satanic element in men [or women] to hinder us from realizing man [or woman]! Let us release speech from its ban! Let us dare, despite all, to trust! (Buber 1957/1974, 239)

Buber's dialogic voice was a consistent call to meet life relationally, seeing the ontological necessity of both self and other finding meaning in the between—meaning is owned by neither partner but co-constituted between them in cooperative interaction.

From this historical standpoint of awareness of metanarrative decline and perhaps collapse, we ask the following question about Martin Buber's work: "How can dialogue in a time of metanarrative crisis offer an alternative to the extremes of individualism and collectivism in a communicative life?" This question points to the common center of Buber's dialogic project. Life is best lived between extremes on the "narrow ridge" (1965b/1966a, 110). Buber's wisdom is discovered between dialogue and crisis.

Martin Buber's Common Center: The Between

Martin Buber's discussion of the between takes us to a window that opens to an ontological reality—life is "best" lived between persons. Remember a moment in which an award was given or a significant passage or event took place in your life. Without a close friend or relative with whom to experience the success, one feels hollow after the event is over. Something happens between persons when genuine joy for another's accomplishment is voiced and together the partners in dialogue enjoy the moment between them. As one of the authors states, "Jealousy steals from both parties, just as lack of relation steals from life itself." Buber understood that genuine joy for another contributes to both communicators. As Buber himself noted: "All real living is meeting" (1965b/1966a, 48).

To interpret Martin Buber's dialogic message, one must understand the philosophical and practical implications of the between as a guiding communicative metaphor. We should not be surprised that Buber was often unclear about the between. He wrote in a poetic fashion, not in a linear and pedantic manner. Buber wrote to understand by pointing through the haze of an early dawn; he did not write in the clarity of sunlight with didactic intent.

Martin Buber's (1967d) writing was consistent with his orientation toward his scholarly task; he considered himself a philosophical anthropologist. A cultural anthropologist looks for cultural implications of societal change, while a physical anthropologist examines the structural and tool foundations of a civilization—each within a historical period. Buber, on the other hand, adopted the stance of a philosophical anthropologist, outlining the philosophical assumptions that guide communicative life between people.

Horizon of the Between

Martin Buber's nonsystematic orientation did not result in clear definitions built upon each other in logical fashion. The meanings of his ideas and concepts are given life and understood in the context of his entire work situated within the historical moment of their formation; the notion of the between is no exception. The reader is left to understand his ideas primarily from one's personal context and the historical necessity of the contemporary moment.

One of the clearest efforts to describe the meaning horizon of the between is in the book that bears the name of this concept, *Between Man and Man* (Buber 1947/1965a). Interestingly, however, we must go to page 203 of his 224-page book to discover an expanded account of this concept, so central to his work. If one forgoes the attempt to read Martin Buber's work systematically and seeks to understand his writings poetically, then finding a central concept buried in one of his essays should not come as a surprise.

The ontological significance of the between is central to Martin Buber's work. The following quotation outlines the meaning horizon of this key term.

The fundamental fact of human existence is neither the individual as such nor the aggregate as such. Each, considered by itself, is a mighty abstraction. . . . The fundamental fact of human existence is . . . rooted in one being turning to another as another, as this particular other being, in order to communicate with it in a sphere which is common to them but which reaches out beyond the special sphere of each. I call this sphere, which is established with the existence of man [or woman] as man [or woman] but which is conceptually still uncomprehended, the sphere of "between." . . . This is where the genuine third alternative must begin.

The view which establishes the concept of "between" is to be acquired by no longer localizing the relations between human beings, as is customary, either within individual souls or in a general world which embraces and determines them, but in actual fact *between* them.

"Between" is not auxiliary construction, but the real place and bearer of what happens between men [and women]; it has received no specific attention because, in distinction from the individual soul and its context, it does not exhibit a smooth continuity but is ever and again re-constituted in accordance with men's [and women's] meetings with one another; hence what is experience has been annexed naturally to the continuous elements, the soul and its world. (Buber 1947/1965a, 202–203)

The notion of the between is at the common center of Martin Buber's work due to the moment of his own historical formation and the commonsense question his work addresses. He sought a concrete alternative to the dangers of the collective (such as Nazism) and the dangers of unconcerned individualism. Buber's response is the ontological reality of the between.

We underscore the following characteristics and implications of the between, central to Martin Buber's dialogic world view. First, the between is ontological or part of being human. Our humanness enables us to come together with others in the between. Second, the between may be seen as a tripartite metaphor for communicative life—pointing to a relational rather than an individualistic or collectivistic view of communicative life, the interdependence of self and other, and a recognition of life as a call to participation. Third, the between is a phenomenological space available in dialogue only through invitation, not demand. Finally, the between is a reminder of our human story—together life is to be lived well, for us, not just for the collective or for me.

The Existential-Phenomenological Nature of the Between

Martin Buber's understanding of the between did not emerge out of a philosophical vacuum; the between is central to his existential phenomenological world view. As the summary chapter of William Luijpen's (1965) work suggested, our being-in-the-world constantly points us to other events and people. Life is filled by intersubjective meaning (Kelley and Tallon 1972).

The concept of the between emerged as a reaction to the overuse of a psychological world view for explaining human action.

> It is basically erroneous to try to understand the interhuman phenomena as psychological. When two men [or women] converse together, the psychological is certainly an important part of the situation, as each listens and each prepares to speak. Yet this is only the hidden event fraught with meaning, whose meaning is to be found neither in one of the two partners nor in both together, but only in their dialogue itself, in this "between" which they live together. (Buber 1965b/1966a, 75)

Martin Buber's work implied a call to the interpersonal importance of intentionality, an awareness of the other as central for understanding dialogue between persons.

Edmund Husserl, the founder of phenomenology, provided the theoretical position from which Martin Buber's use of the between gains some of its philosophical support. The nonpsychological perspective represented by the phenomenological view of "intentionality" was central to the work of Husserl. Husserl described intentionality as "consciousness of" (1931/1969, 114). Intentionality is both the process and the place where one's focus of attention is gathered—between the seer and seen. Husserl noted that intentionality is not in the person or in the object under review, but between person and phenomenon by the subject.

David Stewart and Algis Mickunas, in *Exploring Phenomenology*, provide a clear picture of Edmund Husserl's understanding of intentionality:

> To underscore the phenomenological view of consciousness, Husserl introduced new terminology which would avoid the subject-object dualism of older philosophical views while respecting the polar structure of consciousness. The activity of consciousness he called *noesis* (from the Greek work meaning "mental perception, intelligence, or thought"), whereas the essence to which this mental activity is correlated he called *noema* (from the Greek word meaning "that which is perceived, a perception, a thought"). . . . One would fail to understand Husserl if he identified the noetic with the subject and the noematic with the object. . . . Husserl stressed repeatedly that noetic activity cannot be identified with psychological activity. . . . This unit of meaning is another indication of the importance of the intentional structure of consciousness. . . . One never finds the noetic and noematic in isolation from each other but always correlated; they are two sides of the same coin. (1974, 37–38)

Let us go back to the introductory quotation concerning Martin Buber and the horse. Buber lost consciousness of the horse and placed his focus of attention on his hand in touching the horse. This shift in attention changed the meaning of the event; his focus of attention was moved from the horse to his hand.

To use a baseball example, if a batter is "conscious of" the ball, then his or her focus is on the incoming flight of the object—its speed and direction. However, once a batter's focus is primarily upon his or her own stance, he or she is likely to miss the ball. Focus of attention is the issue that makes moving out of a batting slump so demanding. The batter's focus of attention is often in the wrong location—on his or her stance and not the ball. What one is actually "conscious of" frames the focus and the meaningfulness of the communication. If someone is ill, we send flowers; but if our focus of attention is on how good we are acting in having sent the flowers, then the communication is much different than being "conscious of" the other's needs in a time of crisis.

Six connections between intentionality and the notion of the between can be described. First, both have a nonpsychological

emphasis. Second, both imply an ontological understanding of relation. Third, each points to a reality beyond the common everyday
understanding of the empirical. Fourth, each approach suggests the
importance of the intersubjectivity of phenomenological otherness
and the subject. Fifth, each reveals an alternative focus of attention
beyond self and object. Finally, both announce the ontological
nature of interdependence of the seer and the seen, the listener and
the heard, the knower and the known (Arnett 1986/1997a). Martin
Buber wrote in a historical moment in which a phenomenological
understanding of the world called into question both psychological
and empirical perspectives.

Martin Buber understood the concrete, the particular, and the
unique as requiring dialogue between the historical moment of a
person, or a people, and an event or idea that claims attention.
Even religious faith cannot be understood in isolation from the historical moment. The questions we bring to any moral story outline
the potential answer a religious story can offer in a given moment.

Martin Buber's interpretive existential spin on phenomenology
put him outside the confines of Edmund Husserl's project. Yet
Buber still acknowledged his connection and kinship with Husserl,
who, like Buber, was a German Jewish intellectual.

> Husserl, himself, the creator of the phenomenological
> method . . . [was aware] that the greatest historical phenome-
> non is mankind [or womankind] wrestling for self-understand-
> ing. . . . "Humanity in general is existentially the existence of
> man [or woman] in entities of mankind [or womankind] which
> are bound together in generations and in society." These words
> fundamentally contradict the whole anthropological world of
> the phenomenological school. . . . In these words Husserl says
> that man's [or woman's] essence is not to be found in isolated
> individuals, for a human being's bonds with his [or her] gener-
> ation and his [or her] society are of his [or her] essence; we
> must therefore know what these bonds really mean if we want
> to know the essence of man [woman]. That is to say that an
> individualistic anthropology either has as its subject man [or
> woman] in a condition of isolation, that is, in a condition not
> adequate to his [or her] essence, or in fact does consider man
> [or woman] in his [or her] bonds of community, but regards
> their effect as impairing his [or her] real essence, and thus is
> not thinking of that fundamental communion of which Husserl
> speaks. (Buber 1947/1965a, 159–161)

Buber understood Husserl as conceptualizing the person in relation as the center of a historical story. Buber did not limit Husserl to an individual phenomenological description.

Martin Buber understood the phenomenological essence of the human being grounded in a community and focused on given concrete issues within a historical situation. Buber moved intentionality to a corporate level; intentionality is lived out as the person interprets experiences according to his or her uniqueness, situated and limited by ties to a community of people. While Edmund Husserl wanted to know the phenomenological characteristics of a phenomenon for all time, Buber was content with a historical reading, which would change in accordance with the historical moment.

Maurice Friedman is arguably the primary interpreter of Martin Buber's work, as witnessed in *Martin Buber: The Life of Dialogue* (Friedman 1955/1976) and his three-volume set on *Martin Buber's Life and Work* (Friedman 1981, 1983a, 1983b), along with numerous other articles and books. The following quotation from Friedman (1981) points to the commonality and divergence of Martin Buber from Edmund Husserl:

> Buber related that several times in his youth he wanted to fix an object, to compel it, as it were, in order to find through so doing that it was "only" his conception. Every time that he tried to do this, the object refuted him through the dumb force of its being! This irreducible impact of otherness is what sets Buber apart from Edmund Husserl's philosophy of phenomenology. When Buber wrote in *I and Thou*, "In lived actuality no one thinks without something being thought; rather is the thinking no less dependent on the thing thought than the latter on the former," he sounded very much like Husserl. But when he added: "A subject that annuls the object to rise above it annuls its own actuality," he separated himself . . . from Husserl's Idealist concept of a "transcendental ego." (332)

Buber understood phenomenon grounded in the concrete historical moment, not abstracted from life's events.

Martin Buber's dialogue is not cast in psychology, nor in phenomenology, but in existential phenomenology (Arnett 1981, 1982). Buber was interested in the interpretive task that required knowing, following, and upon occasion carving a new path, in order to continue the aliveness of a given story too valuable to be taken for granted. Such interpretation requires attending to the phenomenon of communicative life and engaging in interpretation of the phenomenon with one's whole being. Life's most profound reality is not "me" or "you," but emerges between one person and another, between us and events of human life. Martin Buber may have been doing existential-phenomenological work, but more importantly he sought to bring tradition and the uniqueness of the interpreter into creative dialogue—inviting a dialogic voice of civilization to emerge. Buber's use of phenomenology had a moral purpose—to call forth dialogic voices willing to listen and to be heard, knowing fully well in an era of Nazi power that both communicative acts required courage and a realistic sense of hope. The existential-phenomenological focus that guided Buber's understanding of dialogue required taking seriously a given story and simultaneously offering a genuine response from the depth of our being to that story.

Ambiguity, Story, and Guidance

Martin Buber wrote to figure out problems, not to simply tell us what he already understood. He intentionally used poetic ambiguity to reveal a positive third alternative to either individualism or collectivism. Without ambiguity, the notion of dialogue is vulnerable to a technique mentality, missing the contribution that dialogue provides for a society unduly focused upon rules, regulations, and emerging new technologies. Buber wanted no more than to point, to suggest, to inquire as a philosophical anthropologist about the communicative life of people. Real communicative living requires taking general ideas and suggestions and applying them to the concrete moment of discourse. Sometimes the clearer the writing of an idea, the more abstract the result.

For instance, we can operationalize the chronological movement out of adolescence into adulthood. We can label the year and the time of different points of maturation. Yet in reality, we all know adults who have yet to emerge out of attitudinal adolescence. Instead of giving us an age in which such a change would take place, Martin Buber might have been inclined to tell a story within the following spirit.

There was a young man who very much wanted to find a pot of gold at the end of the rainbow. He looked everywhere for a rainbow that might have the prize he wanted. One afternoon after the clearing of the rain he stopped and walked to the rainbow that emerged that afternoon. As always, he hoped that this rainbow would have a pot of gold at its tip. This time he was correct and found a large golden container. But to his surprise there was nothing in this golden kettle—it was empty. In great discouragement the young man went home and for years continued to look for the "right" rainbow. One day when feeling utterly empty about his life the young man met an older gentleman. They walked together and talked often. During one of the walks the young man saw a rainbow and said, "That is it." "That is the same rainbow with the empty pot of gold." The two walked together to the rainbow and the young man looked inside the golden pot, finding nothing as he did before. The young man turned and began to walk away, only to have the old gentleman beckon him back with, "Go back one more time. But this time look carefully, not with the eyes of greed, but with prayer of finding direction." The young man went back again scanning the large kettle. This time, however, the kettle that had previously seemed so empty had on its vast floor a yellowed and old rolled up message. The message simply said: *Your task is not to find a pot of gold, but to help fill this kettle. For some, significance is given by birth, but for most, including you and me, **meaningful significance** can only be found in service to the other.*

The two men separated, both knowing that this time the young man had found a genuine pot of gold—his own call to responsibility. The old gentleman then vanished as the young man took his place of responsibility. (Arnett 1996a, 1–2)

Buber was fond of Hasidic tales that pointed the person with direction toward responsibility without dictating. Such stories and tales do not provide the "how," or the means by which one should implement responsibility; historically sensitive implementation is left to the reader. The answer is found between reader, text, and the historical moment of one's living.

Martin Buber understood the concrete nature of a story that guides a listener. The task of a teacher is to point, to give students tools that permit them to adapt ideas and suggestions as appropriate in a given historical moment. A priori answers to historically situated communicative problems bypass what is said, resulting in inappropriate responses to a particular situation. Buber's use of ambiguity as an invitation for concrete and particular application in a given historical moment turned the common understanding of abstract and concrete on their heads. For Buber, a concrete application points and can be adapted to the given moment, but does not dictate particular action. Use of an abstract principle, on the other hand, is a technique that is forced upon a given reality even when it is historically inappropriate. For Buber, stories were more concrete than a priori understandings and uses of technique that he actually considered abstract.

Martin Buber would have agreed with Jacques Ellul (1964) in his warning about the misuse of technique that seeks to live life prior to the needs of the concrete moment. Ellul called the technique mentality the greatest danger of the latter part of the twentieth century, and clearly our current fascination with computers has not lessened such an impulse. Buber's dialogue rebuffs answers that appear too neat and clean, but are actually abstract and miss genuine connections to a given situated moment. This concrete story form of guidance, grounded in intentional ambiguity, is central to Buber's (1967d) approach:

> I must say it once again: I have no teaching. I only point to something; I point to reality, I point to something in reality that had not or had too little been seen. I take him [or her] who listens to me by the hand and lead him [or her] to the window. I open the window and point to what is outside. I have no teaching, but I carry on a conversation. (693)

Buber did not introduce techniques that could be universally applied across various situations; instead, he pointed to concepts that must be applied differently in each historical moment.

Ambiguity combined with direction provides the reader and the hearer a chance to move ideas into appropriate action. Ambiguity serves as a reminder to consider the connection between the necessary companions of ideas and action in a particular situation. For instance, Buber suggests the wisdom of action in a time calling for response, not introspection.

Martin Buber, in *Israel and the World: Essays in a Time of Crisis* (1948/1976), shared:

> "[For one] who studies with a different intent than to act," says the Talmud, "it would have been more fitting for him [or

her] never to have created." It is bad to have teaching without the deed, worse when the teaching is one of action. Living in the detached sprit is evil, and worse when the spirit is one of ethos. Again and again, from the Sayings of the Fathers down to the definitive formulation of Hasidism, the simple man [or woman] who acts is given preference over the scholar whose knowledge is not expressed deeds. (141)

Buber understood the importance of the teacher guiding and the necessity of the reader putting ideas into action in accordance with the demands of the unique historical moment. Buber did not work from the communicative standpoint of a logical syllogism, but rather from the orientation of the enthymeme. Aristotle called "a rhetorical syllogism an enthymeme . . . and all [speakers] produce logical persuasion by means of paradigms or enthymemes and by nothing other than these" (1991, 1356b8). In an enthymeme, the audience provides the final completion of the statement, putting into action a behavior that is sensitive to the unique context. Enthymemes are "the 'body' of persuasion" (1354a3).

Such a view of story/tradition and model of interpretive courage was historically necessary in Buber's era, in which the demonic story of the Third Reich was so dominant that it seemed that we stood at the edge of the abyss of civilized discourse.

It is just the depth of the crisis that empowers us to hope. Let us dare to grasp the situation with that great realism that surveys all the definable realities of public life, of which, indeed, public life appears to be composed, but is also aware of what is most real of all, albeit moving secretly in the depths—the latent healing and salvation in the face of impending ruin. The power of turn that radically changes the situation never reveals itself outside of crisis. This power begins to function when one, gripped by despair, instead of allowing himself [or herself] to be submerged, calls forth his [or her] primal powers and accomplishes with them the turning of his [or her] very existence. (Buber 1966b, 124)

In the terror of collapse of constructive metanarratives, Buber called for courage to attend to the other and respond with one's whole being, permitting the reality of the between to be visible and heard in the discourse.

A Communicative Poetic

In a time of metanarrative collapse some people look for a formula
for survival, others search for "false" firm answers, still others call
for a leader to step forward and speak with such clarity that confusion is no longer an option. Martin Buber did not seek to artifi-
cially cover up confusion and lack of clarity; he did not attempt to
provide "false" clarity. Instead, he rode right into the center of
metanarrative chaos with hope and conviction that someday "common sense" would once again shine—but only if we invited "common sense" to emerge without forcing clarity of vision before its
time. Buber understood that the vision of a poet is sometimes
needed, not the clarity of a writer scripting prose in a compact, linear style. Buber's unique understanding of "concrete" and
"abstract" drove his commitment to intentional ambiguity in an
effort to address the lack of clarity offered by metanarratives
under attack. Buber avoided the swing from chaos to artificial clarity by offering ambiguity coupled with direction. He wrote with a
restless sense of realistic hope that patiently waited for genuine
answers in the between.

Nowhere in Martin Buber's writing is his poetic style more
powerfully present than in his discussion of *I and Thou* (1958).
Buber used his understanding of intentionality to state that there
is no "I" without a "Thou" and there is no "I" without an "It." Both
are connected views of the world, but only one is dialogically relational. "I-It" is how we experience and use the world. "I-Thou" is
how we invite a meeting with the world. Interestingly, if we try to
make all communication into "I-Thou" we are doomed to remain in
"I-It." The "I-Thou" can be invited, but never demanded. Buber
(1958) discussed "I-It" and "I-Thou":

> Here it becomes crystal clear to us that the spiritual reality of
> the primary words arises out of a natural reality, that of the pri-
> mary word *I-Thou* out of natural combination, and that of the
> primary word *I-It* out of natural separation. . . . The world of *It*
> is set in the context of space and time. The world of *Thou* is not
> set in the context of either of these. The particular *Thou*, after
> the relational event has run its course, *is bound* to become an
> *It*. The particular *It*, by entering the relational event, *may*
> become a *Thou*. . . . And in all the seriousness of truth, hear this:
> without *It* man [or woman] cannot live. But he [or she] who lives
> with *It* alone is not a man [or woman]. (24, 33, 34)

Essentially, in the above quotation, Buber is suggesting the following. First, all life is connected. We gain who we are from meeting otherness. Second, both "I-It" and "I-Thou" are fundamental parts of life. We use life and we meet life; one without the other limits the quality of human existence. Third, the "I-Thou" is the realm of dialogue—inviting, not forcing, meeting in the between.

Martin Buber calls for responsible understanding of the ideal and the given, and points with his poetic sense of guidance that does not dictate or force. "The long series of experiences that taught me to understand the problematic relationship between maxim and situation, and thereby disclosed to me the nature of the true norm that commands not our obedience but ourselves" (Buber 1973, 26). Buber was not evasive. He simply understood the difference between reading a significant work and an instruction manual— life for Buber needed to be treated with respect, even when events do not go as we desire. His poetic ambiguity revealed that a person has responsibility to respond to life, but seldom can we force life to do as we command.

Martin Buber's poetic patience was supported by more than a secular understanding of dialogue; it was grounded in a *Believing Humanism*:

> For if I should characterize my own basic view by a concept, it can only be the same as that with which we characterize Erasmus: the concept of a believing humanism. . . . Here humanity and faith do not appear as two separate realms each of which stands under its own signs and under its special laws; they penetrate each other, they work together, indeed, they are so centrally related to each other that we may say our faith has our humanity as its foundation and our humanity has our faith as its foundation. (1967d/1969, 117)

While some call Buber a mystic, we are more inclined to call him a poet of human communication. When clarity is not present, poets point without the "false" sureness of vision presented by a demagogue. Life speaks on its own terms and much can be learned by those with the courage to hear and to respond.

Martin Buber's writing is guided by an unclear destination, an intuitive teleology. Not only did Buber play with ideas in writing, he invited readers to do the same and creatively interact with his poetic and intentionally ambiguous style.

Play itself contains its own, even sacred, seriousness. Yet, in the attitude of play, all those purposive relations which determine active and caring existence have not simply disappeared, but in a curious way acquire a different quality. The player . . . knows that play is only play and exists in a world which is determined by the seriousness of purposes. But he [or she] does not know this in such a way that, as a player, he [or she] actually intends this relation to seriousness. Play fulfils its purpose only if the player loses himself [or herself] in his [or her] play. It is not that relation to seriousness which directs us away from play, but only seriousness in playing makes the play wholly play. (Gadamer 1960/1986, 91–92)

Under these conditions, play is serious without losing the dialectic of innovation and creativity within the horizon or rules of the game—in this case developing the text of a conversation.

Martin Buber's understanding of life was not only relational and dialogical, it was an alternative to metanarrative systems that were under attack in the Germany of his early thought formation. Buber provided a response to human beings living in a time between the collapsing of metanarratives and the construction of new genuine narratives. In *The Minimal Self: Psychic Survival in Troubled Times* (1984), Christopher Lasch stated that in a metanarrative decline the focus upon self is a natural option; it is just the wrong path to take. Focus upon self leads to narcissism and an increase in communicative problems, not a reduction in them. Buber's focus upon life happening between person and person or person and event, offers an alternative to a focus upon self.

Central Concepts in Martin Buber's Work

The general story of Martin Buber's work is understood through terms such as the between, the "great character" (1947/1965a, 116), "unity of contraries" (1965b/1966a, 111), and the "narrow ridge" (1965b/1966a, 110)—all terms that point to the danger of extremes. The complexity of life for Buber is lived out in the confusion of contradictions, not the certainty of YES or NO. Within the fabric of a "unity of contraries," Buber offers a dialogic view of interpersonal communication. The following section introduces some new terms, as well as integrating major points outlined earlier in the chapter.

The Great Character

One of Martin Buber's (1947/1965a) clearest examples of this "unity of contraries" impulse of intentionality is featured in his description of the "great character" (116).

> The great character is beyond the acceptance of norms. No responsible person remains a stranger to norms. But the command inherent in a genuine norm never becomes a maxim and the fulfillment of it is never a habit. . . . Today the great characters are still "enemies of the people," they who love their society, yet wish not only to preserve it but to raise it to a higher level. Tomorrow they will be the architects of a new unity of mankind [and womankind]. It is the longing for personal unity, from which must be born a unity of mankind [and womankind], which the educator should lay hold of and strengthen within his [or her] pupils. Faith in this unity and the will to achieve it is not a "return" to individualism, but a step beyond all the divide of individualism and collectivism. A great and full relation between . . . [two people] can only exist between unified and responsible persons. That is why it is much more rarely found in the totalitarian collective than in any historically earlier form of society; much more rarely also in the authoritarian party than in any character of free association. Genuine education of character is genuine education for community. (Buber 1947/1965a, 114, 116)

Buber's "great character" is the person doing philosophical anthropology who is conscious of the historical moment within a narrative background and takes his or her own uniqueness to a given situation without ignoring the larger text under study. A "great character" knows the story of a people well enough to violate it when necessary to meet the demands of the historical moment, permitting the story to continue to live and nourish a people.

Dialogue

In *Between Man and Man*, Martin Buber (1947/1965a) outlined three basic forms of communication: monologue, technical dialogue, and dialogue. He considered each form of communication necessary and important in its own right for working with people and events.

There is genuine dialogue—no matter whether spoken or silent—
where each of the participants really has in mind the other or
others in their present and particular being and turns to them
with the intention of establishing a living mutual relation
between himself [or herself] and them. There is technical dialogue, which is prompted solely by the need of objective understanding. And there is monologue disguised as dialogue, in which
two or more men [or women], meeting in space, speak each with
himself [or herself] in strangely tortuous and circuitous ways and
yet imagine they have escaped the torment of being thrown back
on their own resources. (Buber 1947/1965a, 19)

Buber stated that dialogue is rare; attending to what emerges
between persons in conversation is not the norm. We live in a time
of technical dialogue that is focused upon information—accentuat-
ing information delivery, information processing, and information
recall in the information age of the twenty-first century. In monologue one is more appreciative of hearing one's own voice than in
making contact with the other or actually sharing information that
might be of value.

Martin Buber's understanding of dialogue was not for those seeking comfort. Dialogue brings us face to face with life as it is, not as
we hope it would be. Buber's philosophy of communication is not to
be confused with a communicative system of comfort or a set of blinders permitting one to ignore the pain of the human struggle. Buber
(1966b) placed dialogue in the heart of human crisis and interaction:

And yet this must be said again and again, it is just the depth
of the crisis that empowers us to hope. Let us dare to grasp the
situation with that great realism that surveys all the definable
realities of public life, of which, indeed, public life appears to be
composed, but is also aware of what is most real of all, albeit
moving secretly in the depths—the late healing and salvation in
the face of impending ruin. The power of turning that radically
changes the situation never reveals itself outside of crisis. (124)

One finds insight walking through a crisis, not around it. Avoidance
and rejection of life's struggles is the antithesis of Buber's view of
human dialogue. One may deeply disagree with life's events as they
are played out and work to change them. Such action is, however,
quite different than pretending problems do not exist. Intentional
blindness to human problems seldom steers us to safety.

We use the term *dialogue* with much ease. Martin Buber's view of dialogue was much more demanding. One must first know the ground on which one stands and then be open to the other's position. Dialogue, for Buber, is not to be confused with expressivism. Two people sharing emotive responses is contrary to his communicative emphasis on content that simultaneously requires openness to the other.

The form of communication that one uses will have a significant impact upon focus of attention or where one looks for communicative meaning to emerge. Like the chicken and the egg, we are unclear which comes first—the form of communication or the focus of attention. These two components work in interactive fashion with one another to enable communication to occur.

Focus of Attention

Dialogue guides the focus of attention between persons. Technical dialogue puts the focus of attention on gathered information. Monologue places the focus of attention upon oneself. Martin Buber saw the importance of each focus of attention. The goal, however, is to be honest about where one's focus is and to appropriately connect that focus to a given historical moment.

For instance, a young girl works very hard to do well on an exam only to receive a B at the end of much labor. The girl's focus upon oneself in such a situation would be normal and appropriate. However, staying in this form of communication too long would be problematic. Eventually, she needs to gather information through technical dialogue about why this happened. Finally, perhaps years later after the young girl has become a woman, she might mentor another young person who is disappointed with her result after long effort. The seasoned mentor can then listen for what emerges between the two of them in dialogue, with full knowledge that a current problem is more fully understood out of the historical material of her own life, situated in that particular moment.

Authenticity

Often when one hears the term *authenticity*, one thinks of a 1960s form of self-disclosure placed upon genuine feelings. This view is contrary to Martin Buber's understanding of being and seeming. Buber connected being to the notion of authenticity. Being is tied, not to "me," but to the complexity of the communicative moment. This suggests that being includes dialogue, technical dialogue, and monologue. Often the notion of being is tied solely to dialogue, leading ironically to seeming—if one forces the appearance of dialogue when it is not called for or possible in a communicative situation, monologue is unleashed.

Seeming is based upon images of what one wants to be. Being is based upon dialogue with the other about what is appropriate in a communicative moment (Buber 1965b/1966a). Authenticity for Buber is not tied to "my" emotive reaction, but a willingness to be in communication with the other in the given historical moment, permitting monologue, technical dialogue, and dialogue to emerge when called forth appropriately in the concrete moments of life.

Historicality and Dialogic Civility

The value of Martin Buber's work is twofold. First, in a time of meta-narrative crisis, the concept of the between works as a metaphor, reminding us that we still need to co-constitutively discover ways to create communicative background in communicative interaction—even if that background has limited history and duration. Second, Buber reminds us in a time of corporate downsizing and increasing concern for "me" that life is still to be lived in relation—sometimes to gather information, sometimes to reflect upon one's own life that has been lived with others, and sometimes in actual dialogue. Life in relation is guided by an interdependent metaphor—the between.

Martin Buber is a needed poet of communication for the twenty-first century. He embraces the necessity of an informational life, while clearly suggesting that real living includes and goes beyond information to the relational meeting of the other. Stories need to guide us as we listen and respond to their insight as well as responding to the needs of the historical moment between us. The following quotation from "Technicians of Goodness: Ignoring the Narrative Life of Dialogue" (Arnett 1996b) articulates the spirit of Buber's dialogic project between persons:

> Dialogue requires one to know the ground on which one stands and argues for, while affirming the other's right to do the

same. There is a philosophical commitment to a dialogic oxymoron—recognition of the importance of the story and awareness of the limits of any given story.

A narrative guides; a technician follows a snap shot, a static picture, failing to understand the lived tradition and story. As we work to assist persons in communication, my hope is for an understanding of narrative that (a) calls more for cautious conviction than ideological certainty, (b) calls more for accountability rooted in compassion than the assurance of the "true believer," and (c) calls more for a willingness to see the person as necessary not sufficient, recognizing the complexity and ambiguity of the narrative guiding one's actions. My hope is that the person in dialogue with a substantive narrative would not fall prey to what Jacques Ellul has called the danger of the 20th century—a technique mentality. (354)

There is no formula for dialogue and there is no excuse for pure expressivism. Both reliance on technique and expressive babble fail to meet the demands of dialogue in the midst of genuine crisis, wherein the between is found between the ground on which one stands and openness to the other.

Martin Buber clearly points to a dialogic civility in a time of metanarrative crisis. He takes dialogue to a more public level between persons. He resists the impulse to privatize communication meaning within the self. The poet is a public figure, writing to be read aloud, with others, in relation—finding meaning between text and person. Buber, a communicative poet, pointed to dialogic civility, calling us to find meaning between people, together. The crisis is met in dialogue, without the answer being found in the one or the collective, but between us in dialogic civility.

Chapter *Eight*

Carol Gilligan

Gender and Moral Voice

Including Woman's Voice —

Listening to women's voices clarified the ethic of care, not because care is essentially associated with women or part of women's nature, but because women for a combination of psychological and political reasons voiced relational realities that were otherwise unspoken or dismissed as inconsequential.

—Carol Gilligan, "Hearing the Difference:
Theorizing Connection"

Voice, Hearing, and Human Connection —

Metaphors of voice and hearing . . . draw attention to human connection—to the relationship between speaker and listener, to the possibility of different language, and thus to the potential for misunderstanding and mistranslation as well as to the ability of people to see and to speak about themselves and the world in more than one way. In short, by suggesting a change in the language and the metaphors of psychology, we imply the need for a metaphysical shift: a change in stance, a new voice, a different perspective, a change of heart.

—Carol Gilligan, Lyn Mikel Brown,
and Annie G. Rogers, "Psyche Embedded"

C arol Gilligan offered a relational/psychological approach to interpersonal experience that opened discussion about gender differences in communication and moral decision making. Gilligan responded to traditional moral theory developed primarily by Lawrence Kohlberg (1958, 1969, 1976, 1981, 1984), who used male subjects and focused on notions of equality, justice, and rights. According to Gilligan, traditional moral theory portrays woman as morally deficient because woman's moral judgments place greater emphasis on relational ideas such as caring, rather than abstract concepts such as justice. In essence, Gilligan introduced woman's relational voice into the discussion of moral reasoning. Like Abraham Maslow, Gilligan offers additive change; to fully understand issues of morality we must listen to both woman's voice and man's voice. Gilligan's work inspired cultural awareness of woman's psychological health, enlarging the study of moral development.

Carol Gilligan addresses a moral crisis, in which exclusion of women's voices was systematically perpetuated by a narrow research agenda. Following a discussion of the historical context that framed Gilligan's writings, we overview her depiction of two distinct moral voices, which prompts a discussion of the biological, social, and cultural differences associated with male and female moral development. Gilligan's work on adolescent development and the moral self, including her focus on connection, responsibility in relationships, resistance, a morality of care, as well as voice and inclusion are addressed. Focusing on women in relationship, Gilligan's work provides important insight about exclusion, which opens the door to routine cynicism in contemporary society. The contribution of Gilligan's work for interpersonal communication comes from her highlighting a relational voice in the moral crisis about human development. Dialogic civility points to a public moral dimension where exclusion based on gender, race, and ethnicity is rejected, while different voices framed from different standpoints are encouraged to contribute to public dialogue.

Introduction

Carol Gilligan examines moral voice and gender in discussions of relational/psychological development and education. Traditional moral theories generally identified stages of a man's development and his application of moral concepts. Gilligan (1995) noted that women were rarely included in early research on psychological development, and when they were included, they were marginalized—male moral development was defined as the norm. Woman's viewpoint, which Gilligan identifies as the care perspective, prioritizes caring and responsibility in relationships. The central premise of woman's morality is that self and others are connected, interdependent (Gilligan 1977, 1982, 1988c, 1995).

Carol Gilligan's research purports a difference between a patriarchal and a relational voice. Her work marks a paradigm shift in psychology, wherein "voice, relationship, resistance, and women become central rather than peripheral in this reframing of the human world" (Gilligan 1995, 120). Gilligan's work generated discussion among specialists interested in moral development theory and generalists who identify with an ethic of care. Joy Kroeger-Mappes (1994) recognized that Gilligan's work has significant import for feminism, social science theory, and moral philosophy; Gilligan's thought shifted the ground not only for psychology, but for philosophy and political theory as well.

As Carol Gilligan's writing became noteworthy, criticism of her research methods as well as the theoretical underpinning of her ethic of care emerged (Davis 1992, Kerber, Greens, Maccoby, Luria, Stack, and Gilligan 1986, Kroeger-Mappes 1994, Wood 1994). Like Carl Rogers, Carol Gilligan was a pioneer. Her task was to reveal the crisis in moral development theory. Gilligan sought ways not to offer the answer to moral development, but to ask how a female voice might add to our understanding of the process. Gilligan, whether one agrees or disagrees with her research methods or conclusions, has enriched and deepened our understanding of moral development and what it means to be fully human. Gilligan's contribution to morality emerged within a historical context where even within a framework of equality, woman's voice could no longer be ignored. From this historical standpoint of awareness of meta-narrative decline and perhaps collapse, we ask the following question about Carol Gilligan's work: "How can dialogue in the midst of the crisis of exclusion encourage voice?" Gilligan addresses the crisis of access and voice in moral development research, with the implications of her work reaching well beyond the field of psychology.

Historical Context: A Window for Cynicism

The historical context that frames Carol Gilligan's work spans the 1950s to the present. Gilligan (1988b) explained that following

Sputnik in the late 1950s, Americans (in an effort to keep up with the Russians) became concerned about the state of math and science education. A psychological rationale for their concern was found in the work of Jean Piaget (1932/1965), who equated cognitive development with the growth of mathematical and scientific thinking. Theories of adolescent development advanced by Jean Piaget (1932/1965), Erik Erikson (1950), and Lawrence Kohlberg (1958) associated development with the ability to think formally by proceeding from theory to fact and the ability to differentiate both the self and moral dilemmas apart from identification with one's childhood world. The inquiry into adolescent development began with a world in which control or mastery seemed more significant than relational caring—the former given to a male public world and the latter to female private caring in the home.

During the late 1960s, student protests focused on the consequences of social inequality and spoke out against unfairness. Student movements included a large number of females, who challenged the existing state of relationships. On January 23, 1973, the Supreme Court ruled in *Roe v. Wade*. Their decision legalized abortion and made it a basic, specially protected right, like free speech. Writing in the wake of this decision, Gilligan lamented that the Supreme Court gave women a legal voice, yet "framed that voice within a discourse of rights which made it impossible to speak about relationship, except in terms of justice . . . [and] in terms of contractual obligation, neither of which had much bearing on many women's situation" (1995, 121).

The student protests of the 1960s and early 1970s, plus *Roe v. Wade*, generated much optimism. As stated before, however, unmet optimism is the seed of cynicism. In this window for cynicism, Gilligan added a positive voice to our understanding of human development including both males and females as participants.

The decade of the 1970s brought disillusionment from the protests of the 1960s. The social movements seeking to inspire change in the social system "degenerated into privatism and retreat, as concerns with both justice and care focused increasingly on the self" (Gilligan 1988a, 156). Simultaneously, global issues such as pollution and the threat of nuclear war revealed the erroneous possibility of solving problems by exit, which drew attention from the reality of human interdependence.

Gilligan witnessed increases in teenage suicide, educational problems, and illegal activity, providing further evidence that new directions in psychological theory and practice were needed. Carol

Gilligan, Lyn Brown, and Annie Rogers identified an irony in psychology: even as psychologists sought to understand interaction or relationships, the language used to describe relationships was filled with "static images of separation" derived from traditional research protocol which attempted to classify, categorize, and ultimately, predict and control human behavior. Concerned with seeing woman's morality defined as deficient by Lawrence Kohlberg (1958, 1969, 1976, 1981, 1984) and other moral theorists, Gilligan began to examine woman's activities and cultural values and the problem of exclusion.

Carol Gilligan heard women speak in a different voice from the male voices that dominated psychological theory at that time. Julia Wood summarized Gilligan's thesis: "women's 'failure to develop' on [traditional moral scales] is actually divergent development. . . . Because women and men develop in different ways, they embrace distinct values and employ distinctive criteria to define situations and guide their actions" (1986, 274).

Carol Gilligan recognized that women construct moral problems differently than men. Instead of comparing women to men within the patriarchal model of morality, Gilligan was interested in understanding what female experience contributes to thoughts about woman's identity and moral development. "What then do women say when asked to construct the moral domain; how do we identify the characteristically 'feminine' voice?" (Gilligan 1977, 485). Gilligan's pioneering efforts required a new approach to developing a relational/psychological theory of moral development.

Moral Voices

In beginning her investigation, Carol Gilligan was aware that "the master's tools will never dismantle the master's house" (Lorde 1984, 112). This meant not relying on traditional research methods and data analysis techniques. Gilligan and her associates created instead "a voice-centered, relational method of doing psychological research" (Brown and Gilligan 1992, 19; see also Gilligan 1988b, Gilligan and Attanucci 1988, Gilligan and Wiggins 1988, Gilligan, Brown, and Rogers 1990). They used an interviewing approach, "responsive to the harmonics of psychic life, the nonlinear, recursive, nontransparent play, interplay and orchestration of feelings and thoughts, the polyphonic nature of any utterance, and the symbolic nature not only of what is said but also of what is *not* said" (Brown and Gilligan 1992, 23). Gilligan relied on the power of storytelling because the process allows the storyteller to continually locate and relocate one's voice within a social and cultural context.

Steven Spielberg's (1993) production, *Schindler's List*, reminds us that only decades ago Germany, considered one of the most highly educated and cultured of nations, demonstrated an indescribable capacity for moral atrocity. Given this historical background, Carol Gilligan understood that any isomorphic association of morality with culture, intelligence, or education is immediately suspect. She suggests such associations "may have opened the way for the current revival of religious fundamentalism and of terrorism, as well as for the present skepticism about nineteenth century ideas about development or progress" (1988b, xvi).

Carol Gilligan recognized that any discussion of morality carries with it institutionalized social norms and cultural values. Gilligan (1977) reminded us that choice making and one's willingness to accept responsibility for one's choices is the essence of moral decision making. In considering what is moral in any given context, each person reflects on how she or he should or would like to act in relationships. Scholars interested in moral inquiry *In a Different Voice* (Gilligan 1982) investigate questions of relationship and emphasize issues of inclusion (how to connect with oneself and others) and exclusion (how to avoid being detached or turning away from others in need).

In Carol Gilligan's investigations, she discovered that woman holds a moral conception different from that described by Sigmund Freud (1905/1962), Jean Piaget (1932/1965), or Lawrence Kohlberg (1958, 1981). Traditional research conceived of morality as abstract fairness and connected moral development to the understanding of rights and rules. Joy Kroeger-Mappes explained:

> In this logic, morality consists of a hierarchy of rights and rules used to resolve moral conflicts or problems by weighing claims and judging which is the heavier claim. Images of winning and losing are common. There is potential for violence resulting, in part, from seeing others as opponents and seeing oneself in contest to obtain, or win, one's rights and to maintain them. Individual rights are primary and universal. (1994, 110)

In traditional approaches to moral dilemmas, the solution is rationally conceived by abstracting from the interpersonal situation, so that anyone following reason will arrive at more or less the same right or rule.

Underlying the ethic of rights is the premise that individuals are separate from one another. Relationships are understood on the basis of reciprocity between separate individuals, grounded in the duty and obligations of their roles. Reciprocity is defined in terms of maintaining standards of justice and fairness. "The values of justice and autonomy . . . incorporated into definitions of morality and self, imply a view of the individual as separate and of relationships as either hierarchical or contractual, bound by the alternatives of constraint and cooperation" (Gilligan 1988c, 8).

In response to traditional moral theory of justice and theoretical fairness, Carol Gilligan recognized a conception of morality concerned with "activities of care" (1988a, 151), which center moral development around the understanding of "responsibility" (1982, 21–22) and "relationships" (1982, 170–171). These two moral standpoints (justice and "care") offer people a choice of perspective from which to approach moral problems. Gilligan noted that having a choice of "moral voice or standpoint" (1988b, xviii) brings a new dimension to understanding the role of the self in moral decision making.

In the historical moment during which Carol Gilligan's early work emerged, traditional moral theory was understood as universal. Gilligan undertook the task to get woman's voice heard in studies of moral development. We read Gilligan's work with the knowledge that other writers, such as Julia Wood, continue to join the conversation that seeks to understand woman's voice.

Carol Gilligan suggests that there are two psychological voices, situated in but not dependent on biological sex, which emerge in crises and influence one's moral development:

The different voice I describe is characterized not by gender but theme. Its association with women is an empirical observation. . . . But this association is not absolute, and the contrasts between male and female voices are presented here to highlight a distinction between two modes of thought and to focus a problem of interpretation rather than to represent a generalization about either sex. In tracing development, I point to the interplay of these voices within each sex and suggest that their convergence marks times of crisis and change. No claims are made about the origins of the differences described or their distribution in a wider population, across cultures, or through time. Clearly, these differences arise in a social context where factors of social status and power combine with reproductive biology to shape the experience of males and females and the relations between the sexes. (1982, 2)

Throughout Gilligan's work, she associates a justice perspective with man and she associates a care perspective with woman. Julia Wood suggested, "[I]t is more appropriate and more useful to recognize that distinct understandings and motives may guide how individuals perceive and deal with their relationships. To appreciate these differences as legitimate is a prerequisite to coordinated communication" (1986, 299). A "male" or "female" style of communication is not biologically determined, but relationally chosen when situationally appropriate. In connecting Gilligan's psychological theory of voice to relational communication, Wood does not bifurcate justice and care, but acknowledges both perspectives as vital to authentic relationship.

Julia Wood (1994) recognized that Gilligan writes in two authorial personas, or voices—that of scholar and that of partisan. Although not mutually exclusive roles, they are not entirely harmonious in Gilligan's works. Wood sought to unravel connections between biological sex, psychological gender, and moral voice that present an interpretive challenge in the development of Gilligan's ideas. Gilligan identified a developmental sequence of levels in an ethic of care. Wood's (1994) careful analysis of Carol Gilligan's (1982) work recognized that Gilligan did not demonstrate a sequential progression among the levels in moral development. Further, Gilligan does not address any possibility of regression to less mature levels. Wood's insight suggests this sequence of levels in the ethic of care may better be conceived as types of caring that are not necessarily sequential. Each type of caring acknowledges a relationally and situationally appropriate connection of self and other. Consistent with Gilligan's commitment to broadening our views, Wood's (1994) observation echoes Gilligan's (1990) correction of her own work.

Carol Gilligan (1982) asserts that women judge themselves in terms of their ability to care, their ability to take responsibility for their own destiny, and their ability to maintain interpersonal relations. Julia Wood responded:

In encouraging women to continue caring for others because it is good, it needs to be done, and no one else will do it, Gilligan invites women to participate—or to continue participating—in their own subordination. In effect, Gilligan's ideas in no way challenge the structure of our culture, which establishes the meanings and consequences of the role she advocates for women. Given this, Gilligan emerges as a distinctly conservative voice, one that endorses the existing social organization and women's conventional place within it. She suggests in fact, that *because* caring and relationships are not esteemed in Western culture, women have a special mission to be the ones who preserve these values within the pockets and margins of a social order they are not invited to collaborate in creating. (1994, 167)

Wood situates women within a social history in which advancing oneself means having the right to choose how to live one's life.

Carol Gilligan responded to her critics by centralizing relationship between persons, rather than differences in moral voice, in her feminist ethic of care. Connection with others is recognized as primary and fundamental to human life. Gilligan (1995) notes that autonomy, rather than providing a solution to psychological and moral problems, is itself the problem. Reframing psychology to accent connection, rather than autonomy, changes that way we understand the world. Connection through relationship has moved to the foreground in her discussion of moral voices.

Julia Wood and Carol Gilligan each addressed a different historical moment. Gilligan pressed the female voice to almost a caricature form so that it could be heard. Wood now calls us to a human moral development in which issues other than gender can encourage choice of voice—justice or care.

Central Concepts in Carol Gilligan's Work

Carol Gilligan's work centers around the experience of girls' adolescence—the crossroads between being a girl and becoming a woman. She considered problems of connection that occur at this time, and noted how responsibility and care in relationship are central to woman's voice.

Female Adolescence

Lyn Mikel Brown and Carol Gilligan, in *Meeting at the Crossroads: Women's Psychology and Girls' Development* (1992), reminded us that the edge of adolescence is a time of heightened psychological risk for girls. During adolescence,

> the interpretive schemes of the culture, including the system of social norms, values, and roles, impinge more directly on perception and judgment, defining within the framework of a given society what is "the right way" to see and to feel and to think, the way "we" think. (Gilligan 1988b, xxiii)

Adolescence is the time when girls' thoughts and values clash with structures composing a patriarchal social system.

Developmental changes that occur in girls' bodies visually disconnect them from their childhood. Girls become identified by others as women and become all too familiar with advertisements and cultural images that identify physical and moral perfection as the standard of female beauty and goodness (Spitzack 1990). Lyn Mikel Brown and Carol Gilligan address adolescence as a time when girls become looked at, talked about, and judged against standards of perfection and relationship ideals. They remind us that girls approaching adolescence are often victims of incest and other forms of sexual abuse. Further, adolescence is a time when girls may experience eating disorders, poor body image, a loss of self-worth, and suicidal thoughts and gestures. During adolescence, girls may lose their vitality, their resilience, their immunity to depression, and their sense of themselves. Gilligan's work advances our understanding of girls' crisis by examining the psychological dimensions of adolescence.

Disconnection. During adolescence, girls try to maintain their own thoughts and feelings while trying to fit an image—an artistically airbrushed, static representation—that is not real. A division occurs between what girls know in their personal experience and what has been socially constructed as "reality." Aware of this contradiction, a girl may "lose" her own voice:

> Thoughts and feelings which expose that reality as unreal often seem too dangerous to speak out loud, and are retracted, taken inside, moved out of sight and hearing: hidden from all

but the most trusted relationships or perhaps not spoken at all. Feelings are felt, thoughts are thought, but when no longer spoken, they are no longer heard—no longer endangered but also no longer exposed to the air and the light of relationship. (Brown and Gilligan 1992, 168)

For a girl to take on the "problem of appearance" (Gilligan 1990b, 4) in adolescent development by trying to connect her life with society, she must enter a tradition in which human generally means male.

Adolescence is a critical time when girls are in danger of losing their own voices—when they choose not to speak to avoid revealing that their voices might not match societal standards of perfection.

Girls develop a sharp eye and ear for the disparity between what people say and what is really going on. But underneath there is a deeper and more confusing split: not between appearance and reality but between their experience and reality as it is generally constructed by other people. Then girls speak of feeling crazy or insane. (Brown and Gilligan 1992, 170)

Adolescents have the capacity to hold and coordinate a variety of perspectives—both hypothetical and abstract. Brown and Gilligan recognized that during this time, girls risk losing touch with their bodies, their feelings, their relationships, and their experience: girls "are in danger of losing their ability to distinguish what is true from what is said to be true, what feels loving from what is said to be love, what feels real from what is said to be reality" (1992, 215). During adolescent development, girls becoming young women face the danger of losing their ability to know the difference between authentic and inauthentic relationships.

Lyn Mikel Brown and Carol Gilligan (1992) recognized that in one sense girls progress steadily, moving from childhood into adolescence, a stage of developmental crisis. Adolescent female development is characterized by a struggle for girls to listen to their own voices in conversation and respond to their feelings and thoughts. In the process of girls becoming women, girls reach a crossroads marked by disconnection. This time of development leaves them psychologically at risk and involved in relational struggle.

Carol Gilligan identified problems of connection—attachment and detachment—as central concerns in girls' accounts of their experiences in adolescent years. To develop one's identity and achieve moral growth, one must separate both from parental authority and from the authority of social conventions. During girls' adolescence, they renegotiate issues of attachment which include sexuality and perspective in relationships—which introduces new complications and depth to the human connection. Gilligan noted that "conflicts of attachment that arise at this time are exemplified by the problems that girls describe when they perceive the inclusion of themselves (their views and their wishes) as hurting their parents, whereas including their parents implies excluding themselves" (1988a, 148). This insight illustrates a paradox many girls live with: when a girl speaks her voice, this will limit others from achieving what they desire; for a girl to include others means she, herself, will not be included.

Re-Connection and Care. As girls discussed conflict and choice, Carol Gilligan (1988a) heard a moral dimension in activities of care; one's ability to care is both a source of empowerment and a standard of self-evaluation. Girls' vision reveals cognitive and affective dimensions of care. Care is grounded in the ability to perceive people in their own terms and to respond to their needs. Because this knowledge generates the power both to help and to hurt, the use of care becomes a measure of responsibility in relationships.

The reality of relationship is that persons are connected and interdependent. Life can only be sustained by care in relationship. At the time of Carol Gilligan's early writing, many self-help books touted the dangers of dependence and co-dependence. Contrary to popular sentiment, Gilligan contrasted separation, equality, and independence with connection, inequality, and attachment. Gilligan recognized a "psychological ambiguity and ethical tension" (1988c, 14), which emerge in the concept of dependence. Dependence is not the opposite of independence; isolation is the opposite of independence. This realization shifts the concept of dependence:

> Being dependent, then, no longer means being helpless, powerless, and without control; rather, it signifies a conviction that one is able to have an effect on others, as well as the recognition that the interdependence of attachment empowers both the self and the other, not one person at the other's expense. The activities of care—being there, listening, the willingness to help, and the ability to understand—take on a moral dimension, reflecting the injunction to pay attention

and not to turn away from need. As the knowledge that others are capable of care renders them lovable rather than merely reliable, so the willingness and the ability of care becomes a standard of self-evaluation. (Gilligan 1988c, 16)

When girls get disconnected, they rely on others to tell them what they feel, think, and know. Their shock and resistance to disconnection reveals the strength of their connection to childhood. This relational voice is needed in a time of self-help individualism, revealing the importance of Gilligan's historical contribution to dialogic civility.

Responsibility in Relationship-Grounded Caring. When a girl comes into relationship with herself, and recognizes her responsibility for taking care of herself, the way she is connected with others changes. These changes set the boundaries of the moral conflict girls describe when responsibility for oneself conflicts with her responsibility to others. Girls seek to resolve two perceived conflicts: first, how to be responsive to themselves without losing connection with others; and second, how to respond to others without abandoning themselves. A woman then seeks to be responsible for herself *and* others, thus reconciling the disparity between hurt and care.

The exercise of such responsibility requires a new kind of judgment, whose first demand is for honesty. To be responsible for oneself, it is first necessary to acknowledge what one is doing. The criterion for judgment thus shifts from goodness to truth when the morality of action is assessed not on the basis of its appearance in the eyes of others, but in terms of the realities of its intention and consequence. (Gilligan 1982, 82–83)

In her analysis of Carol Gilligan's work, Julia Wood identified passages that "suggest that responsibility involves experiencing others' needs as one's own, which . . . is one of the requirements of caring and has the potential to diminish a caregiver's autonomy and sensitivity to her or his own motives, needs, and goals" (1994, 76). To remain responsive to one's own needs, a woman must practice resistance to social and cultural conventions that mute her own voice. Caring has a dialectical set of responsibilities—toward self and the other.

A Dialectical Dance. For a girl to remain responsive to herself, she must resist the conventions of feminine goodness; for a girl to remain responsive to others, she must resist the values placed on self-sufficiency and independence in North American culture. She must consider what relationship means to herself, to others, and to the world (Gilligan 1990a).

In clinical psychology, resistance means to bury psychological truths or avoid key memories and emotions. In adolescence, a girl's development may hinge on resisting the loss of knowledge gained in the experiences of her childhood. As a girl's body and experiences change in adolescence, she is more likely to discount her childhood experiences or group them together and hide them from herself and others. At the center of the relational crisis of girls' adolescence is a resistance to giving up the reality of relationships for the cultural image of an ideal relationship. Girls are encouraged at adolescence to adopt images of perfection and to become the perfect woman.

Girls have a healthy resistance to connection, which emerges at the edge of adolescence—against a culture in which separation is encouraged, choices are dominated by logic, and honest, genuine relationships are not seen as possible. Lyn Mikel Brown and Carol Gilligan (1992) shared the story of Anna, who describes psychological resistance in her attempt to suppress her feelings of hurt or anger. This resistance will lead Anna to become a "nice" girl who is successful. At the same time, Anna experiences political resistance in her realization that she can not allow cultural messages to overtake her will. Her resistance will inevitably create conflict in her relationships with others. At adolescence, girls' psychological development becomes inescapably political.

Carol Gilligan, Annie Rogers, and Deborah Tolman (1991) believe resistance is a mark of psychological strength and courage. For girls to be psychologically healthy, they must resist inauthentic or false relationships. We must all work through challenges and strive to maintain authentic relationships with others. We all need a dialectic counter to our interpersonal strengths, otherwise a strength may become so exaggerated that it becomes a liability. Indeed, caring requires learning a dialectical dance in which one not only follows, but one can lead.

A Morality of Care

The morality of care situates responsibility within the context of relationship or connection with others. Carol Gilligan (1982) offers the image of a web that ultimately connects everyone. Joy Kroeger-Mappes (1994) equated Gilligan's view of responsibility with the "need to respond" (110) and the "moral imperative to care" (110). Relationships are understood as a response to the other through a morality of care. A morality of care "implies principles of equity, flexibility, and responsibility in dealing with particular situations, needs, and people" (Wood 1986, 275). From this perspective, moral dilemmas are conceived as conflicting responsibilities within the context of relationships. In the morality of care, this focus on multiple responsibilities "affirms" human connection.

Carol Gilligan (1977) identified the developmental sequence of the ethic of care as comprised of three levels: individual survival, goodness as self-sacrifice, and the morality of nonviolence. Gilligan identified two transitions, which connect the levels: repairing relationship by self-correction from selfishness to responsibility and moving from goodness to truth. The first level in the ethic of care involves caring for one's self to ensure survival. This is followed by a transition wherein the judgment to care for oneself is conceived as selfish. A new understanding of the connection between self and others is found in the concept of "responsibility" (1982, 74) for others. In the second level, caring for others is equated with what is good. Goodness occurs only when others are the recipients of the woman's care. Yet, when the woman excludes herself from relationship, problems emerge. During the second transition the woman reconsiders the relationship to sort out the confusion between self-sacrifice and care in the concept of goodness. The third level relieves the tension between selfishness and responsibility by a new understanding of the relationship between self and other. In this level, "care" (1982, 74) is selected as the preferred response, condemning any exploitation and hurt of others. This sequence is informed by an understanding of the psychology of human relationships wherein self and other become increasingly differentiated. The "ethic of care" (1982, 74) is centered in relationship—self and other are interdependent and the activity of care enhances both self and others when the activity is chosen for appropriate historical and situational reasons.

In her later writing, Carol Gilligan noted that this developmental sequence was not supported in observations of younger girls: "the sequence that I had traced by following adolescent girls and adult women through time and through crisis did not seem to be rooted in childhood. Instead it seemed a response to crisis, and the crisis seemed to be adolescence" (1990a, 9–10). In this realization, the foundation of the sequence shifts. The sequence is no longer seen as an occurrence of developmental progression, but rather occurs in response to the crisis of adolescence. Adolescence is the field where the dialectic dance begins; those who genuinely meet this moment and successfully move through it will be at different points of historical development in their sense of morality and responsibility of care.

Voice and Inclusion

Carol Gilligan (1988a) cited Albert Hirschman's *Exit, Voice and Loyalty: Responses to Decline in Firms, Organizations, and States* (1970) wherein he addresses the problems of attachment that are part of modern society. Hirschman offers the notion of loyalty as a correction to the exit option as a sole means for effecting change. Girls define loyalty as attachment to others; a relationship in which one's voice is silenced is not a relationship in any meaningful sense. Girls who resist the exit option may recognize that dilemmas of attachment are best solved by voice. In deciding when to stay or leave, when to remain silent or speak, the interplay of exit, voice, and loyalty are illustrated.

Because voice is embodied, it connects psyche and body. Because voice is in language, it joins psyche and culture. Voice is inherently relational. The sound of one's voice changes depending on the relationship—whether one is heard or not, how one is responded to (Brown and Gilligan 1992, 20). Exit and voice are seen as "modes of response and recuperation" (Gilligan 1988a, 143). Exit offers an alternative to silence where one's voice has failed. Realizing the costs of detachment from oneself and others is important in girls' development; this recognition encourages voice while sustaining exit as an option of last resort (Gilligan 1988a, 155). To be in relational care with another permits the voice of self and other to be heard.

Historicality and Dialogic Civility

Carol Gilligan argues for an expanded conception of adulthood that integrates woman's voice into developmental theory. Out of the crisis of exclusion, Gilligan made public another perspective, *In a Dif-*

ferent Voice (1982). "Women's thinking about moral conflict and choice reflects an image or web or network—of multiple, simultaneous, and overlapping relationships and responsibilities that connect people and are sustained through processes of communication that assume and affirm connections" (Wood 1986, 275). Gilligan's work contributes important insight for our understanding of communication and relationships. For us, she penned a new chapter to the background moral call to care that now impacts interpersonal communication theory.

Women struggle in relationships to accommodate both an ethic of care and an ethic of justice. Women who feel they cannot trust their own voice may not trust others' communication either. Rather than asking people directly what they feel or think and then listening to what they say, women interpret beyond the appearance of what is said and done—becoming experts at translation. Lyn Mikel Brown and Carol Gilligan report that girls

> talk about seeing, seeing through, seeing into, as if one must step outside of relationships to know what is going on. And with this move, they align themselves with a long tradition that separates knowing from feelings, self from relationship, mind from body, voice from desire. By-passing relationship as a way of knowing, they attempt to become all-seeing, omniscient. (1992, 173)

In the futile attempt to become all-knowing, we can easily see how routine cynicism may emerge as a response to the differences between reality and illusion.

Women's sensitivity to disenfranchised voices leads to a difficulty about what to think and do as they struggle to understand and reconcile conflicting perspectives in the determination of a good and fair solution. Women's efforts to reach fair solutions can be difficult because of a complex standpoint on issues. Standpoint theory (Harding 1991; Hartsock 1983, 1985; Wood 1992) offers a means for repositioning Gilligan's theory of morality.

By adopting a distinct standpoint, an understanding of relationship and the world can emerge. Gender must be understood within the culture whose structural and discursive base comprise it (Wood 1992). We must situate moral standpoints in the material, social, and historical conditions from which they arise. A theory of care as an ethic for interpersonal relationships must not be associated wholly with women; instead we should focus on the relational conditions in which caring is needed and appropriate.

Carol Gilligan responded to a historical moment that called for inclusion of another voice in the crisis of moral voice exclusion. Her voice is not the last to speak, as Julia Wood and others continue the conversation. We are, however, indebted to this courageous and pioneering voice that called attention to the exclusive nature of moral development. Gilligan is prophet calling us to listen to those not heard, so that they may enlarge their own worlds and our own. Gilligan's dialogic response to crisis is based on inclusion, relational voice, dialectical tension between self and other, and the additive reminder that to be fully human requires not only a sensitivity for justice but a responsibility to care. Dialogic civility as background narrative for public discourse has at its center both justice and care. In a time of ethnic, religious, and social diversity, each voice is important to this approach. Both justice and care need to be part of the public arena of dialogic civility. Dialogue and crisis through Gilligan's voice remind us of the value of an ethic of care in the public arena, bringing into the light relational care, the action of dialogic civility.

Chapter Nine

Paulo Freire

Dignity and the Limits of Inclusion

On Authority and Freedom —

The dialogical theory of action opposes both authoritarianism and
license, and thereby affirms authority and freedom. There is no
freedom without authority, but there is also no authority without
freedom. . . . In the theory of dialogical action, organization
requires authority, so it cannot be authoritarian; it requires freedom, so it cannot be licentious. Organization is, rather, a highly
educational process in which leaders and people together experience true authority and freedom, which they then seek to establish in society by transforming the reality which mediates them.

— Paulo Freire, *Pedagogy of the Oppressed*

On Liberating Education —

One of the radical differences between education as a dominating
and dehumanizing task and education as a humanistic and liberating task is that the former is a pure act of transference of knowledge, whereas the latter is an act of knowledge. As expected, both
of these radically opposite tasks, which also require opposing procedures, revolve around the relation between consciousness and
world. . . . In its relation to consciousness and world, education as
a dominating task assumes that consciousness is and should be
merely an empty receptacle to be "filled"; education as a liberating
and humanistic task views consciousness as "intention" toward
the world.

— *The Politics of Education*

Paulo Freire, a Brazilian educator, is best known for his work *Pedagogy of the Oppressed* (1970/1974). In this work, he brought dialogue and crisis together as he discussed the importance of fighting for the literacy of oppressed people. Freire outlined a nontraditional style of instruction guided by an important dialogic/interpersonal insight—we uphold human dignity by connecting learning to the historical situation in which the person lives. By connecting education to the learner's own historical situation, education becomes an additive rather than a substitutional enterprise that requires forfeiting something in order to gain something. One does not have to give up "old ways" to learn new ideas. The rationale for this form of educational face saving is not to be nice or exhibit excellent interpersonal manners, but to invite both the courage and the insight needed to look at and participate in the world anew. Freire does not make the learner feel inadequate for what he or she does and does not know; he allows what is known by the learner to be melded with new learnings.

If a person who is being taught to read works in the construction environment, the first place to begin education is with the immediate tools of the environment (e.g., hammer and nails) that permit the accomplishment of one's craft. Paulo Freire is an educational builder. He builds upon what is present, not what he wishes the other person knew. He begins an educational dialogue with what is familiar to the other; his goal is to make contact with the other in an additive fashion, not simply to demonstrate how much he, as the teacher, knows and how little the other understands a topic. Freire's teaching style invites the other to learn in his or her unique historical situation, restraining the temptation to teach another according to one's own or the other's psychological formation. Freire's key is to be in dialogue with the historical moment which includes the other, oneself, and the social practices and institutional constraints that impact a communicative exchange.

Paulo Freire has a dialogic voice that pragmatically protects the dignity of the other, permitting the learning process to proceed. Freire invites learners in interpersonal communication environments to meet new ideas and concepts without fear of humiliation and loss of face. Attending to the common historical situation, not one's own or the other's psychological makeup, drives Freire's interpersonal pedagogy.

Paulo Freire's work with nontraditional students situates learning within the historical moment. We address his grounding of dialogue in historicality, not technique—and review his perspective on limits inherent in the metaphor of "inclusion." Education provides dignity and a sense of hope that one can make a difference, by adding a genuine voice to community discourse. Following a discussion of Freire's interpersonal pedagogy, we discuss the contemporary relevance of his ideas for dialogic civility.

Introduction

Paulo Freire, out of pragmatic necessity and documented success, points to the importance of a dialogic mode of learning that is historically sensitive and works to preserve the other's sense of face. Freire is not simply offering education in a nonauthoritative fashion by following "pop psychology" precepts. On the contrary, Freire is using a philosophical perspective that has deep practical implications. He enters dialogue between socioeconomic cultures, is sensitive to the historical moment, and understands differences in educational needs in order to permit the other to learn what is offered and to give the other a concrete place of application for such learning.

In his interpersonal pedagogy with nontraditional students, Paulo Freire points to learning as a form of praxis—theory-informed action—not just the act of memorizing abstract concepts with limited historical connection to lived experience. A major contribution of Freire's work is that he provides a dialogic and civil voice that saves face for the other within a philosophical understanding of historicality. Freire's voice is informed by a nonpsychological philosophical perspective. Freire's perspective is not framed by trying to do good; goodness emerges as a byproduct in offering pedagogy appropriate for the historical moment of teaching and learning.

Paulo Freire, in educational praxis, has outlined a dialogic style of education for oppressed persons. The hermeneutical key for Paulo Freire is one that many of us in interpersonal communication and those of us interested in the issue of diversity (Makau and Arnett 1997) may find hard to ignore: inclusion, yes—but not at any price. Freire's understanding of dialogue is not for the fainthearted.

From this historical standpoint of awareness of metanarrative decline and perhaps collapse, we ask the following question about Paulo Freire's work: "How does a dialogic teaching style offer assistance to persons in an illiteracy crisis without glorifying inclusion?"

Freire understood the difference between a false dialogue and a genuine dialogue; such insight lessened the chance of communicative harm coming to communicators in need of leadership. Freire finds dialogue in the crisis of genuinely oppressed persons in need of guidance and literate voice.

Interpersonal Pedagogy

Education in Paulo Freire's dialogic pedagogy does not ask the student to give up anything, but rather to bring his or her concrete historical person to the learning event between teacher and student— adding one's own experience to the information offered. This form of dialogue permits learning to genuinely address the historical moment of learner and place education in a concrete situation.

Humility

As the following quotation suggests, Paulo Freire grounds his concern for the other not in sympathy, but in a philosophical conviction based upon historicity, limits, and the practiced virtue of humility:

> I am constantly open, precisely because of the limits of the act of knowing. I am sure that knowing is historical, that it's impossible to *know* without the history of human beings. . . . It means that it is in the social experience of history that we as human beings have created knowledge. It's because of that we continue to recreate the knowledge we created, and create a new knowledge. If knowledge can be overcome, if the knowledge of yesterday necessarily does not make sense today and then I need another knowledge. It means that knowledge has *historicity*. That is knowledge never is static. It's always in the process . . . my first position has to be a humble one vis-a-vis the very process of knowing, and vis-a-vis the process of learning. . . . I am humble not because I want to be agreeable. I don't accept being humble for tactical reasons. (Horton and Freire 1990, 193–194)

Freire's pedagogy teaches in a face-saving fashion out of a humble conviction that knowledge is ontologically tied to the historical moment. If we cannot escape our situatedness, how can we expect the other to do so? Instead of lamenting the limits and situatedness of our human condition, Freire works within the historical moment as a particular teacher with a particular student—permitting each to educate the other. He does this, not out of psychological conviction, but out of a philosophical conviction about the way in which life is ontologically lived by all of us—within historical limitations.

The philosophical grounding of Paulo Freire's dialogic model of education comes from his work with phenomenology, in opposition to a psychological world view. When this distinction is understood, his educational pedagogy moves from sensitivity to the other to respect for the historical moment of teacher, student, and ideas under discussion. Face saving, a byproduct of historical sensitivity and concern for the other, is only appropriate when it is a response to the historical moment which assists the other. If a student could "only" be educated by withdrawing the face-saving environment, Freire would do so immediately.

> [Paulo Freire:] The student needs to know that in some moments freedom must be punished, when it goes beyond the limits of democratic authority. And the punishment has to be made by the authority. . . . [Ira Shor:] The teacher is different from and not equal to the students, even as we practice democratic relations in the classroom. . . . The dialogic teacher is more intellectually developed, more practiced in critical scrutiny, and more committed to a political dream of social change, than are the students. We have to acknowledge these differences between the teacher and the students. (Shor and Freire 1987, 93–95)

The historical moment, not abstract theory, drives Freire's instruction. One might want teacher and student in theory to be equal, but in the historical moment of learning a teacher needs to guide—both cannot lead simultaneously. Freire does what is needed and what is called for in a given historical situation.

Praxis

Paulo Freire uses praxis-oriented pedagogy, which combines both theory and action within the confines of the historical limits of a given task. Freire's understanding of praxis is grounded in the work of Karl Marx. Freire penned the Preface to Moacir Gadotti's (1996) *Pedagogy of Praxis: A Dialectical Philosophy of Education*, which outlines Marx's view of praxis as theory-informed action. Marx was opposed to ideal philosophical speculation; he moved philosophy to action—praxis.

> One can notice . . . that Marx is not referring to the idealistic German philosophy nor to political bourgeois philosophy. He is instead referring to all philosophy. He is trying to show the limits of philosophy, which are the very limits of reflection, by underlining the need for a *praxis*. However, in doing this, he doesn't deny the value of philosophy and theory in the class struggle, but shows the limits of philosophical speculation. (Gadotti 1996, 83)

Freire affirms the other with a sense of care aimed at encouraging the learning of new material and the application of that learning in one's given situation.

Paulo Freire seeks to find ingredients in dialogic pedagogy that encourage human dignity and invite the opening of one's vision beyond submission to authoritarian information dispersion. One significant benefit of Freire's praxis philosophy is that he is unlikely to get caught in the danger of routine or unreflective reliance upon techniques that offer an answer a priori to the actual educational moment met by teacher and learner. William Barrett's *The Illusion of Technique* (1978/1979) and Jacques Ellul's *The Technological Society* (1964) both express concern about the misuse of technique. The historical moment, not some abstract method or technique, needs to guide action and education between teacher and learner.

Being in dialogue with students permits Paulo Freire to avoid getting caught in the contemporary communicative problem of entitlement. Freire is accustomed to working with people who are grateful for the concern of a teacher and who are willing to address the needs of the historical moment. In entitlement, the receiver of the gift of learning is unlikely to be appreciative; gratitude is no longer present. From a perspective of entitlement, the learning is possessed and held to the self, not passed on to the other. Entitlement gives birth to narcissism and an emphasis on possession; gifts become more important than the act of gift giving. When working with a student who holds an attitude of entitlement, Freire confronts him or her, feeling little need to save the face of such a learner. People in genuine historical need are invited to learn in a situation where face saving occurs, but those eager to take on the self-preoccupation of an oppressing class can be dealt with in a swift and different manner. Face saving for Ira Shor and Paulo Freire (1987) is based in the historical demands of the situation, not an ideology that compels one to apply some a priori technique of caring uniformly to all students.

> Because I am a teacher, I am not obliged to give the illusion that I am in agreement with the students. . . . The dominate ideology makes its presence in the classroom partly felt by trying to convince the teacher that he or she must be neutral in order to respect the students. This kind of neutrality is a false respect for students. On the contrary, the more I say nothing about agreeing or not agreeing out of respect for the other, the more I am leaving dominate ideology in place. (174)

Existential phenomenological insight into the historical moment, not psychological goodwill, moves the work and education of the other in Freire's interpersonal pedagogy.

Affirming the Other

Paulo Freire provides the philosophical background to understand and meet the nontraditional student in education that is rooted in interpersonal communication praxis.

> Marginality is an option with all that it involves: hunger, sickness, rickets, pain, mental deficiencies, loving death, crime, promiscuity, despair, the impossibility of being. In fact, however, it is difficult to accept that 40% of Brazil's population, almost 90% of Haiti's 60% of Bolivia's about 40% of Peru's more than 30% of Mexico's and Venezuela's and about 70% of Guatemala's would have made the tragic *choice* of their own marginality as illiterates. If, then, marginality is not by choice, marginal man [or woman] has been expelled from and kept outside of the social system and is therefore the object of violence.
>
> In fact, however, the social structure as a whole does not "expel," nor is marginal man [or woman] a "being outside of." He [or she] is on the contrary, a "being inside of," within the

social structure, and in a dependent relationship to those who we call falsely autonomous beings, inauthentic beings-for-themselves. (Freire 1970/1988, 10–11)

Those outside any system—whether they are on the wrong side of power and influence, from the "other" side of the tracks, or simply had unconventional timing for their entrance into the higher educational system—have felt some kinship with the disadvantaged of whom Freire speaks.

Connecting the work of Paulo Freire to a nontraditional Saturday educational program on a university campus may at first glance seem too far of a stretch. After all, many students entering a nontraditional educational track are employed and have their education partially or fully paid by their companies. Few, if any, of these students live the demanding and demeaning lives of many of Freire's oppressed pupils, in which literacy campaigns were implemented. However, the connection with nontraditional Saturday college students is suggested in the following conversation between a traditional and nontraditional student overheard at a coffee shop before class.

The traditional student asked, "Why are you going to school at your age? What good is an undergraduate degree to you?" The nontraditional student offered a response that would have made Paulo Freire proud. "We can document that the degree assists with employment. But what I did not expect was to have the education affect my vision, my perspective on the world." One of the authors walked with the student to class and said, "I have heard no better way to differentiate the accumulation of information from a quality education than to suggest that an education alters one's vision!" Indeed, the world will never look quite the same way again after a genuine education.

While in exile in Chile, Paulo Freire wrote often to his niece, Christina. His words to her are supportive of the above comments from the nontraditional student from the "former" steel city of Pittsburgh.

Information is communicative, or generates communication, when receivers learn the content of what was communicated in such a way as to transcend the act of receiving. They do this by recreating the received communication and transforming it into knowledge concerning what was communicated. The receiver becomes the subject of the process of communication, which, in turn, leads to education as well. Education cannot take place within the suffocating limit of specialization. Education can only take place when we go beyond the limits of purely utilitarian knowledge. (Freire 1996b, 99)

Freire educates for life, not just the accumulation of data; he lives educational praxis; he affects and effects the vision of the learner.

There is a second component that distinguishes the nontraditional group of students with whom one of the authors works. They speak their minds; they disagree with one another, the faculty, and the administration. An almost unwritten rule that they live by is, *Education, yes. But, not at any price!* Clearly, each of these students wants to get his or her money's worth. But there is yet another unstated cry from this population: "You can have my effort, but not my soul." Perhaps it is because Pittsburgh's population of nontraditional students are often from blue collar and lower-middle-class family structures in which pride and integrity are so important. However, we suspect that the desire to "protect one's soul" is fueled by a much larger issue than the city itself. Traditional students also speak their mind, but from a position of entitlement. Traditional students often perceive that a degree is needed to get a job and, as such, focus on the diploma rather than the learning process itself.

Nontraditional students know that to a degree they already have "made" it in the world without an education that is formal in nature. They know that not all education happens in a formal classroom. They want to learn more, but they do not want to forgo the hard lessons of the blue collar family—we may not have much, but no one can take away our family name, our integrity, or our soul. Nontraditional students are led to face saving out of a historical conviction—the formal classroom is not the only place of learning. To allow another person to suggest that formal education is the only context in which knowing can occur violates common sense.

The Limits of Inclusion

Both nontraditional students and Paulo Freire assume a posture contrary to the popular understanding of interpersonal learning and interaction—inclusion is not the primary goal of a good communicative life! Like nontraditional students, Freire does not want inclusion in the communicative process at any price. Freire rejects inclusion that requires denial of oppression. In fact, if asked to choose between exclusion and inclusion that requires acceptance of oppression, he would choose separation as the necessary communication goal in such a relationship. Freire's (1970/1974) warning is simple: Inclusion is important, but it is not the highest of human aspirations and cannot be the goal above all goals in the pursuit of communicative connection.

This major point of Paulo Freire's work, the limits of inclusion, needs to be held in tension with his deep caring and love of people.

> I feel my incompleteness inside me, at the biological, affective, critical and intellectual levels, an incompleteness that pushes me constantly, curiously, and lovingly toward other people and the world, searching for solidarity and transcendence of solitude. All of this implies wanting to love, a capacity for love that people must create in themselves. This capacity increases to the degree that one loves; it diminishes when one is afraid to love. Of course, in our society it is not easy to love, because we derive much of our happiness from sadness; that is, very often for us to feel happy, others must be sad. Under these circumstances it is difficult to love, but it is necessary to do so. (Freire 1985, 297–298)

Note that even as Freire speaks longingly about inclusion he offers a dialectical reminder—many in our culture are unhappy; they try to find happiness by inflicting sadness upon others. Freire, on the other hand, in the words of Martin Buber, is a "great character" (1947/1965a, 116) who in his idealism walks with both feet on the ground—a place where both joy and oppressive pain live.

When the goal of any interpersonal exchange is inclusion, a relativistic view of the world without any sense of a moral good life is required from interactants. If a person is grounded in a value system, one puts at risk a sense of face when a "universal" demand for inclusion is acted upon. At this juncture it is important to mention Freire's kinship with Martin Buber. For Buber (1958), dialogue does not begin with the conversation at hand. Instead, it begins with the ground of conviction that one takes into the conversation. Buber did not call for complete openness, but rather an openness that is historically appropriate and within the limits of conviction; openness linked to a creative response to crisis guides one's entrance into dialogue. If a person does not work from the ground of a historical moment, then the conversation is wrapped in fiction, "awash in 'existential weariness' and 'historical anesthesia'" (Freire 1992/1996c, 137).

As teachers, we have great respect for Paulo Freire's dialogic voice. He walks the line between inclusion and principle that is necessary for a quality education. He reminds us that relational connection cannot be the only motivator for our communicative lives. People, young and old alike, invite trouble when they believe inclusion is the only communicative goal worthy of pursuit. A person needs to keep dialectic inclusion and principle as part of communicative action. Knowing when to be separate from others is as important as knowing when to invite others to join in communication.

Education requires a sensitivity to the other and a willingness to enter a life-long pursuit while wrestling with identifying the principles needed to offer a communicative background to one's relational interaction in a given historical moment. Granted, there is danger in overreliance upon principle; moral rigidity will not serve us well in the twenty-first century. However, neither will a predisposition to follow the herd—doing whatever is necessary, just to be accepted and included. Dialectically, both inclusion and adherence to principles guide Freire's understanding of a quality communicative life. Such a message is consistent with an education that inspires one to ground a life on principled soil (out of one's wisdom within in a given historical moment) and an education that seeks to include and to join with others whenever appropriate.

Paulo Freire's dialectical reminder is fundamental to those of us who study interpersonal communication. Inclusion cannot be the ultimate goal of human life. We court confusion and problems when we offer the message of inclusion as an ultimate good to young people; the message becomes ideological without a dialectical counter. For instance, let us suggest that a message of inclusion is consistently heard by a young person at school, at home, and at church. If this theme is dominant, how can we expect a young person to choose well when faced with the choice of following problematic friends or not being included in a group of people? If messages about inclusion are powerful enough and not countered dialectically with conversation about other principles, we provide a limited communicative background for a young person to reject the invitation to drug use—at the expense of friendship and inclusion.

One of the authors met with a group of parents in preparation for their children's final season of a sporting event. Much of the discussion centered around the inappropriate behavior of some of the parents. The group of parents began to ask how a small group of parents could so easily make things difficult for a much larger majority. The answer emerged that no one wanted to question the negative statements of a small number of parents; they were afraid that if they did they and their children would not be included in the social functions of the organization.

Finally someone in the group got the parents to discuss how the notion of inclusion is not always an appropriate guide for decision making. If one is certain that the actions of another are wrong and destructive, one must pose questions and counter the other's ideas or actions, even if some forms of inclusion are sacrificed. Shortly thereafter, in the spirit of Paulo Freire, the parents began to permit themselves to go beyond inclusion questions. At the next meeting some parents called attention to the fact that fairness, to the coach, was more important than their own social inclusion. In that existential moment, Freire's message was understood and people acted in defense of another. Where genuine oppression raises its ugly head—toward persons of different ethnicity, race, gender, religion, or even an athletic coach—the wisdom of Freire's voice needs to be heard. Freire's understanding of dialogue does not accept the oppression of another to keep all included.

Paulo Freire is willing to forgo "cheap" inclusion. He does not want false charity used to give the impression of inclusion when in actuality deep oppressive systems are maintained to keep the "outsider" or the person of "difference" in his or her place.

> True generosity consists precisely in fighting to destroy the causes which nourish false charity. False charity constrains the fearful and subdued, the "rejects of life," to extend trembling hands. True generosity lies in striving so that these hands—whether of individuals or entire peoples—need be extended less and less in supplication, so that more and more they become human hands which work and, working, transform the world. (Freire 1970/1974, 29)

Freire wanted inclusion with a genuine voice, not inclusion in the form of a handout cloaked in the demand to know and keep one's place. Freire advocated genuine inclusion, not the mere appearance of inclusion.

More than any other author that we discuss in *Dialogic Civility in a Cynical Age: Community, Interpersonal Relationships, and Hope*, Paulo Freire calls for caution when communication between persons of unequal power is present. He accepts differences in authority, while rejecting authoritarianism. Freire reminds us that some communicative environments are best escaped, not entered. This message sets his dialogic voice above others who unknowingly confuse dialogue with relational inclusion at the price of human dignity and displace commonsense truth from the historical moment of a given action.

Central Concepts in Paulo Freire's Work

Paulo Freire understood that education was fundamental to giving the poor and oppressed a voice. Education carries with it a sense of hope that one can make a difference in the culture in which one lives. Freire places education within a spirit of liberation; education allows silent oppressed voices to be heard—both in writing and in speech.

At the commencement of a group of nontraditional students, one of the authors offered the following to the graduating class. "We thank you because you remind us what an education is, what education can do, and the **HOPE** education can bring to the human community. Your presence here reminds us to use education with care; education is important; education is a major sense of **HOPE** for you, me and our survival as a human community" (Arnett 1996a, 2). A sense of hope tied to education may be less visible in today's educational industry, which serves primarily middle- and upper-middle-class students. However, a much different reminder about education is present when one teaches nontraditional students who are excited about being in school, learning, and advancing their voices on the job and in their communities. One can feel hope in the air when a voice is being built to replace the gulf of silence.

Paulo Freire, who masterfully connected dialogue to pedagogy in the concrete moment of oppressed/oppressor struggle, saw the fundamental nature of hope.

> The idea that hope alone will transform the world, and action undertaken in that kind of naivete, is an excellent route to hopelessness, pessimism and fatalism. But the attempt to do without hope, in the struggle to improve the world, as if that struggle could be reduced to calculated acts alone, or a purely scientific approach, is a frivolous illusion. To attempt to do without hope, which is based on the need for truth as an ethi-

cal quality of the struggle, is tantamount to denying that struggle is one of its mainstays. . . . [H]ope, as an ontological need, demands an anchoring in practice. As an ontological need, hope needs practice in order to become historical concreteness. (1992/1996c, 9)

Freire connects hope to his interpersonal pedagogy, but with a careful and thoughtful dialectical reminder of hope's call within realism and struggle. Hope that is grounded in historical reality does not go out of fashion.

Rejecting a Culture of Silence

Paulo Freire is concerned with the other. His interpersonal pedagogy works to save face for the other in a historical moment by lessening a "culture of silence" (1970/1974, 13). A culture of silence keeps another from speaking, from looking critically at the world, thereby maintaining an oppressive system. Much of traditional education is largely socialization into an ongoing world view, not participation in the critical examination of such a perspective. Freire works to alter the meaning of education.

Nontraditional students at one point in their life received messages from others that submerged them into an educational culture of silence. Someone may have told them that their abilities were too limited. Someone may have suggested that only part of the family could go to college. Someone may have stated that there was no time to waste on this thing called college—immediate employment was demanded in the family. And, of course, some had the responsibilities of younger siblings, parents, and their own children to take care of—submerging their own desires for a college education into a genuine "culture of silence." For these people, college becomes the unspoken, hidden hope. For traditional students, attending college is often expected by one's family and friends.

This culture of silence can only be broken as one begins to understand the "cultural-historical" (Freire 1970/1974, 71) constraints that have been imposed on one by a cultural superstructure. For some the message in a given historical moment is, "College is not for you—college is for others!" A dominant culture can ignore groups of people, keeping them from achieving by expecting them to be silent. When asked why their current historical-cultural moment is so different, one nontraditional student offered an answer that would warm Paulo Freire's heart: "Colleges and universities now pay attention to us. They need the revenue and the numbers we bring. They can no longer afford to ignore us." In short, the historical-cultural moment for their education is now here. These students understand the "consciousness historically conditioned by the social structures" (Freire 1985, 74) that now drives their educational opportunities. This consciousness is unleashed and altered as the historical-cultural conditions change; major universities are in need of student numbers and revenue. Seeing differently permits education to begin. "*Conscientizaçao* . . . [makes] it possible for men [or women] to enter the historical process as responsible Subjects" (Freire, 1970/1974, 20). Freire does not ask the student to follow, but to walk beside the teacher—both keeping their eyes open to the genuine consciousness of a given historical situation.

Narrative Sickness

In order to assist the other in seeing, Paulo Freire rejects what he terms the "banking" (1970/1974, 58) concept of education that puts material into a person's head and then asks for that information to be repeated back to the instructor. Freire wants the learner to begin to recognize the "deep structures" (1970/1974, 14) of a culture, not repeat the ongoing message that permeates the surface of discourse.

At this point, Paulo Freire connects narrative with the banking concept. Before discussing his critique of bad narratives, we recall the following. First, there is no such thing as only a good or only a bad narrative. Second, an unreflective narrative that does not permit participation and change can become a rigid ideology. Finally, Freire is attempting to offer a story of liberation and a practical new vision as an alternative; he does not reject narrative, just unreflective and oppressive narratives that become oppressive ideologies.

Education is suffering from narration sickness. As Paulo Freire stated:

> The teacher talks about reality as if it were motionless, static, compartmentalized, and predictable. Or else he [or she] expounds on a topic completely alien to the existential experience of the students. His [or her] task is to "fill" the students

with the contents of his [or her] narration—contents which are detached from reality, disconnected from the totality that engendered them and could give them significance. Words are emptied of their concreteness and become a hollow, alienated, and alienating verbosity. (1970/1974, 57)

Freire's view of narrative is not identical with the way in which this work would point to the use of narrative. However, his understanding of the term is very much in agreement with popular consensus.

The authors understand narrative as an open and participatory process that is developed in evolutionary stages. First, a person engages in a speech act that is heard by others. Second, this person begins to move the speech act into telling a story that has a past, drama, main characters, and a teleological direction. Third, if people begin to interpret episodes of life in accordance with this story and there is seeming agreement between the story and reality of their lives, numbers of people begin to believe the story. At this juncture, the story is held corporately and is a narrative. Both capitalism and Marxism are narratives that guide a body of people. However, when the narrative ceases to permit participation and dictates action a priori to an event under consideration, the narrative lapses into an inflexible ideology and needs to be critiqued and opened up for participation again.

Our language is somewhat different than Paulo Freire's; however, we agree with his sentiment. He is working under conditions where the narrative of a people has become rigid—where the narrative has become an ideology that oppresses the learner. His task is to open up the narrative of knowledge by permitting the participation of the learners, forgoing the temptation to push rigid learning into the minds of the learners, which he equates with a banking view of education. Concern for the limits of a banking form of education make his interest in "critical consciousness" and "dialogue" appropriate for this historical moment. The interpersonal face saving he does is rooted in a hope of opening the narrative of knowledge for oppressed people. We contend that Freire's work offers a competing narrative structure.

Critical Consciousness

Paulo Freire examines "critical consciousness" in each of his works. However, Freire's *Education for Critical Consciousness* (1969/1996a) outlines this approach to education well. The following quotation places his opposition to a rigid narrative in perspective, as he brings his critical consciousness to education in Brazil.

> The starting point for the Brazilian transition was that closed society to which I have already referred, one whose raw material export economy was determined by an external market, whose very center of economic decision was located abroad—a "reflex," "object" society, lacking a sense of nationhood. Backward. Illiterate. Anti-dialogical. Elitist. (Freire 1969/1996a, 9)

The way to open society for participation is to call into question its very foundation or deep structures. In education, the first necessary rejection is that of the "banking concept" (Freire 1970/1974, 58). The historical need for an interpersonal style that saves face for the learner and invites him or her to look at society with a different eye propels not only Freire's writing, but his life project as an educator.

Paulo Freire rejects what he terms a "sectarian" (1969/1996a, 11) perspective on education. Whether this approach is motivated by the left or right; a sectarian perspective is the implementation of action taken as predetermined within a paradigm, void of any critical consciousness. The "sectarian" is provincial and wants to pass on his or her psychological formation without discussion of events. Others are not allowed into the act of change and participation in a future history of the people; their job is implementation and memorization.

Paulo Freire wanted people to be educated—to move from "naive transitivity" (1969/1996a, 20) to eventual critical consciousness. If this educational process is successful, then "humanization" (1969/1996a, 20) of the learner and an opening of the narrative for participation becomes possible. But there are two dangers that require attention: first, curtailing change through participation in a live narrative; and second, countering rigidity with an equally rigid counterperspective.

> [A] . . . crucial step from naive transitivity to critical transitivity would *not* occur automatically. Achieving this step would thus require an active, dialogical educational program concerned with social and political responsibility, and prepared to avoid the danger of massification. . . . [The person] falls into a *fanaticized consciousness*. . . . To the extent that a

person acts more on the basis of emotionality than of reason, his [or her] behavior occurs adaptively and cannot result in commitment, for committed behavior has its roots in critical consciousness and capacity for genuine choice. (Freire 1969/1996a, 19–20)

Freire does not want what Alasdair MacIntyre calls "emotivism" (1981/1984, 1–14) to guide his or her behavior. One needs to be propelled by more than the emotion of personal choice. Freire wants a freedom, but connected in conversation and dialogue to a knowing narrative that involves "critical consciousness" (1970/1974, 81).

Paulo Freire wants a person to move from naive acceptance to reflection grounded and tested in "experience" (1969/1996a, 36). Critical consciousness is both theory and action. The ability to apply, to connect, to use information is essential to his interpersonal pedagogy. Freire does not hold the "intellectual" (1969/1996a, 39) as the end goal of education. Such a person can perpetuate the naïve and lead people astray through what Jean-Paul Sartre would call "bad faith" (1953, 86–116)—lying to oneself, lost in a world of ideas alien to the test of everyday events. Action is a way to test and connect ideas to human life and projects that can make a difference.

Dialogue

"Dialogue" (Freire 1970/1974, 75) is the historically necessary interpersonal skill needed for opening narratives, developing human consciousness, and re-humanizing people. Indeed, this is no small task—but in order to break a system of domination, a narrative system or "communicative ethics" (Habermas 1973/1975, 75–90; see also Benhabib 1992) is necessary. In chapter 3 of *Pedagogy of the Oppressed* (1970/1974) Paulo Freire outlines his understanding of dialogue as central to a revolutionary view of education. When life is confused, keeping the conversation going is at times one's most important contribution.

Dialogue is fundamental to Paulo Freire's interpersonal pedagogy. Freire saves the face of the learner to invite him or her to walk into a different arena of consciousness, out of oppression and into participation, action, and contribution. In *Pedagogy of the Oppressed*, Freire connects the notion of dialogue to "reflection" and "action" (1970/1974, 75). Such a perspective is appropriate in light of his commitment to praxis—theory-informed action. Dialogue can transform the world—through reflection and action, dialogue enables us to determine the type of world we want to constitute together.

Dialogue calls for a love of the other, a humility to learn from the other, and faith in the ability of dialogue co-constituted between persons to shape the world. Dialogue is guided by trust between persons and propelled by a deep sense of hope. Paulo Freire connects dialogue to attitudes of "love, humility, . . . faith . . . mutual trust . . . [and] hope" (1970/1974, 80). Dialogue between persons is not possible when one seeks to oppress the other. The above attitudes clearly point to an orientation similar to a mentor, a friend, a parent—forgoing the action of oppression. Freire makes it clear that

> dialogue [cannot] exist without hope. Hope is rooted in men's [or women's] incompleteness, from which they move out in constant search—a search which can be carried out only in communion with other men [or women]. Hopelessness is a form of silence, of denying the world and fleeing from it. The dehumanization resulting from an unjust order is not a cause for despair but for hope, leading to the incessant pursuit of the humanity denied by injustice. (1970/1974, 80)

This sense of hope and conviction in "critical thinking" (Freire 1970/1974, 81) moves Freire to get the other to think and to use one's voice. Freire saves face for the learner until the learner has a sense of his or her own voice; at that juncture the learner takes on the responsibility to save the face of another in the ongoing dialogue of learning.

Paulo Freire offers dialogue that accepts a person as a text (Gadamer 1960/1986) that needs to be opened up. The question that one takes to the opening task is central. In the limits of this historical moment, Freire brings us the question, "What is possible for you?" He acknowledges limits and then helps the other walk through the situation. "It is not the limit-situations in and of themselves which create a climate of hopelessness, but rather how they are perceived by men [and women] at a given historical moment: whether they appear as fetters or as insurmountable barriers" (Freire 1970/1974, 89). For a person in dialogue, the focus is on the historical moment for the other.

Paulo Freire gives the teacher a reason, a why, to be in dialogue with the student—the call of the historical moment to break the chains of oppression. He also offers the learner a why to be in dialogue with the teacher—this is a relationship that can be trusted, a person of genuine (not demanded) "authority" (Freire 1969/1996a, 149). Dialogue, Freire's interpersonal pedagogy, seeks to educate both the pupil and the teacher—each is learning *roles*. As learning occurs, information is acquired and relationships are supported—the participants educate one another and co-constitute a learning community forgoing the temptation of individualism and simple enhancement of self.

> This movement of inquiry must be directed towards human-ization—man's [or woman's] historical vocation. The pursuit of full humanity, however, cannot be carried out in isolation or individualism, but only in fellowship and solidarity; therefore it cannot unfold in the antagonistic relations between oppres-sors and oppressed. No one can be authentically human while he [or she] prevents others from being so. Attempting *to be more* human, individualistically, leads to . . . [egotism]. (Freire 1970/1974, 73–74)

Freire's understanding of humanization bespeaks our connection to one another not out of compassion but out of a philosophical con-viction similar to that of Martin Buber (1958)—real living requires the meeting of persons in dialogue. To be human is fundamentally a social, not an individualistic activity.

Historicality and Dialogic Civility

Paulo Freire offers a historically grounded model involving saving face for the other that does not rely upon psychological technique. He would not mistake the use of historically appropriate self-esteem enhancement of the other with an unreflective technique that equates every learning problem as a deprived sense of self-esteem. The message from Freire is straightforward and powerful. Saving face is the core to this form of education—as long as it is his-torically situated and necessary. A psychological technique of caring that is carried out a priori to the meeting of the other will miss the educational moment and contribute to an attitude of entitlement. Entitlement encourages the entitled to objectify others and use them for personal gain.

Paulo Freire would caution people against slogans and mottos that get in the way of genuine attention to the historical needs of a teaching moment. The teacher must pay attention to this historical moment or the teaching will be framed by "me" and "my formation," not the genuine needs of a real person, in a unique moment, in a particular interpersonal exchange. As communicators we are called to meet what is before us, not only what we desire. Christopher Lasch warned us of a *Culture of Narcissism* (1978/1979) grounded in too much self-reflection. Freire offers a model of interpersonal pedagogy that does not place reflective concentration on self or other, but on the historical moment. Ironically, out of this focus comes saving face, dialogic civility as a way to lessen routine cynicism. He does not purport to deliver more than he can offer and he never loses focus on his task—to educate in dialogic connection with the other. The goal is to liberate the other, not feed one's own narcissism about being good, or to confuse consistency of communicative style in every communicative setting with historical appropriateness.

Paulo Freire's contribution to dialogic civility centers on his connection of saving face to the public requirements of a historical situation, not private psychological need. Freire does not confuse caring with inclusion at any personal price or societal cost. He is deeply concerned about the other and what the other can do in the public arena of work and societal influence—not out of abstract technique, but out of concrete meeting of the other. Freire permits voices of critical consciousness powerful enough to alter rigid and oppressive social systems to shape narrative commitments.

Chapter Ten

Sissela Bok

Crisis and Ethical Imagination

On Hope—

The sense of hopelessness that many voice at seeing the spread of humanitarian emergencies, and the inadequacy, to date, of efforts to cope with them is nevertheless premature. To reverse the present development may well take many persons and groups, on as many fronts, and with as much ingenuity and courage, as went into the work against segregation, apartheid, and the nuclear balance of terror of which Martin Luther King, Jr., spoke. . . . In 1964, too, many were ready to give up all hope of peaceful resolutions to those evils. Three decades later, we have more reason than ever to heed his conclusion:

> I have the audacity to believe that peoples everywhere can have three meals a day for their bodies, education and culture for their minds, and dignity, equality, and freedom for their spirits. I still believe we shall overcome.

> —Sissela Bok, *Common Values*

Disrupted Practices—

Powerful new techniques of storing and of probing secrets increase the need for careful debate. From the miniature cameras that can be hidden in a pen to the invisible wire-tapping devices and electronic mechanisms for overhearing conversations at a great distance, from the "truth serums" and mind-altering drugs, new means beckon to anyone who would abuse either openness or secrecy. . . . The new techniques and the changes they make possible join with the long-standing personal and professional conflicts over secrecy to raise practical moral problems for us all.

—Secrets

S issela Bok is, perhaps, best known for her work *Lying* (1978/1979). In her writing, she offers a call to walk a line between hope for a better world and the danger of undue optimism. She addresses head on our concern about the formation of routine cynicism. She reminds us of the importance of limits and the need to control the impulse to lie. However, Bok rejects an "absolute" (1978/1979, 48) position on the ethical communicative question, "Should I ever lie?" Her answer is offered with great reflective care—lying can only assist a society when reasons for the action can later stand public scrutiny. Bok's work cannot be placed in an extreme camp of unrealistic hope or excessive optimism. Even if one contends that her writing rests on the brink of optimism, she does not fall from her balanced position.

Sissela Bok's work is marked by thoughtful balance. For instance, *Secrets* (1983/1984) cautions against the use of such communication while simultaneously recognizing the importance of limited disclosure in the maintenance of human freedom:

> [People believe] secrecy and controls are neutral, that they carry no risks of their own to commerce, no dangers to judgment and to character, and no risks of encouraging official negligence and corruption.
>
> But why accept this course as inevitable? We need not hasten to give up hard-earned freedoms through indifference or panic. The very hostilities and technological advances that threatened security also challenge us to reassess the complex role of secrecy in [both] containing or escalating their danger. (1983/1984, 285)

Bok wants the world to be a better, more ethical, place; her hope for such a reality is tempered by the historical moment of today, not an abstract wish for a better tomorrow. Bok discusses human honesty in a time of routine cynicism and lack of trust. She examines reasonable arguments from multiple sides of issues—pointing us in the direction of a communicative ideal without confining us to a rigid ideology that is unresponsive to contrary arguments.

Sissela Bok contributes to dialogic civility in a postmodern era. Her approach to lying, secrets, peace, and common values undergirds her conversational ethic, searching for practical ways to negotiate minimalist metanarratives that ground dialogic civility. Bok reminds us of the oxymoronic nature of much of life—yes, we need a common ground of values; no, we cannot impose values on another. Thus, she searches for minimalist values that emerge in various cultures and societies across historical moments. From a title of one of Richard Bernstein's books we find the key to Bok's efforts—*Beyond Objectivism and Relativism* (1983). She rejects extreme positions, more content to carve a third alternative to obvious choices. Bok's response to the crisis of ethics is found in the dialogue between extremes, not in emphasizing opposition.

Introduction

Sissela Bok suggests we are losing a sense of ethical coherence in everyday life. Her scholarly task is twofold. First, Bok asks her readers to admit and understand problems central to this historical moment, such as lying (1978/1979), peace (1989), and a minimalist foundation for ethics and values (1995). Second, Bok begins a conversation about implications that such problems hold for our contemporary historical moment. Her suggestions do not offer a metanarrative substitute; Bok's agenda is more modest and humble. She functions as a philosopher in dialogue with our contemporary ethical crisis who seems to state, "We must be wary of absolutes, while simultaneously finding a minimal common ground on ethical issues." Her project is to keep an ethical conversation alive concerning important and fundamental issues that impact how we interact with one another.

One of the authors was at a conference on issues related to higher education. He was asked what was the most important concept to teach a communication student today. The answer was twofold: first, why the other is important; and second, why respect for the other is necessary for inviting conversation. Sissela Bok accents these two areas of communication in her understanding of ethics: why and respect.

In the opening to *Secrets: On the Ethics of Concealment and Revelation*, Sissela Bok offers insight into her search:

> In thus exploring secrecy and openness, I have come up against what human beings care most to protect and to probe: the exalted, the dangerous, the shameful; the sources of powers and creation; the fragile and the intimate. Such an inquiry must of necessity be incomplete. I hope nevertheless, that it will help to shed light on the crucial moral issues that secrecy and openness raise in every life, and invite the debate that these issues now require more urgently than ever. (1983/1984, xvii–xviii)

Bok understands that she writes about subject matter that is impossible to finalize in any era, let alone in a postmodern moment of narrative confusion; thus, she has significant philosophical reasons for not offering a final answer to ethical problematics and one pragmatic reason for working to keep ethical conversation alive— such conversation is essential if rampant individualism, domination, and power are not to destroy us.

One of the authors asked a class in Interpersonal Communication the following question, while examining the notion of "standpoint theory" (Wood 1992, 12–18): "If you were to define life from the standpoint of a competitive swimmer, what might you say through using an illustrative metaphor?" A number of answers, of course, emerged about staying afloat and not drowning. The students were then asked to offer a swimming metaphor about life in the spirit of a traditional society, then modernity, and finally a postmodern existence consistent with the standpoint of each respective historical era.

The student statements emerged in the following fashion. In a traditional culture, swimming is tied to bathing and, at times, enjoyment in open water; swimming is organically connected to how life is lived in a village. The metaphor for a traditional society is *open water swimming* in a familiar place. In modernity, swimming is tied to laps and a pool; one tries to make progress in swimming more and faster laps. The metaphor for a modern society is *lap swimming*. In postmodernity, all of the above is going on at the same time and numerous people are getting in one another's way as swimming goes on without clear rules; the metaphor in this case is an oxymoron: *crowded "open" swim*. There is a conceptual irony at many public pools that call such swimming "open swim." We contend that Sissela Bok understands the swimming chaos presented in a crowded "open" swim environment. She would not lament the existence of such swimming. Her scholarly response can be placed within another swimming metaphor, *treading water*. Bok's scholarly project helps us tread water—in a time of postmodern confusion she keeps the conversation alive about important ethical issues that impact our communicative lives together, permitting us to tread water until the fog clears and we can see the direction we need to swim.

Sissela Bok is willing to get in the water, not to tell others how to swim, but to model treading water as we try to figure out appropriate narrative structures that will guide us in postmodernity. From this historical standpoint of metanarrative decline and perhaps collapse, we ask the following question about Sissela Bok's work: "How do we search for minimal ethics and values that might support human beings in living, raising families, and working together in a world of difference and narrative crisis and confusion?" Bok does not waste time in romantic lament; she moves ahead with sensitive dialogue tied to ethical questions central to our historical moment of ethical crisis.

Ethics and Postmodernity

Sissela Bok invites us to consider issues related to ethics and the notion of the good life in our current era—marked by postmodern metanarrative decline and the routine presence of unreflective cynicism in daily discourse. During our prevailing time of narrative confusion, Bok asks us to reconsider basic ethical issues such as lying, secrets, peace, values. Her scholarly project is propelled by understanding that in a postmodern culture such issues cannot be taken for granted; agreement cannot be assumed. Reexamining questions about what is ethical and virtuous in a time of narrative confusion makes good philosophical sense—unless one gives up completely on such ideas, which is a position clearly rejected by Bok. She is concerned about the practical implications of trying to work together without basic ethical guidance held in common by both parties. She takes the reality and significance of postmodernity seriously as she offers a counter to despair. Bok points us toward hope without ignoring the serious results, practically and philosophically, of living in a postmodern world that lacks a clear and undisputed set of communicative agreements about what it means to be ethical and dialogically civil.

The reason we suggest that Sissela Bok understands the postmodern condition while not being a postmodern writer is that she openly declares that her scholarly project is conversation about a minimal ethical/value system that can undergird our working relationships with one another. She, like other authors highlighted in this work, points to the importance of "humble narratives" (Arnett 1997b, 45) that offer background support for the implementation of ethics in interpersonal discourse. This background informs us of limits and options available in our foreground implementation of ideas in interpersonal decision making. Bok's task is to keep before us the search for *Common Values* (1995), permitting us to work constructively together. The following quotation points to the nature of her common minimal ethics project.

> As we near the end of a century in which the three gaps mentioned above—between haves and have-nots, rhetoric and reality, concern and indifference—continue to widen, the full scope and difficulty of these questions are only beginning to be taken into account in international and domestic debates. Answers still elude us, even as they elude the field workers and policy makers who confront these dilemmas daily. The search for answers will be central to the debate over the role of ethics in the century to come, engaging collaborators and adversaries the world over. They will have at least a starting point from which to begin to the extent that they acknowledge a minimalist set of common values. (Bok 1995, 9)

Bok does not claim to have the answer to issues of lying, secrets, peace, common values, and ethics; however, her scholarship keeps before us the need to identify ethical background issues that might assist human beings working with one another in both commonality and difference. Calvin O. Schrag, in *The Self After Postmodernity*, stated "Heterogeneity, multiplicity, diversity, difference, incommensurability, and dissensus become the chief interpretive categories of the postmodern mind" (1997, 8). Bok would concur and then simultaneously call for discourse on minimal value agreements. Within the metaphor of creative contradiction lives the contribution of Sissela Bok.

Communication without Ethical Coherence

People have lost confidence in metanarrative systems to guide our ways of interacting with one another. The significance of postmodernity for the contemporary communicator is pointed to by Kenneth Gergen in *The Saturated Self*:

The relatively coherent and unified sense of self inherent in a traditional culture gives way to manifold and competing potentials. A multiphrenic condition emerges in which one swims in ever-shifting, concatenating, and contentious currents of being. One bears the burden of an increasing array of oughts, of self-doubts and irrationalities. The possibility for committed romanticism or strong and single-minded modernism recedes, and the way is opened for the postmodern being. (1991, 80)

Gergen suggests that the person living in a postmodern historical moment does not abide by one major narrative system; the postmodern person is open to multiple possibilities in the communicative environment. Bok concurs and then begins to work out a minimal foundation that does not have us languishing in postmodernity forever.

Sissela Bok (1983/1984) intends to keep alive conversation about a minimal set of ethical agreements; otherwise, she contends, we lay the groundwork for secret societies that work to combat any narrative that guides and moves people in a given direction. Let us first flesh out Bok's idea with an example and then explain her intent as related to the notion of practice. One of the authors was surprised to find on a small campus a group that was bound together in critique of the historic direction of the university. What was so confusing was that the group of critics offered no alternative vision, only open hostility toward the current direction. This was the first time that one of the authors had met a postmodern argument in the flesh. The communication offered by persons in opposition did not point in a different direction than the university, but was aimed at reminding everyone that no direction can be permitted to gather momentum in an era of metanarrative controversy. The aim of the argument was not to have one's own side win, but to make sure that no side could gather momentum to move the institution. This group did not fear a particular direction, but any direction. If one examines such a situation with the notion of practice as an interpretive guide, an interesting sense of irony emerges.

We can set up an environment in which antinarrative groups form out of the simple practice of binding together to discuss secrets to be used against a given status quo. The practice of contending with the given narrative structure of another emerges out of a *Culture of Complaint* (Hughes 1993). The unreflective group's disagreement with another group's narrative perspective results in the practice of routine complaint, which then takes on the appearance of a group bound by a common agenda. However, in this case the agenda is an antinarrative—it ironically binds people together in opposition to another's narrative framework.

The irony is that the antinarrative agenda in practice becomes a narrative created via complaint, without any direction except opposition. Only as we work consciously to understand the power and danger of "irony" (Niebuhr 1952, 153) can we see results of the practice of opposition giving way to a new narrative formed as an antinarrative. This antinarrative begins to shape the communicative life of both groups as secret glances and comments and then public contention permits the current narrative structure to be torn asunder.

What is dangerous is that those using unreflective communicative practice may not see the irony in a group based on secret perspectives offering consistent critique of an ongoing narrative direction. This reflective ability permits Sissela Bok, like Robert Hughes (1993), to applaud difference and still focus on the importance of some form of common agreement—otherwise small groups begin to separate us from one another. Somehow we need to lean in two directions simultaneously—toward a small number of core values and toward appreciation of difference. If we fail this dual motion, we open the world to constant strife, which might be considered one of the unfortunate learnings gained from observation of the continuing deterioration of countries that were formerly part of the Soviet Union. Some common value commitment is needed to curtail the power and pain of ethnic dispute. Cultural diversity calls for common principles that permit us to respect the other; we should not confuse this social good with separatism that most often begins in the practice of secret meetings.

> Separatism is the opposite of diversity, and it can also make unholy alliances. Nearly thirty years ago Malcolm X's Black Muslims and George Lincoln Rockwell's American Nazi Party staged a joint rally at Madison Square Garden to dramatize their mutual hope of splitting the United States into segregated zones, one for blacks, the other for whites. (Hughes 1993, 149–150)

Neither Hughes nor Bok is a conservative writer, but both see the need for some agreement on a common agenda about what constitutes the good life between persons. They simply reject the extremes of both total agreement and total disunion.

Sissela Bok embraces two contrary and equally compelling issues—lack of ethical agreement and the need for some minimal ethical foundation for a common discourse about the future of human life. Bok offers no one answer, but calls us to begin conversation about "a minimalist set of common values" that can bring us together in a time of increasing difference and diversity (1995, 9). Bok does not despair of, nor does she romanticize, our postmodern era. She goes about her business, examining the need for some, not complete, agreement on ethics that can point to constructive coherence as we work with one another in both commonality and difference.

Central Concepts in Sissela Bok's Work

Sissela Bok's contribution to an ethical background can assist dialogic civility between persons. Communication is an act of implementation in foreground action, but it is the background narrative that guides, restrains, and shapes discourse shared between persons. How should we, in this historical moment, communicate as we address questions of lying, secrets, peace, and minimal core values between us? To address a time of ethical crisis, Bok offers an ethical background that directs action without dictating communicative behavior a priori to a decision grounded in the historical moment. This section examines her communicative ethics background suggestions for dealing with such common problems in a postmodern culture.

Lying

In a time of Watergate and Vietnam, Sissela Bok began to question how we were going to address the issue of lying. She rightly sensed that the aftershock from those events would shake the foundation of confidence in truth telling. Indeed, Watergate became a metaphor for why a social epidemic of unreflective cynicism was unleashed upon us.

From 1966 to 1976, the proportion of the public answering yes to whether they had a great deal of confidence in people in

charge of running major institutions dropped from 73 percent
to 42 percent for medicine; for major companies from 55 percent to 16 percent; for law firms from 24 percent (1973) to 12
percent; and for advertising agencies from 21 percent to 7 percent. (Bok 1978/1979, xviii)

The practical and the social need for examining the question of
lying was evident to social observers who understood the event of
Watergate as more than a political mistake; it became a defining
moment for the legitimate use of routine cynicism in American culture.

Watergate was a wakeup call for the historical necessity of cynicism. Such a communicative reality has been necessary before and
will be called upon again. Upton Sinclair's (1905/1960) Lithuanian
labor hero, Jurgis, was portrayed as a victim of early industrialized
life in the United States. He pointed to the necessity to learn the
danger of undue optimism and the historical appropriateness of
cynical suspicion necessary for dealing with the misuse of power.
Jurgis lost his freedom through jail, his wife to illness, his son to an
accident, and his wife's cousin to prostitution, while discovering the
dishonesty of politicians, owners, and managers—discovering the
rightful place of cynicism in a life. Sinclair then offered socialism as
an alternative to complete cynicism. Sinclair seemed to suggest
that it is necessary to see the historical need for cynicism and then
one needs to discover an alternative narrative, or one simply
becomes lost.

Sissela Bok, like Upton Sinclair, focuses on the historical need
for cynicism and then offers an alternative to routine cynicism. Bok
has a basic guide that frames her approach to the question of
lying—veracity needs to be our goal, without viewing truth telling
in an absolute or dogmatic fashion. Only in a moment when such a
defining event (Watergate) provided a platform for the legitimate
use of cynicism is it necessary to remind us that veracity is a good
idea. Of course, Bok makes sure we do not limit ourselves to an ideological and closed understanding of veracity. Bok clearly states
that her primary objective is to rekindle a commonsense background assumption—lying is generally not a social good and it
needs to be done with the greatest of care and only after appropriate reflection. This approach guides her in discussions of terminal
illness, the public good, and crisis management. Bok contends that
a rationale for a lie needs to meet the test of "justification"
(1978/1979, 105) in the public arena with a group wider than one's

conscience and open to anyone that the decision may impact or potentially concern. One must justify a lie not only to ourselves or believers in a given cause, but to a much larger constituency of concerned persons. As a general rule, "justification" requires understanding the broader context that places limits on lying.

Sissela Bok goes through one moral and practical example after another following the guideline: veracity with a small window of escape. Bok's reminder to readers is a simple but important message. "Trust and integrity are precious resources, easily squandered, hard to regain. They can thrive only on a foundation of respect for veracity" (1978/1979, 262). Truth that has no exception would be an ideology permitting no discretion. Bok recalls the great moral tradition of truth: truth is an essential social good that must be guarded with care and practiced regularly, ignored seldom and only when justifiable to the larger social good—well beyond one's companions, compatriots, and persons of agreement. Bok understands the irony about the notion of truth: "It is only the cynic who claims 'to speak the truth' at all times and in all places to all men [or women] in the same way" (1978/1979, 304).

Sissela Bok further considers the resultant implications of a postmodern culture that has little to join people together and little to call us to be accountable to one another. Postmodernity is a practical environment for the prospering of individualism that may not look for ways to assist the larger good or protect veracity as a general principle for guidance.

> The very stress on individualism, on competition, on achieving material success which so marks our society also generates intense pressures to cut corners. To win an election, to increase one's income, to outsell competitors—such motives impel many to participate in forms of duplicity they might otherwise resist. The more widespread they judge these practices to be, the stronger will be the pressure to join, even compete, in deviousness. (Bok 1978/1979, 258)

Lying is a natural extension of looking out for "me" in an era in which the narrative structures that pull us together are not clear or in place. Bok expresses a concern for the "we" as she calls for reasonable veracity with a window for exceptions. She seeks to assist not just "me," but the social fabric in which "we" live and communicate. The metaphor that guided modernity was "self." Postmodernity does not claim the notion of self or agency as primary, but calls us to a time of questions. Instead of falling prey to a reinvestigation of self and languishing forever in questioning, Bok moves in a corporate or "we" centered fashion—looking for minimal points of narrative agreement.

Secrets

A lie is based upon incongruence between action and expression. Secrets are more subtle; they involve not what we do or say, but what we withhold and do not say.

> The word "secrecy" refers to the resulting concealment. It also denotes the methods used to conceal, such as codes or disguises or camouflage, and the practices of concealment, as in trade secrecy or professional confidentiality.
>
> Accordingly, I shall take concealment, or hiding, to be the defining trait of secrecy. It presupposes separation, a setting apart of the secret from the non-secret, and of keepers of a secret from those excluded. The Latin *secretum* carries this meaning of something hidden, set apart. It derives from *secernere*, which originally meant to sift apart, to separate as with a sieve. It bespeaks discernment, the ability to make distinctions, to sort out and draw lines; a capacity that underlies not only secrecy but all thinking, all intention and choice. The separation between insider and outsider is inherent in secrecy; and to think something secret is already to envisage potential conflict between what insiders conceal and outsiders want to inspect or lay bare. (Bok 1983/1984, 6)

In typical fashion, Bok guides us through the dialectic of secrets—their use can both assist as well as hurt a person, an organization, and a society.

The unique component that is offered in the above quotation is the awareness of secrets separating "insiders" and "outsiders." In an era of concern for diversity, questions about what might unknowingly pull us apart need to be addressed—for Sissela Bok the question of "secrets" is such an issue. In-group and out-group members are clearly identified by what is concealed from whom.

The terms "inside" and "outside" do not only generate a feeling of connection, they are also terms necessary for "privacy" (Bok

1983/1984, 11) and for group "loyalty" (Bok 1983/1984, 145) to exist. Both privacy and loyalty are social goods and, of course, both are potentially dangerous. Actions such as "gossip" (Bok 1983/1984, 89) and "whistle blowing" (Callahan and Bok 1980, 280) begin to take place as a counter to inappropriate uses of "privacy" and "loyalty." Additionally, Bok cautions against making openness into a technique; openness can both assist and hurt persons and organizations by the ideological use of disclosure.

Sissela Bok keeps a conversation alive about both the need for and the danger of secrets—reminding us of the error of falling on either side of the extreme. For instance, Bok would fight to protect the right of a whistle blower. However, she also knows that some persons might use such a role for the wrong reasons. "No society can count itself immune from the risk that individuals or groups in power might use whistle blowing for their own purposes. . . . From the moral point of view, there are important differences between the aims, messages, and methods of dissenters from within" (Bok 1983/1984, 213). Secrets are a social concern, but living a good life without them is impossible. Bok's goal is for us to use secrets with care and to realize that secrets bond those that share the information and separate those that do not have similar access. Any time an action of private bonding and separation of in-group and out-group members is encouraged by a communicative action, it must be used with care, caution, and concern.

Peace

Concerns about lying and secrets, which are often at the center of any war between "insiders" and "outsiders," paved the way for Sissela Bok's next major work—*A Strategy for Peace: Human Values and the Threat of War* (1989). The common theme that runs throughout all her work is getting a person to think beyond "me"— to ask how a decision might impact the larger public, and social good. In this work, Bok makes this case by critiquing what she terms the "pathology of partisanship" (1989, 6).

The following quotation outlines Sissela Bok's (1989) concern about partisanship:

> In time of war or other intense conflict, partisanship can foster a pathology all its own. When this happens, partisanship

goes beyond the emphasis on loyalty and cohesion needed for the well-being of any community and leads people to become obsessive and heedless of their group's long-range self-interest, even of its survival. Communities, like living organisms, can succumb to stress, internal weakness, or contagion. These factors heighten the risks that the pathology of self-destructive partisanship will take over. Only with the help of strong leadership and institutional safeguards can communities prevent or withstand such deterioration. (6)

Bok offers a clear alternative to "the pathology of partisanship" (1989, 6). She suggests that we cannot afford to lose the capacity to imagine ourselves in the shoes of another person. When we can only imagine our own view we succumb to what Arthur Koestler called "revolutionary ethics" in *Darkness at Noon* (1941, 78). The darkness in this case comes from partisanship that permits no light but its own. One can experience threats to another, not just oneself; empathy is tied to such a belief and action. One can think beyond "me" and include others; we can travel in time. Generational sensitivity is grounded in our reaching beyond our own time frame. "We then try to envisage how recent conflicts may affect beings not yet even born, and consider our responsibility toward the past as well—what many have called our stewardship of resources that are not ours to use up or destroy at will" (Bok 1989, 28). Bok's suggestion is to move us beyond the "insider" group of those focused only on partisanship and to offer a wider perspective of the world in which we all belong and for which we have a common responsibility.

Sissela Bok works from a dialectical position. She rejects the highhanded comments from "moralists" (1989, 119) that ignore complexity of issues. Yet on the other hand Bok calls for a commitment to peace. Bok brings much of her early work to bear in advocating "genuine self-defense with the public desire for a principled foreign policy . . . [that seeks to both protect and] reduce excessive, debilitating distrust" (Bok 1989, 143). The notions of a "public" beyond one's own provincial group and "justification" of one's actions are central to her call for the restraint of war and the invitation of a peace that keeps our collective responsibility before us.

There is a maturity about Sissela Bok's *Strategy for Peace* (1989) that is present in her obvious call for hope and her disdain for simple solutions to complex crises. There is the wisdom of François Marie Arouet de Voltaire's (1962/1966) *Candide*, who wants to embrace the optimism of Pangloss but eventually discovers it necessary to simply get to work—to "cultivate our garden" (124). *Candide* is full of irony, which calls us to look at life as it is, not as we would want it to be. The "do-gooder" who finds that simple help can actually, at times, cause harm could benefit from a reading of both *Candide* (Voltaire 1962/1966) and *A Strategy for Peace* (Bok 1989).

In Sissela Bok's own words, if genuine peace is to be an international reality, we must seek the "common good" (Bok, 1989, 148) beyond "me" and a limited sense of "us." She calls for open and lively debate, the protection of free speech, and a willingness to enter into conversation with the other as a minimal foundation for peace between persons.

Common Values

Sissela Bok's work *Common Values* (1995) is necessary for her other insights to have a lasting impact. Lying, secrets, and peace need to be implemented in a way that can be understood and appreciated by the other. In short, what is needed between persons is a commitment to basic *Common Values* (Bok 1995). "The search for answers will be central to the debate over the role of ethics in the century to come, engaging collaborators and adversaries the world over. They will have at least a starting point from which to begin to the extent that they acknowledge a minimalist set of common values" (Bok 1995, 9).

In typical fashion, Sissela Bok works dialectically. She does not embrace a deep structural set of common values, but rather calls for a minimal set of agreements that permit cultural diversity efforts to succeed. Bok's caution is that we are in "compassion fatigue" (1995, 4). Bok does not want us to work as "do gooders" (1995, 114) who provide simple answers to complex problems. She is convinced that only those people who are willing to work, study, and act to understand "complex humanitarian emergencies" (1995, 123) will be able to assist us in the twenty-first century.

Sissela Bok (1995) offers four assumptions that she considers necessary for a realistic effort to articulate a minimal core of common values for a diverse public.

1. Basic minimal values are needed for the survival of all humans.

2. Acceptance of basic minimal values is necessary for coexistence.

3. Basic minimal values do not preclude an appreciation and respect for diversity.

4. Common ground for cross-cultural dialogue is needed.

Bok offers not a major set of ideas, but points to a common ground upon which one can have dialogue, debate, and critique.

> A constructivist basis for morality thus interpreted calls for no extra human or superhuman guarantees of objectivity or absoluteness. To the extent that is a minimalist basis, it offers, rather, common ground or footing upon which to undertake dialogue, debate, and negotiations within and between otherwise disparate traditions; a set of values that can be agreed upon as a starting point for negotiation or action. (Bok 1995, 76)

Bok rejects the idealism of maximal value agreement and moves in the direction of a conversational ethic. When conversation is possible—to speak, to be heard, and to respond—a minimal ethic is offered. Bok is working philosophically in a fashion similar to the anthropological work of Clifford Geertz. Geertz (1973) understood the value of both the insider engaging in unreflective practice and the outsider with a specialized vocabulary. Bok in a similar manner understands the need for local and translocal or particular and common ground values.

Historicality and Dialogic Civility

The relevance of Sissela Bok's writing in a postmodern culture rests with her acceptance of the historical moment in which we are located and in her simultaneous effort to search for practical ways for us to negotiate this time of metanarrative confusion and crisis. Her work has a dialectic tone of acceptance and realistic hope.

Whether examining the question of lying, secrets, peace, or common values, there is a consistent sound to Sissela Bok's voice. First, we can no longer assume agreement on everyday practical ethical issues. Second, we need to keep the conversation alive about such important human themes. Third, the answer to any of these human problems lies in guidance and conversation, not in dictate or inflexible ideology.

Sissela Bok is a teacher of ethical issues who wants us to communicate with her and with one another about human themes that impact our daily living and the future of the human community. Her work has significant implications for the quality of our daily lives together. The teacher in Bok is clearly present in the conclusion to the book *Ethics Teaching in Higher Education*: "Our only claim is that a 'higher education' that does not foster, support, and implement an examination of the moral life will fail its own purposes, the needs of its students, and the welfare of society" (Callahan and Bok 1980, 300). Bok does not understand moral education as propaganda, nor as relativism, but instead as conversation about central human ethical issues that must be worked out in the practical context of the given historical situation.

Sissela Bok's voice is relevant today in her dialectical warning of the danger of too much and equally too little moral agreement and guidance. As Bok takes on the practical problems before us, she models the skill of discernment of real danger and a realistic hope grounded in tenacity and action. Bok rejects hopelessness; she calls for action that is both realistic about the complexity of human problems and emergencies and fueled by a common value of concern for the other. She grounds such a call in flexibility, not rigidity and self-righteousness.

> The posture of standing by one's convictions "unflinchingly," for example, hints at moral heroism; but exactly why *should* such an unflinching stance be a mark of civilization? Surely, both the nature of the convictions and what is done to uphold them must matter. Otherwise, might not a Caligula or a Goebbels qualify as civilized rather than barbarian? And why should anyone be so presumptuous as to label as "barbarian" the vast majority of human beings who either believe their convictions to be fully valid or whose stance, regardless of whether or not they do, is less than unflinching? Attributing moral worth as inherent in an unflinching stance for one's personal convictions proves nothing by itself. (Bok 1995, 68)

Bok seeks to overcome a tendency to routine cynicism, despair, and the other extreme of moralism, and calls us into action, work, and a life of hope.

Indeed, Sissela Bok is a scholar willing to address the ethical crisis of this historical moment. She reminds us of our common values of concern for people beyond the self if we are to live in some form of constructive social arrangement. She does not resolve the issues of lying, secrets, peace, or common values. The task of an invitational scholar is not to end the conversation, but to keep us interested in the topic. This conversational effort is what Bok does well and with care. She reminds us that hope and action of care are not just idealism, but are tied to the quality of a human life.

Sissela Bok is a practical philosopher who is working with ethical crises in a postmodern era. Her work rings with the consistency of Walter Brueggemann's *Hopeful Imagination: Prophetic Voices in Exile*. Brueggemann suggests that in time of serious change and chaos three major themes emerge for the human trying to cope— "denial," "utilitarianism," and "amnesia" (1986, 132). For the "hopeful imagination" of the human to be given voice and action one must counter the above three themes that collectively point to ignoring our historical moment. She reminds us over and over again in each of her books of her unwillingness to let amnesia guide our inaction. As Brueggemann suggests, denial, utilitarianism, and amnesia keep us in exile—and Bok would concur. She reminds us of common values—walking in the midst of the human community with our eyes wide open and our realistic discernment abilities honed—yet still offering hope and practical concrete action for the other, thereby continuing to shape our own human face.

Sissela Bok points to a dialogic civility as she embraces values and rejects moralism in a time of ethical crisis. Bok will not let us deny the importance of ethics in dialogic civility. She points to dialogic civility as she looks for the particular and for common ground. She enhances dialogic civility as she rejects the crisis of extremes and keeps a particular human face attached to even the most minimal of values that might bind us together. Flexibility within the historical moment guides Bok's voice and points us toward dialogic civility.

Chapter Eleven

Viktor Frankl

Meaning, Displacement, and Courage

On an Alternative to Psychologism —

Everywhere, psychologism sees nothing but masks, insists that only neurotic motives lie behind these masks. Art, it asserts, is "in the final analysis nothing but" flight from life or from love. Religion is merely primitive man's [or woman's] fear of cosmic forces. All spiritual creations turn out to be "mere" sublimations of the libido or, as the case may be, compensations for inferiority feelings or means for achieving security. The great creators in the realm of the spirit are then dismissed as neurotics. After we have been put through such a course of "debunking" by psychologism we can with complete complacency say that Goethe or St. Augustine, for instance, was "really only" a neurotic. This point of view sees nothing for what it is; that is to say, it really sees nothing. Because something at one time was a mask, or somewhere was a means to an end, does that make it forever a mask, or nothing but a means to an end? Can there never be anything immediate, genuine, original?

Individual psychology preaches courage, but it has apparently forgotten the humility that should accompany courage. Humility in the face of the spirit's powers, in the face of the spiritual realm as a sphere in itself whose nature and values cannot simply be projected psychologistically down into the psychological plane. Humility, if it is genuine, is certainly as much a sign of inner strength as courage.

—Viktor Frankl, *The Doctor and the Soul*

207

On Meaning in Suffering—

It is different with what I call the *homo patiens*, the suffering man [or woman], the man [or woman] who knows how to suffer, how to mold even his [or her] sufferings into a human achievement. The *homo patiens* moves on an axis perpendicular to the success/failure axis of the *homo sapiens*. He [or she] moves on an axis which extends between the poles of fulfillment and despair. . . .

Only if we recognize that there are two different dimensions involved is it possible to understand how on one hand we can meet people who in spite of success are caught in despair . . . while on the other hand we come across people who in spite of failure have arrived at a sense of fulfillment and even happiness, because they have found meaning even in suffering.

—*The Unheard Cry for Meaning*

Viktor Frankl's life and work provide insight into the continuing crisis of existential meaning in life. Frankl pointed to the importance of meaning as necessary background to meet the foreground challenges of everyday existence. His material has even greater credibility when one considers the historical moment in which he constructed his work and theory. Frankl framed many of his ideas during Adolph Hitler's attempt to destroy the lives and meaning structures of non-Aryan people. Frankl's insights were given birth when the narrative meaning of a people was put at risk by genuine evil. He understood the significance of what it meant to have one's meaning background meet the severest of tests and survive. Frankl (1959/1974) was fond of quoting Friedrich Nietzsche, "He who has a *why* to live can bear with almost any *how*" (ix). Frankl's major contribution to our historical moment is his tenacity to call upon meaning structures (*why*) that many people had naturally begun to doubt during the Nazi atrocities. In what was for many people a time of crisis riddled with "bad" stories, Frankl found meaning. Such a voice can speak to us in our present historical moment.

This chapter presents the contribution of Viktor Frankl to understanding dialogic civility. We examine concepts central to Frankl's work in logotherapy. We also review the process of discovering meaning and address how self-actualization and the pleasure principle can lead to a false sense of optimism. Frankl's existential understanding of meaning enables life to be lived in a particular circumstance with thoughtful and meaningful action. Finally, we address the importance of his ideas for this contemporary historical moment.

Introduction

Viktor Frankl's life and scholarship were shaped by his firsthand experience of the savagery of one human to another. Frankl, a Jewish intellectual, witnessed the face of evil in the guise of the Third Reich, making it impossible for him to conceptualize the human as innately good. Yet in the same breath Frankl reminds his readers of the noble potential of the human. Frankl's view of the human is grounded in what Martin Buber called the "unity of contraries" (1966b, 111). Frankl neither demeans the potential of the human, nor glosses over the darker side of human life. As a psychiatrist who lost his own family to the death march of the concentration camps, Frankl discovered the practical necessity for having a psychological why to endure—to bear the often painful how of life's trials (Allport 1974).

The following quotation from Viktor Frankl points to this complex view of the human, central and formative in his work.

> In concentration camps . . . we watched and witnessed some of our comrades behave like swine while others behaved like saints. Man [or woman] has both potentialities within himself [or herself]. . . . Our generation is realistic, for we have come to know man [or woman] as he [or she] really is. After all, man is the being who has invented the gas chambers of Auschwitz; however, he [or she] is also that being who has entered those gas chambers upright, with the Lord's Prayer or the *Shema Yisrael* on his [or her] lips. (1959/1974, 212–213)

Frankl witnessed the dialectical nature of the human as good and evil. Yet, his interpersonal voice is one that offers meaning, not hopelessness in the face of such a stark reality.

The insight of Viktor Frankl bestrides two different historical moments—World War II and the present. Frankl's scholarship was shaped within the historical era leading up to and during the atrocities of World War II by both his academic training and his religious commitment to Judaism. Frankl's historical moment of formation as a scholar embraced a time of enormous contradiction in which there was both ideological clarity (Nazism) and one of the boldest attempts in the history of the Western world to destroy not only a people, but the narrative structure (Judaism) of a people. Frankl understood first hand the potential danger of ideological meaning structures (for example, Nazism) and simultaneously the necessity of narratives for carrying the meaning of a people (for example, Judaism). Narratives guide; ideologies dictate. Nazism was not a narrative, but a rigid ideology that dictated a particular vision. Narratives are altered as people contribute new insight to an ongoing narrative through ideas and action. In the drama of Nazi atrocity, while the background narrative of Judaism was being unraveled, Frankl moved closer to an existential and individual sense of meaning. Note that we do not use narrative and ideology as synonyms. A narrative is a corporate story that guides a people. Narrative guidance requires active participation of people who interpret and through their actions reshape the narrative. An ideology, on the other hand, dictates action for people a priori to the event; it forces life within a script.

Viktor Frankl, like many of his contemporaries in the era of World War II, placed faith in individual existential meaning structures, not the corporate structure. Our work with Frankl lifts up his view of existential meaning while suggesting a more important role that corporate narratives play in individual existential meaning structures. Narratives can be both good and bad, constructive and evil. In the face of a Nazi ideology, looking to individual existential meaning was understandable. For Frankl, meaning is discovered not in the abstract, but through a unique person in a given historical moment. We dialectically affirm the importance of individual existential meaning, understanding the danger of evil narratives while calling attention to the ontological fact that narratives carry meaning for the human. We make sense of the world together through stories created in common experience.

Viktor Frankl's insights from his own suffering offer assistance to the contemporary communicator living in a time of disrupted meaning structures. In spite of his rejection of bad narrative structures, such as Nazism, Fascism, Communism, and the "blind faith" (Camus 1960/1974, 1–32) of nationalism, Frankl called the human being to meaning beyond self-preoccupation. Like the contemporaries of his intellectual moment, Frankl was fearful of corporate or group life. Nazism called people to question a narrative structure rooted in *Life Together* (Bonhoeffer 1954) in service to the other. On the other hand, Frankl clearly understood the limits of self-preoccupation.

Narratives that frame our background experience provide an interpretive screen for foreground discovery of the unique, existential, individual meaning. As any photographer knows, background makes it possible to focus upon foreground. People orient themselves in how they define the meaning of experience, which is guided by background. For Frankl, the individual discovery of meaning is explicit, and we suggest that the carriers of meaning, narrative structures, are implicit.

Viktor Frankl conceptualized meaning as individual, unique, and discovered in the existential moment by a particular person at a particular time. However, even as Frankl moved in an existential direction, he did not forgo a narrative base or the story-laden nature of life. He assumed the background significance of narrative. Frankl envisioned logotherapy or meaning therapy at a time in which many people called the meaning of life itself into legitimate question. For Frankl, stories are manifested in concrete ways—the story of a cause, a love, or God.

> Man [or woman] is never driven to moral behavior; in each instance he [or she] decides to behave morally. Man [or woman] does not do so in order to satisfy a moral drive and to have a good conscience; he [or she] does so for the sake of a cause to which he [or she] commits himself [or herself], or for a person who he [or she] loves, or for the sake of his [or her] God. (Frankl 1959/1974, 158)

The background narrative propels one to deal with a foreground event, guided by one's convictions.

The following section outlines the basic concepts central to Viktor Frankl's work. He constructed a usable and understandable way to endure tragedy and crisis. From this historical standpoint of awareness of metanarrative decline and perhaps collapse, we ask the following question about Frankl's work: "How can a human being, even in crisis, discover unique existential meaning in a given historical moment?"

Lived Life as Thoughtful Action

The value of Viktor Frankl's work is multifaceted. He not only wrote with authenticity, but with insight that speaks across cultures and historical moments. Frankl's courage is displayed in his thoughtful effort to refuse to be psychologically destroyed by the concentration camp experience, discovering within that environment a value for the person in search of meaning. His insight was supported by an integration of academic training and praxis of theories under the most severe of human trials. He reminded us that each person must discover his or her own meaning in the existential situation that claims one's attention and action.

Another way of describing what Viktor Frankl did philosophically can be explained using the language of philosophical hermeneutics (Gadamer 1960/1986). The given situation is the text in an existential dilemma. The interpretive possibilities in an event are limited by the historical moment and to some degree expanded by the background narrative that the person brings to the interpretive event. Simply put, interpretation requires us to take a text seriously and to bring to bear upon the text our own interpretive background. A narrative background permits one to move from technician to craftsman. The technician needs to follow a given set of rules. The craftsman, however, has a background of knowledge that permits him or her to make necessary alterations in accordance with the demands of the job. A background narrative operates as a pool of interpretive options and possibilities—it must be adapted to a given historical circumstance.

Perhaps this interpretive richness of the text enabled Viktor Frankl to state how men and women with an inner depth could survive the physical hardship of the concentration camp experience. Frankl understood the wisdom articulated by Elie Wiesel, another survivor of the camps: "In the Talmud . . . when someone's head is pained—in other words, when he [or she] feels anguish—there are several possible solutions: first he [or she] looks within himself [or herself], then he [or she] reflects upon his [or her] other occupations, trying to put them in perspective, and finally he [or she] studies" (Wiesel and Saint-Cheron 1990, 160). Meaning emerges not only by what a person is doing. More importantly, meaning is given birth by the attitude one takes into an action and event.

At best, the liberal arts are a way for us to understand questions of meaning as we go into professions such as medicine, engineering, and law. The liberal arts provide the background for understanding foreground issues of action appropriate for a given profession. The two integrated together (liberal arts and a profession) point once again to a "unity of contraries," requiring a life of thoughtful action.

The meaning of the doctor's work lies in what he [or she] does beyond purely medical duties; it is what he [or she] brings to his [or her] work as a personality, as a human being, which gives the doctor his [or her] peculiar role. For it would come to the same thing whether . . . [the doctor] or a colleague gave injections, etc., if he [or she] were merely practicing the arts of medicine, merely using the tricks of the trade. Only when he [or she] goes beyond the limits of purely professional service, beyond the tricks of the trade, does he [or she] begin that truly personal work which alone is fulfilling. (Frankl 1946/1973, 119)

For Frankl, life is meant to be lived both in action and thought. Meaning is made present in a life through a combination of action and study—the very model Frankl gives us in his own life and scholarship.

The difficulty many people have in discovering existential meaning for their own lives is reflected by Viktor Frankl's use of a concept that provides a metaphorical picture of this concern—"ontological blindness" (1969, 9). The fact that we are often blind to meaning suggests that meaning is not always visible to us, although meaning is always present. The old question of whether or not a tree falling in the forest makes a "noise" when no one is present is akin to Frankl's concern about meaning. What is indisputable in the above example is that the tree is present—whether a sound is heard or not. What is needed for the tree to be visible is for a person to discover the noise of the falling timber. For Frankl, the existence of meaning is like the tree; it is without dispute. He realizes, however, that for "meaning" to make a difference in a life (to make a noise and be heard) a person must uncover the meaning—someone must listen. Until the existential discovery of meaning takes place, the person rests, like many of us, in "ontological blindness"—unable to see what is present or hear meaning in the existential moment.

In a lesser fashion, some of us are now in a crisis that calls into question a previously accepted pattern of work in an industrial society. The number of unemployed executives that find themselves hanging a shingle with the engraved title CONSULTANT points to such disruption in many large cities.

To be sure, we also have to cope with unintentional leisure in the form of unemployment. Unemployment may cause a specific neurosis—"unemployment neurosis," as I called it when I first described it in 1933. But again, upon closer investigation it turned out that the real cause was the confusion of one's being unemployed with . . . being useless and, hence, his [or her] life's being meaningless. Financial compensation, or for that matter social security, is not enough. Man [or woman] does not live by welfare alone. (Frankl 1977/1978, 25)

The direction and end results of societal change are simply unclear. Many people who were previously untouched by challenges to narrative structures of the problematic other (people different than oneself) now join the ranks of those who have been struggling for meaning in the midst of confusion and change. For many of us, it is not the routine, but the crisis that calls us to uncover a sense of meaning for life by overcoming our blindness.

If one is unable to cope with disruption of the routine, the organization will need to be very stable for such a person to be happy. In today's market, where firms that make changes quickly are applauded, such a person will be less likely to find happiness. The irony is that in a time in which we need flexible workers who can meet change well, many people continue to look for meaning in stability, a sense of place; such meaning is not possible in a workplace that values rapid change. People seek security in the meaning of their routine, simply because other meaning structures are not visible.

Today the communication crisis (Arnett 1986/1997a) of a lack of meaning is in need of attention again. The routine provides a sense of place by practice through repeated and dependable action. Communication crises seldom emerge during stable times, but rather in times of unpredictable change. We then are required to look to something other than repeated action to sustain meaning in a life. In times of crisis, we need to find a definition for meaning that is more complex than repeated pattern (Watzlawick, Beaven, and Jackson 1967).

The contemporary nature of Viktor Frankl's work is pointed to in "Existential Homelessness: A Contemporary Case for Dialogue" (Arnett 1994), which makes the case similar to that above. Finding meaning in life is no longer just a task for the oppressed; lack of meaning has become a malaise for the middle and upper-middle classes in a changing narrative structure. The need for a sense of meaning in an era of change and uncertainty is not new; only the socioeconomic groups that cry out for meaning are new.

Oppressed people throughout civilization have had to muster personal resources to discover meaning in demanding times; such people have witnessed the destruction of their own narrative structures. Now the middle and upper-middle classes will have their turn.

Indeed, the reality of change in the lives of the middle and upper-middle class is now before us. The industrial revolution displaced many laborers and now the information revolution is doing the same to the upper classes—who once thought themselves exempt from concerns about displacement. Indeed, the first wave, second wave, and third wave of Alvin and Heidi Toffler's (1993) view of change can be translated into agrarian, industrial, and information ages. Such changes are being played out before our eyes as one company after another finds ways to do more with fewer white collar workers. This disruption of the routine makes Viktor Frankl's message both relevant and needed—calling us to shed blinders that have confused routine with genuine meaning.

The ability to mask the need for meaning is a well-honed art in our contemporary culture. Hours spent at work long after the workday is over can sometimes signal an aversion to going home and meeting a lack of meaning in the midst of one's own quietude. A desire for material things that seems unquenchable, even after we have more than we need, points to an attempt to fill a meaning void. The quest for youth and a seemingly endless future can sometimes hide us from asking, "What do I want this life, my only life, to represent?" "What am I called to leave behind?" In the quest for youth, we live with the unexamined exploration of the meaning of our life and the inevitability of our own death.

What great civilization or philosophy has moved people and given meaning and direction without taking seriously the notion of death and the need for some form of accounting? "In time and in finiteness man [or woman] must *finish* something—that is, take finiteness upon himself [or herself] and consciously accept an end as part of the bargain. . . . There is, then, no necessity to somehow exclude death from life; rather, it belongs quite properly to life! Nor is there any way to 'overcome it'" (Frankl 1946/1973, 66–67). For Viktor Frankl, meaning can only be found with one's eyes wide open. Life needs to be met on the terms before one, not in accordance with one's wishes and infinite hopes; he calls us not to despair, but to discover meaning grounded in the existential possibilities before us, in this historical moment.

Central Concepts in Viktor Frankl's Work

Viktor Frankl's assumption that logotherapy assists with the problem of "loss of meaning" in life and his forthright embracing of suffering as ontological sets his work apart from other writers. Frankl's voice called out two different messages: "In spite of suffering the human is a meaning seeking creature," and "Because of suffering we must find meaning in life." The human is both defiant and realistic, both courageous and humble, both an idealist and a pragmatic. This person of contradiction has a basic assumption—to live and to survive with dignity. "What then is man [or woman]? . . . He [or she] is a being who continuously decides what he [or she] is: a being who equally harbors the potential to descend to the level of an animal or to ascend to the life of a saint" (Frankl 1967, 110). Ideals and reality combine in each situation, providing the text for dialogue from which individual existential meaning can be discovered.

Pragmatic Spiritualism

Viktor Frankl sought to describe the person as more than a "surviving being." He understood the importance of the spiritual dimension of humanness. Frankl began with the assumption that attention needs to be directed to meaning in connection with the human spirit "termed *logotherapy*. In this connection, *logos* is intended to signify 'the spiritual' and, beyond that, 'the meaning'" (1946/1973, xi). Frankl stressed not only meaning, but with the word *logotherapy*, he introduced the personal dimension of "spiritual action."

Viktor Frankl believed the quality of life is carried by what we make of life, not just what happens to us. He wanted to encourage an attitude or spirit that seeks meaning as we productively meet life's events. *The Doctor and the Soul* (1946/1973) reminds us of this fundamental dimension of the human. The spiritual or the soul of the human is that which urges a particular stance or attitude toward life. One does not just walk through life; one knowingly assumes a stance toward life's events.

> [Karl] Jaspers calls the being of man [or woman] a "deciding" being, not something that simply "is" but something that first decides "what it is." . . . The meaning of concepts like those of

merit and guilt stands and falls on our belief in man's [or woman's] true capacity for not simply accepting as fated limitations . . . on his [or her] capacity for seeing them instead as challenges bidding him [or her] shape his [or her] destiny and . . . life. (Frankl 1946/1973, 21)

Frankl wanted us to meet life with our eyes open to fulfillment and disappointment, as well as acknowledge our responsibility in meaning discovery.

The human being is born with an impulse to seek meaning beyond survival; Viktor Frankl stressed this practical human dimension of spiritual action. He did not want us to miss the symbolic nature of life's events that point to meaning beyond the raw experience. He understood spirituality to be an innate impulse that craves meaning beyond sense data, the self, and survival. Frankl's view of spirituality is practical in nature. He did not confuse spiritual with a religious position; his understanding of spiritual is a philosophical/practical conviction. Frankl's view of spiritual is not meant for contemplative leisure, but for practical living.

Viktor Frankl would like the saying on the back of the shirts of the High School team on which the son and daughter of one of the authors swam: *Know your limits, then surpass them.* The logo did not reflect a macho view of the world, but was a call for quiet courage. The team was comprised of great kids, outstanding students, and good athletes. As the season progressed, the great kids and outstanding students discovered their athletic limitations and then surpassed them. The athletes used everything to their advantage—starts, turns, and long hard workouts. Unlike the team of the prior year, which was ranked third in the country, this team was not even ranked as the season began. Frankl might remind us, however, to watch the kind of leaders that emerge from such a group: *Know your limits, then surpass them.* Perhaps at the age of thirty-five the practices at 5:30 AM, then after school, then on Saturday—during summer and winter—will witness the emergence of people who with quiet courage *Know your limits, then surpass them* in daily acts of leadership. Ultimately, the girls' team lost the regionals but came back to win the state championship and the boys' team came in second at the regionals and fifth in the state—not bad for great kids and only good athletes. More importantly, Frankl and the authors are interested in the team members' leadership abilities twenty years hence.

Viktor Frankl would not equate the above spirit with arrogance, but with a humility that must accompany quiet courage. First, one does not ignore limits; and second, only quietly does one attempt to surpass them. In the mixed setting of courage and humility the spirit does its work; an attitude toward life is embraced that meets the challenges of daily existence. Of course, not all limitations can be overcome; yet only with quiet courage can we determine what is unmoveable and can only be endured. "Humility . . . in the face of the spiritual realm is a sphere in itself whose nature and values cannot simply be projected psychologically down into the psychological plane. Humility, if it is genuine, is certainly as much a sign of inner strength as courage" (Frankl 1946/1973, 19). Indeed, Frankl would approve—*know your limits and then surpass them*. One will not always succeed, but quiet courage provides the foundation for enduring both success and failure.

Meeting Disappointment and Suffering

Logotherapy, as envisioned by Viktor Frankl assists the person in deciding what attitude or spirit he or she wants to assume toward life. In the above example, we suggest it is not enough to simply swim; the question is, "With what attitude or spirit do you swim?" Even in the midst of discovering a genuine limitation that cannot be altered, we still have a final freedom—"What attitude will I take into my meeting of unmoveable realities?" Frankl's understanding of spiritual was not "otherworldly" or a form of escapism; rather, his approach is just the opposite. He was concerned about the attitude we take on as we meet life's events, even those painful events that cause us to suffer.

Disappointment and pain are not often associated with interpersonal approaches to communication. Suffering, however, is reflective of a basic uniqueness of Viktor Frankl's writing. One of the authors recalled a conversation with a colleague. This woman had suffered greatly and survived, had completed a Ph.D. in psychology, and had led a most productive life. During a lengthy conversation, the author asked her to explain the difference between paternalism or maternalism and the action of a mentor or a genuine friend who is more knowledgeable in a given area. The woman was asked not to give a textbook definition, but to describe the differences between the two terms in terms of her own association with members of Alcoholic Anonymous (AA). Her statement resonated ideas central to Frankl's view of suffering. She stated that paternal and maternal instincts are used to protect, comfort, and lessen life's dangers. Paternalism or maternalism invites a life that "should be," failing to give the person life tools for dealing with the inevitable tragedies of life. Only when the paternal or maternal figure is present does the person feel comforted, protected, and "safe." But a mentor takes every suffering and mistake as a opportunity to assist the other to grow. The mentor does not protect against suffering, but assists in understanding what the suffering means and how one might find increased insight and wisdom from its occurrence. The mentor frees the other for singular living and for the eventual mentoring of another.

In her description of a mentor, this colleague pointed to the kind of person Viktor Frankl's theory of logotherapy seems to encourage—a person of quiet but intense strength, even in the midst of disappointment.

> My friend has hope that education and people can make a difference and she fights attempts to placate students, allowing them to learn from disappointment, frustration, and pain. But most students know that if they are in trouble and need a teacher to walk with them in disappointment, helping them once again find hope, that they must knock on my friend's door. The people who might be called purveyors of a managed smile, who offer an unrealistic sense of optimism grounded in expectations of ease and comfort, not work and commitment, are nowhere to be found when intense pain enters a student's life. Dialogic education is grounded in a realistic sense of caring—one in which hope and the tools for meeting pain and disappointment can assist the life of a graduate. (Arnett 1992/1997c, 113–114)

A mentor meets the stuff of life with another, helping the other discover meaning in the wake of disappointment.

Meaning does not come to us in only positive gifts—sometimes a gift is wrapped in suffering, rather than ease, comfort, and joy. Frankl shared this story:

> A rich and mighty Persian once walked in his garden with one of his servants. The servant cried that he had just encountered Death, who had threatened him. He begged his master

to give him his fastest horse so that he could make haste and flee to Teheran, which he could reach that same evening. The master consented and the servant galloped off on the horse. On returning to his house the master himself met Death, and questioned him, "Why did you terrify and threaten my servant?" "I did not threaten him; I only showed surprise in still finding him here when I planned to meet him tonight in Teheran," said Death. (1959/1974, 89)

For Frankl, suffering, like eventual death, is inevitable. The human needs to meet suffering, not with surprise, but with a question, "Where have you been and why have you been away so long?"

Let us conclude this section by emphasizing once again that Viktor Frankl did not want a person to pursue pain. The task of a logotherapist or mentor is to help the other reframe the meaning of suffering—to find meaning that goes undetected in everyday looking. The following story points to how Viktor Frankl reframed suffering for another person:

For what matters above all is the attitude we take toward suffering, the attitude in which we take our suffering upon ourselves. Let me cite a clear-cut example: Once, an elderly general practitioner consulted me because of his severe depression. He could not overcome the loss of his wife who had died two years before and whom he had loved above all else. Now how could I help him? What should I tell him? Well, I refrained from telling him anything, but instead confronted him with the question, "What would have happened, Doctor, if you had died first, and your wife would have had to survive you?" "Oh," he said, "for her this would have been terrible; how she would have suffered!" Whereupon I replied, "You see, Doctor, such a suffering has been spared her, and it is you who have spared her this suffering; but now, you have to pay for it by surviving and mourning her." He said no word but shook my hand and calmly left my office. Suffering ceases to be suffering in some way at the moment it finds a meaning, such as the meaning of a sacrifice. . . . I could not change his fate, I could not revive his wife. But in that moment I did succeed in changing his *attitude* toward his unalterable fate inasmuch as from that time on he could at least see a meaning in his suffering. (1959/1974, 178–179)

Frankl did not seek to alter the fate of suffering, rather he focused his energy on changing people's attitude toward the fate that meets us. All human beings suffer. How one meets the suffering that greets him or her at various points in life's journey determines the quality of one's life.

Discovering Meaning

Meaning does not emerge out of the abstract, but from concrete happenings before us. The task of the person is to uncover the meaning present in ordinary and extraordinary events of life.

Tripod of Meaning. Meaning emerges out of what Viktor Frankl called the "tripod of meaning" (1967, 15). Congruent with the whole of his work, this view of meaning is tied to concrete everyday action. "Life can be made meaningful in a threefold way: first, through *what we give to life* (in terms of our creative works); second, by *what we take* from the world (in terms of our experiencing values); and third, through *the stand we take* toward a fate we no longer can change (an incurable disease, an inoperable cancer, or the like)" (Frankl 1967, 15). Frankl met life as it was, not as one might hope it to be. All components of the tripod are needed for a complete life. Granted, we will not experience each (giving, taking, and the stand against the inevitable) with equal intensity at any one moment. Throughout life each form of meaning is made present to us. At times, some of us have more opportunities for giving. On other occasions, we are fortunate to get. And at some junctures, life is primarily a stand against the inevitable.

Each of us experiences all three basic forms of meaning in various quantities and at different stages of life, but some people seem to have more opportunities in one area than the other two. If we permit jealousy to move us to envy another person's life of meaning, we will miss great opportunities for our own lives, as we lament what is not given and ignore the historically situated meaning before us. For instance, suppose a great teacher, who has an opportunity to find meaning through giving, spends an inordinate amount of time lamenting that he or she is not "recognized" as a great scholar (getting). If one chooses this stance, then the opportunity for meaning is missed and deep unhappiness is unleashed. There is nothing wrong with wanting to be something one is not or attempting to earn something one does not have—unless one ignores the things that could make life significant and becomes fixated upon lament. The cliche that the grass is always greener on the other side of the fence is more correct than many of us might want to admit. However, if one overlooks the grass in one's own yard and lives life in a fantasy, then meaningful opportunities right before us will go unseen.

Missing what is before us results from what Viktor Frankl called *"hyper-intention"* and *"hyper-reflection"* (1969, 33). We become so attached to a particular goal or success that we actually decrease our performance. Witness a baseball player who desires to hit a home run so badly that he or she can only think of the cry of the crowd after the achievement. However, if one is so focused before swinging upon the response of the crowd, it is unlikely that the needed attention on the baseball will be present. The result of not attending to the needed action at hand is simple—a missed opportunity.

Our task is to decide to focus upon that which is right before us—otherwise we miss much of the meaningfulness of human life, lamenting that life is not what we ordered! In the course of a life we discover meaning in giving, getting, and our stand against the inevitable. Our task is to look to the right carrier of meaning for this historical moment—for instance, finding meaning through giving when there is a chance to care. Such an attitude is essential, if we are to bypass a life of despair—looking for greener pasture on artificial turf. A person who is always looking for a "better" life as a youngster wants to be old, as a student wants to teach, as a parent wants to be free of responsibility, and as an aging, dying form desires to be young, to learn again, and to hear the voices of children. Such a life misses meaning—always looking for what is not, instead of finding meaning in the demands of the given historical situation.

Tragic Triad. Viktor Frankl additionally outlined what he called the "tragic triad" of pain, death, and guilt (1967, 15). These three items are central to a life of suffering and need to be met with the recognition that each can only be absent for a brief time in a life; a visit from one or more of the triad members is inevitable. Pain generates suffering. Death reminds us of our mortality. Guilt reminds us of our fallibility and calls us to responsibility. The pain of suffering will meet us, death will claim us, and mistakes will mark one's life. Such insight is common sense, but this wisdom is often avoided in a culture so busy pursuing comfort. Frankl not only did not ignore the tragic triad, he attempted to give us tools to learn from them and to find meaning in them.

Freedom. Freedom was central for Viktor Frankl. He emphasized the vitality of human agency and the ability of a person to choose an attitude or stance from which to understand the events of life. Freedom is not just what happens to us; our interpretive processes are central to our freedom. Freedom is not only physical; it is attitudinal. Frankl wanted the human to work to uncover freedom in finiteness. Life's answers are often no more than finding freedom within the unchangeable. As Frankl so often stated, death cannot be altered. Our freedom is in how we live and in how we die. Our final freedom is our stance against what we cannot change, alter, or wish away.

Problematic Assumptions

Viktor Frankl outlined problematic assumptions about life that counter a realistic sense of hope—we are too easily led astray by false optimism and comfort. Two terms in particular lead to a false sense of optimism: self-actualization and the pleasure principle. Both concepts are fundamental terms in popular discourse about the person.

Self-Actualization. For Viktor Frankl the notion of "self-actualization" (1969, 38) was like a boomerang. The more a person focuses primarily upon actualizing the self, the less likely such a result will occur. The problem with "hyperreflection" on the notion of self-actualization is the narrowing of one's focus of attention. Just as the baseball player who is in a slump is unable to follow the flow of the ball when it is pitched due to one's focus on his or her stance (not the release of the ball from the pitcher), a person can miss the events of life when unduly engaged in self-preoccupation.

One of the reasons Viktor Frankl was so positive about the use of humor is that it offers "self-detachment" (Frankl 1969, 17). Taking oneself too seriously loses a fundamental premise of life—we are necessary but not sufficient for meaning to emerge. Other people, events, and activities contribute to individual existential meaning as one interacts with life's activities. As one of the author's father-in-law stated: "A sense of humor is indeed a lubricating facet of life." A good sense of humor is a practical life skill.

Viktor Frankl also stressed the notion of service to others, a cause, or a project for a similar reason. Frankl spoke of "self-transcendence" (1969, 18), the ability to focus beyond oneself—which, ironically, permits the self to grow while encountering others and activities worthy of being done. Self-actualization is a byproduct of an active life well lived, not a goal unto itself.

Contrary to the Pleasure Principle. Sigmund Freud's assertion that the human being is propelled by a pleasure principle and tension reduction has been absorbed into contemporary taken-for-granted assumptions about human communication. Viktor Frankl witnessed human beings doing good for others in spite of their own lack of pleasure and he saw human beings engage in action simply to increase their tension. For Frankl, the human is more complex than common assumptions such as the pleasure principle suggest. Granted, some people are propelled mainly by pleasure and others seek primarily to reduce tension. However, there are people moved by acts of goodness that are not in their own best interest; additionally, each of us has been on a vacation in which we brought tension to the forefront, just to lessen the boredom.

Viktor Frankl recognized sacrifice and tension as necessary ingredients in discovering human meaning.

> Today, people are spared tension. First of all, this lack of tension is due to that loss of meaning which I describe as the existential vacuum, or the frustration of the will to meaning. . . . It is true that young people should not be subjected to excessive demands. [However,] . . . in an age of an affluent society, most people suffer too few demands rather than too many. The affluent society is an underdemanding society by which people are spared tension. (1969, 45)

The assumption that the good life is to be lived for "me" alone and that tension is to be avoided on all counts was rejected by Frankl as an illusion that invites problems for the individual and his or her communicative partner.

Choosing Meaning

Viktor Frankl contended that we can choose to look for meaning. We cannot always choose what will be meaningful in life, but we can choose to look for the meaning that is around us in daily living. The human does not invent meaning; we can, however, join the search and "discover" (Frankl 1969, 60) meaning that is particular to a given existential moment.

To choose meaning as fundamental to the good life requires us to look for it in life's basic actions—we discover meaning in suffering, love, and work (Frankl 1946/1973, 105–175). For Viktor Frankl, we each have a responsibility to look for meaning in the daily acts of life. When a person is unable to find meaning in daily events, he or she might be assisted with "dereflection" (1946/1973, 105–175) and "paradoxical intention" (1969, 99–113)—both techniques have a similar result. Dereflection moves one to another point of focus—it redirects one's attention to another area to find meaning, upon reflection, in the first event—similar to a doctor trying to check one's reflexes and asking a person to touch his or her nose to get the knee to move when bumped. "Paradoxical intention" requires someone to do something for so long he or she loses any interest in the task. When a person loses interest, meaning about another task may emerge. In both cases the goal is to move the person from a destructive obsessed focus to a point of openness to life in which meaning might reemerge.

Viktor Frankl's basic assumption is clear—humans have an ontological need for discovering meaning in both the common and extraordinary events and experiences. When we communicate we do not begin with the communicative event itself. We walk into a communicative event with a unique and undiscovered sense of meaning that guides what we consider important and significant. Not all conversation taps a sense of meaning—but when a topic, person, or environment awakens our latent desire to understand a meaning structure, the importance and value of the communicative event is dramatically increased.

> In spite of all the enforced physical and mental primitiveness of the life in a concentration camp, it was possible for spiritual life to deepen. Sensitive people who were used to a rich intellectual life may have suffered much pain (they were often of a delicate constitution), but the damage to their inner selves was less. They were able to retreat from their terrible surroundings to a life of inner riches and spiritual freedom. Only in this way can one explain the apparent paradox that some prisoners of a less hardy make-up often seemed to survive camp life better than did those of a robust nature. (Frankl 1959/1974, 56–57)

Meaning for Frankl is ontological and a basic practical implication for how life is lived—the quality of life is not enhanced or lessened by the data of life, but by what that data means to us.

All of us have met successful people who are deeply unhappy. Additionally, we have all met those who suffer one pain after another, only to offer a spirit of joy and service to others. Upon meeting people who serve with joy in spite of their own pain, we are left with a fundamental question—why? What is different in the lives of such people? Some who are in pain only exude sadness while others in pain can increase a sense of joyfulness in others. Why does a person with so much success walk with pain while the person with seemingly so little going right offers light and insight into the lives of people with whom he or she connects?

Viktor Frankl understood that more than the events of life, it is our attitude toward life that separates "despair" from "triumph." "Let us take the lessons from both San Quentin and Harvard. People sentenced for life or waiting for death in gas chambers may 'triumph,' whereas the successful people . . . fell in 'despair'. . . . Despair is well compatible with success—as compatible as fulfillment of meaning is compatible with dying and suffering" (Frankl 1969, 77). Meaning, for Frankl, holds together the data of a life. For instance, suppose a man or a woman does manual work that is perceived to have little societal dignity attached to it, and yet those around this person are amazed at the grace and good will this person brings to the job every day. The job alone is not what moves this person to quality action; the person may be moved by the conviction that his or her children need a role model of what it is to work with dignity, even in circumstances that are considerably inconvenient. If a job is demanding, one may change jobs or find a way to correct the problems in his or her life. But on some occasions, change or newness is not what is needed or what is possible. What is required is a reason, a *why* for doing what one is needed in a given moment.

> Carl J. Rote, resident chaplain in a state institution of 4,300 mentally retarded patients . . . [explained why he continued to do what many considered a very depressing form of ministry]: "The retardates have taught me more than I can ever tell. Theirs is a world where hypocrisy is banished; it is a kingdom where a smile is their passport to your affection and the light in their eyes will melt the coldest heart. Perhaps this is God's way of reminding us that the world must rediscover the attributes which the mentally retarded have never lost!" (Frankl 1969, 139–140)

Where most of us would see despair and hopeless work, this chaplain was able to see opportunities for ministry and a reminder about our own humanness. Such voices come from unexpected corners in life's journey. One's task is to have the courage to discover the unique meaning that experience holds for oneself in a given historical situation. Even though we live in what Frankl called an "existential vacuum" (1967, 126)—a time without a clear sense of meaning—meaning can and must be invited for a high-quality life to be possible.

Perhaps, in an information age that is changing the nature of work, place, and relational contact, Frankl, again, has a message that needs to be heard: meaning is needed to guide our lives in the transition of change and the inevitability of suffering and disappointment. What makes Frankl's message enduring is his call for meaning in spite of a changing narrative and his call for encouraging the good of the other in spite of his vivid awareness of evil. He not only embraced the historical formation of his time, which explicitly pointed to evil; he reminded us of the more quiet and courageous voices of the human spirit. Somehow, in such a demanding historical moment, Frankl provided a balanced view of the potential of the human spirit—a spirit capable of both great good and enormous tragedy.

Historicality and Dialogic Civility

Today's crisis of change calls forth Viktor Frankl's voice of clarity. Indeed, ours is a different historical moment than when his ideas were formed, but his insights are no less valuable. For Frankl, the notion of "meaning in life" permits us to make sense of change and disruption in taken-for-granted routines. He pointed to meaning as not only ontological—part of our being—but as an essential need for the human, at least in the crisis of dislocation from a sense of place and self. The question of meaning becomes paramount when pattern and routine are disrupted. The movement from the farm to industry and now to the information age has generated incredible change and is fertile soil for Frankl's focus on the "search for meaning" (1977/1978, 17).

In the reality of narrative change, we are in a postmodern historical era. However, human reserves are found not just by heroes of great tragedy, but by common people who with a quiet courage add grace and dignity to the world they touch.

Most often real courage is quietly determined. Such courage propels prayer behind closed doors. This quiet courage embraces not only one's own ability, but one's own limitations. This thoughtful sense of courage works to make a difference; yet when asked why only utters a sincere, BECAUSE. Somehow isn't that how life is to be lived? I deeply admired such courage in a neighbor, as I was growing up. Her husband died and there were still three children to feed. Up she went to work outside the home, for the first time in a lifetime. The job was not glamorous. She was a nurse's aid. Every tough job was given to her that no one else wanted to do. But somehow this lady was able to take care of three kids, teach Sunday school class, and work to get the neighborhood children to go to Sunday School with her. Nobody has given her a medal. She is the model of COURAGE upon which we build healthy families, businesses, communities, and nations. (Arnett 1995, 4–5)

The neighbor referred to above never read Viktor Frankl, but they were linked in spirit. The demands of both their lives were met with courage and those around them witnessed what human agency can do.

As Mahatma Gandhi was fond of saying—"the *means* of life are the *end* in the making" (Duncan 1972, 42). Frankl's contemporary voice calls for agency, will, and the courage to make a difference— no matter what the environment or the changes before us. His call is not just one of courage, but also one of pragmatic wisdom when met with "the awful," "the unchangeable," "the painful." What other choices do we have other than capitulation or an act of will? William Barrett (1978/1979) quoted William James: "my first act of freedom will be to believe in freedom [of will]" (291).

Viktor Frankl's insight is not only contemporary, but grounded in long-stated advice about the importance of service in the invitation of a quality life. "We had to teach the despairing me, that *it did not really matter what we expected from life, but rather what life expected from us.* . . . Life ultimately means taking the responsibility to find the right answers to its problems and to fulfill the tasks which it constantly sets for each individual" (Frankl 1959/1974, 122). Frankl calls us to see the importance of being charged with a task that reaches beyond the self.

Ordinary people often discover extraordinary courage as they go beyond their own sense of self to live in service of others. One need not reflect long to understand the number of deaths that occur after the winter holidays. Somehow the sick are often able to marshall their resources to see relatives for one last time and to make it to Christmas or Hanukkah—revealing the power of hope in the face of terminal illness (Scannell 1993, Douville 1994).

> To be charged with the task to fulfill the unique meaning assigned to each of us is neither to be avoided and feared . . . human existence is essentially self-transcendence. . . . It cannot consist in self-actualization; man's [or woman's] primary concern does not lie in actualization of his [or her] self, but in the realization of values and in the fulfillment of meaning potentialities which are found in the world rather than within himself [or herself]. (Frankl 1967, 68)

Each person needs to find meaning beyond oneself, not out of religious or moral impulse, but out of ontological necessity.

Central to Viktor Frankl's work is the idea of being pulled by a task or act of service that needs to be done. Frankl's reach beyond the self to task and service is more akin to a classical view of happiness, rather than our contemporary understanding of happiness, which is closer to Aristotle's view of pleasure. Happiness in the classical sense is action or labor worthy of being done. Happiness involves study, virtue, and, finally, action for its own sake and, of course, some external good fortune that we do not control (Aristotle 1985). Frankl's orientation is grounded in teleology, which pulls the person to an action appropriate for the existential moment and invites a sense of meaning. This meaning cannot be forced on another; it must be discovered as one finds projects that call to be completed or attempted.

Viktor Frankl highlighted the power and the courage of the human spirit. In the worst of human situations, the concentration camps, he witnessed great acts of courage, generosity, and boldness of spirit. Frankl showed the potential of humans—even under the most painful of circumstances. Frankl's voice may not speak to all people; but to those that have felt the pain of life's events and have fought to conquer the dual limitations of cynicism and naivete, he offers a voice worthy of listening to anew as we experience the challenges of a postmodern age.

Viktor Frankl's life and scholarship have contributed to dialogic civility. Instead of constant self-indulgent lament, Frankl calls for realistic engagement in the public arena, consisting of both joy and pain. As one meets the historical moment, even in crisis, our task is to do something, to make a difference, to offer civility and human hope as we meet life on its own terms in dialogue and with courage.

Section 3

Narrative Construction:
Interpersonal Dialogue and Story

Chapter Twelve

Nel Noddings

Re-Storying an Ethic of Care

On Stories—

Not only are voices set free to speak to others and among others in live classrooms and counseling centers; they resonate with the sense of seeking, struggling to name, striving to find language for what was repressed and suppressed over the years. Also, they are marvelously multiple. There is, as will be realized, a common theme: the ways in which stories—and myths, and diaries, and histories—give shape and expression to what would otherwise be untold about "our lives."

—Maxine Greene, *Stories Lives Tell*

Developing an Orientation Toward Caring—

How can we help children to develop a capacity for interpersonal reasoning? Many of us believe that it develops in the actual activities of care, and if it develops there, our worries about the moral status of its outcomes are considerably reduced. People develop a moral orientation of caring, we suggest, through direct contact with those who need to be cared for. In contrast to what [Simone] Weil believed, this is *not* a capacity that develops in isolated study. It requires sustained interpersonal contact.

—Nel Noddings, *Stories Lives Tell*

Nel Noddings begins her work with a basic assumption: any application of an ethical code has limitations. Noddings recognizes limitations in the use of ethical codes to guide social action. Alternatively, she suggests renewing the story-based life of community through relational ethics framed in our individual and collective dramas. Caring is central to the ethical story Noddings tells.

Caring is concerned first with human beings and their suffering. Problems and promises of science, religion, and law only become important as they address humans and their suffering. Developing a story based in caring requires a person to hold an attitude wherein the relationship is more essential than the individual. A healthy community requires characters who model caring, relational lives, hopefully encouraged by educational processes in the community. Three major action terms guide Noddings's insight into caring: story, individual, and community. A story informs both individuals and community; "I" and "we" are story-formed. Dialectically, "I" and "we" work to keep the story healthy. Noddings's offers a dialogic story-framed understanding of interpersonal caring.

This chapter explains Nel Noddings's ethic of caring as distinct from a traditional view of ethical codes. Concepts comprising her perspective are traced through her writings addressing women and evil, intuition, caring, and relational understanding. As a professional educator, Noddings situates her ethic of caring in educational settings, emphasizing caring relations between people in the praxis of learning. Responding to the demands of the historical moment, Noddings brings an action-filled story of caring relation into our era of educational individualism. Throughout her work she discusses ways educators can contribute to a renewed sense of moral action and dialogic civility between persons.

Introduction

Nel Noddings's writing is framed by her commitment to an "ethic of caring" (Noddings 1984, 79–103) and moral education. In *Caring*, Noddings wrote, "Human caring and the memory of caring and being cared for . . . form the foundation of ethical response" (1984, 1). Our lives are shaped by personal participation and involvement in the educational experience, which greatly influences our moral life. The process of lifelong learning creates one's personal stories, which are later used as vehicles for reasoning. Carol Witherell and Nel Noddings, in *Stories Lives Tell*, recognized that, "stories invite us to come to know the world and our place in it. Whether narratives of history or the imagination, stories call us to consider what we know, how we know, and what and whom we care about" (1991b, 13). Stories comprise the backdrop for dialogic civility.

Nel Noddings is distinctly aware of social problems that plague our society. Responding to the demands of the historical moment, Noddings brings both the action and metaphor of caring relation into an era of educational individualism. Initially, her work stemmed from a recognition of the limits of traditional approaches to the study of ethics. From this historical standpoint of awareness of metanarrative decline and perhaps collapse, we ask the following question about Noddings's work: "How might the story of relational caring address cynicism and metanarrative decline?"

Re-Storying Ethics

In everyday life, morality is often associated with how people live their lives, at home and work. Nel Noddings, in *Philosophy of Education*, explained that philosophers hold a broader range of meaning for morality, "referring to how we should conduct our lives and, especially, how we should interact with others" (1995, 136). Traditional approaches to ethics recommend a scientific application of codes to human dilemmas—establishing guiding principles and discerning values and behaviors that can be logically derived from them. From this perspective, ethical decisions are made on the basis of abstract reasoning which appears to be governed by logical necessity.

Nel Noddings carefully explained how a relational story-formed ethic is different from scientific ethical codes:

[Persons acting from a relational ethic] do not judge their own acts solely by their conformity to rule or principle, nor do they judge them only by the likely production of preassessed nonmoral goods such as happiness. A consideration of both principles and utilities may influence the thinking of such ethical agents, but neither can be decisive. What we must also consider is the relation, not only what happens physically to others involved in the relation but what they feel and how they respond to the acts under consideration. (1989, 184)

An ethic of caring recognizes the place of principles and in addition emphasizes ethical discussions made in caring, relational interactions with those affected by the discussion.

Daniel Taylor recognized scientific reasoning to be "the great competitor with *story* [italics ours] as a way of knowing" (1996, 28). Because science is recognized as the standard bearer for all forms of knowledge, many people feel we do not "really" know something until it has been "proven" scientifically. In scientific approaches to ethics, scientific analysis results in invariant formulas for application to human behavior. While Nel Noddings agrees analysis is necessary, she notes that an adequate analysis will not end in formulas. "On the contrary, [analysis] will reveal the hopelessness of formulaic approaches. Caring cannot be achieved by formula. It requires address and response; it requires different behaviors from situation to situation and person to person" (Noddings 1992, xi).

Codes are guidelines or principles that specify preferred action and are useful shortcuts to reliable conclusions. Codes that specify a set penalty for a legal infraction inhibit social anarchy. Unfortunately, the narrative base that inspires a code is often forgotten. People forget that the code was generated as a useful conclusion and implementation tool within a given historical context. As Daniel Taylor reminds us, "rationality itself is a culturally shaped approach to life that is dependent on a long history of stories" (1996, 167). Stories help us understand our personal and collective experiences. Each story or narrative is composed of characters, choices, actions, and meaning. An ethic of caring is connected to a narrative and rooted in dialogue between persons in relationship.

In American society, characterized by an individualistic focus that can result in self-promotion and self-protection to the extreme, two common responses to codes have emerged. First, a person may cling to the code as a form of refuge, fully accepting and rigidly adhering to guidelines due to a distrust of others. From this perspective, if one cannot trust other people, at least one can rely on the unchanging code. The converse is also true. Second, because of a distrust of others, some people believe certain codes do not apply to them. From a distrusting person's perspective, he or she did not make the rules nor should he or she have to follow them. In both cases, an abstract principle enables distrusting people to disengage from communication and accountability with others. Even more importantly, distrust is perpetuated; tenets of the code seem disconnected from their lives because the underlying narrative is missing.

Stanley Hauerwas and David Burrell (1977) explained that what makes the abstract code significant is the original narrative context in which it was formed. The code is historically dependent on the narrative that gave rise to it. Moral principles do not offer the actual "ground for conduct" (Hauerwas and Burrell 1977, 26)— the original narrative which inspired the moral principle is the ground for the why of conduct; the code itself is only how or implementation. The usefulness of the code depends on stories out of which the abstraction emerges. Once the moral principle is removed from the code or story that carries it, the power of the story to inspire us to apply it to our own lives is lessened (Taylor 1996).

Missing Stories

In discussions, we hear people apply codes to best suit their needs, depending upon their interpretation of the situation. For example, most people agree "stealing" is wrong. Yet, "borrowing" office supplies from work to take home for personal use may not be interpreted by some people as "stealing." One person interprets the situation in a given fashion and applies one set of principles. Another person interprets the situation differently and applies a different set of principles. In contemporary society, in which an attitude of relativism is rampant, each person's interpretation is recognized as equally valid. People shrug their shoulders with ambivalence and accept the other person's interpretation rather than engage in discussion. Fear of offending the other person and potentially suffering some consequence "worse" than the initial offense guides interactions: "Better safe than sorry." Such acts of relativism remove us from a call to responsible dialogue with each other. Dialogue does not presuppose certainty, but neither does it permit each one of us to make our own rules. The meaning of rules or guidelines must be co-constituted to be given life.

If all interpretations of how codes should be applied are equally valid, then our choices are unimportant.

[However,] the choices we make *are* important. All stories and all choices are not equal. One of the enemies of story and of a healthy society is an uncritical relativism that says that truth and goodness are entirely subjective opinions, that everyone's stories (and values) are radically different and incommensurable, and that affirming some stories and rejecting others is by definition intolerant. Such knee-jerk relativism pervades our society and is often the unacknowledged basis for the fatalistic shrug of passivity, paralysis, and cynicism. . . . But unless we are prepared to argue that injustice is as desirable as justice, racism and sexism as acceptable as equality, and hatred and greed as honorable as love, then we must insist on the need for wise choices and on the existence of something like truth. (Taylor 1996, 2–3)

Stories, based in historical experience, give us the confidence to make wise choices. Living and understanding one's stories is a form of praxis; stories are a form of social theory which inform action.

Caring as Story

Nel Noddings responded to the suggestion that an ethic of caring may itself be an ethic of principle, potentially interpreted as a traditional approach to ethics:

As a descriptive principle, one that describes how carers look to observers outside the caring relation, we hope it will be generally accurate. But it need not be the guiding force behind the carer's response, nor can we derive other principles and rules from it. Carers must rub elbows with the recipients of their care. Guiding questions arise, but even these change with the situation, and there are no recipes for caring. Cultural and personal differences will result in different manifestations of care. (1995, 188)

A code offers principles historically disconnected from the narrative of origin. An ethic of caring is not a principle, it is a story! Stories are guided by some moral principle and then applied with situational care, not a priori technique. During times of difficulty, "instead of turning to a principle for guidance, a carer turns to the cared-for" (Noddings 1995, 187). The carer considers what the cared-for needs and offers appropriate information and support, often through a story. A mentor listens carefully to what the person being mentored is saying—and what he or she is not saying. Often, a mentor shares a story recounting similar circumstances, which offers guidance to the person being mentored. A mentor can be an educator in an "ethic of caring" (Noddings 1984, 79–103) who frames education as both content and relationship development—a moral task.

Moral Education

Nel Noddings is acutely aware of social problems in contemporary society. When relationships are neglected, separation results. Separation, which is fundamental in creating enemies, may present itself in forms such as rival gangs or workplace competition. The neglect of relation lies at the root of the cultural evil of routine or unreflective cynicism. Daniel Taylor commented,

> We have made disunity into a virtue. Not only do we have much less consensus about the fundamental nature of things than has been traditional in human societies; we have lost much of our belief even in the desirability of consensus. [Consensus] is often associated with stifling conformity, authoritarianism, denial of diversity, or compromise of principle. To be in broad agreement with others is to sacrifice one's sacred individuality at the altar of the herd. (1996, 140)

Nel Noddings (1989) traced the origins of relational neglect to several areas, including faulty or incomplete analysis of virtues, the dominance of individualism, rigid religious systems, and the fear of being like a woman. She maintains that these four factors have contributed to creating social structures that perpetuate our neglect of relation "A relational ethic prescribes attention to the relational situations in which we find ourselves, and it makes significant use of imagined relations and situations in testing its decisions" (Noddings 1989, 204).

Teachers have a responsibility to create relations in which they care for others and also assist students in developing the capacity to care. As stated earlier, Martin Heidegger (1962) recognized that care is inevitably ontological; all human beings care. However, not everyone may develop the capacity to care for others. Caring is a complex activity requiring practice and patience. The educational setting provides an important opportunity for modeling an ethic of caring in human relationship and telling the story of caring.

Nel Noddings (1984) identified four components of moral education centered around an ethic of caring: modeling, dialogue, practice, and confirmation. The first component of moral education is "modeling" (Noddings 1984, 179). Modeling is vital in any approach to education that advocates an ethic of caring. Modeling does not mean simply applying principles to problems. Instead, teachers have to model caring in their relations with cared-fors. Student development of a capacity to care may depend on the student's experience in being cared for (Noddings 1992).

Stories and narratives are important tools for educators in modeling caring. "The use of narrative and dialogue can serve as a model for teaching and learning across the boundaries of disciplines, professions, and cultures" (Witherell and Noddings 1991b, 2). Stories represent experiences with practical ethics. They reveal dilemmas of human caring and conflict, reliving situations in the continuous attempt to make sense of the meaning of life in interaction with others.

The second component of moral education is "dialogue" (Noddings 1984, 182–187). Nel Noddings (1992) draws from Paulo Freire's (1970/1974) understanding of dialogue in her ethic of caring. Dialogue provides us with knowledge of the other, which forms a foundation for caring. Genuine dialogue is open-ended, in which neither party knows at the outset what the outcome will be. Dialogue offers students a chance to question "why," helps both parties arrive at well-informed decisions, connects us to each other, and helps to maintain caring relations. While dialogue is generally comprised of words, dialogic interaction is also exhibited through nonverbal communication, such as a touch, smile, supportive sound, or respectful silence.

Genuine dialogue offers an important foundation for learning. If an educator believes a student has engaged in a wrongful act, one does not enter into dialogue with the student to determine whether or not the act is wrong. Such dialogue would not be genuine. Educators can, however, engage in dialogue with the student about the possible reasons for opposing positions regarding the act, the likely consequences of such acts to oneself and others, and the personal history of one's position through stories. Dialogue requires time and caring for trust to develop. Dialogue enables us to better relate to oneself, better relate to others, and better relate to one's cultural communities through the "negotiation of meanings" (Witherell and Noddings 1991b, 7).

The third component of moral education is "practice" (Noddings

1984, 187–193). An attitude of caring is shaped, at least in part, by experience. "When we live in caring relations, we teach each other gently by example and by confirmation—not by accusation, confession, forgiveness, and penance" (Noddings 1992, 95). We must practice acts of caring to instill this orientation in others.

The fourth component of moral education, from an ethic of caring, is "confirmation" (Noddings 1984, 193–197). Confirmation involves affirming and encouraging the best in others. In *Nichomachean Ethics* (1985), Aristotle identified friendship as central in a moral life. The main criterion of friendship is that one friend wishes another friend well for his or her own sake. When we are friends with others, we want good things for them because they are our friends, not because that thing will in some way enhance oneself. As educators, we want students to learn so they will have insight to make informed decisions about their behaviors. Teachers' actions should be driven by the well-being of students rather than some other motivation.

The four aspects of moral education are all highly interactive and illustrate how interpersonal reasoning is framed by a story and action of caring. Teachers model and elicit interpersonal reasoning by "asking questions, following leads, and conjecturing rather than presenting faultless products" (Noddings 1990, 17). Such teaching requires a command of content knowledge as well as pedagogical skill: teachers must guide a learning environment that truly leads to reasoning, rather than relativistic solutions.

The role of the teacher is to influence. A teacher cannot engage in genuine dialogue with students in the project of learning if he or she selects aspects of the world ingenuine to him or her. The teacher selects aspects of the world to present while stretching the student's abilities and encouraging an ethic of caring in students. The teacher realizes that the student (as ethical agent) will select from the presented possibilities. The teacher must be prepared to put energy in the service of these projects. However, one's task as one-caring must have the highest priority. Most importantly, one-caring must nurture the other's "ethical ideal" (Noddings 1984, 120–124) through dialogue and inviting the other into an ongoing story of caring.

Central Concepts in Nel Noddings's Work

Nel Noddings has written extensively on subjects of women and evil, intuition, caring, and interpersonal reasoning. She addresses the problem of evil by offering a relational ethic of caring. She suggests how an educational environment tells a relational story by discussing intuition and interpersonal reasoning.

Reducing Evil

Society has long associated evil with women, who were considered inherently inferior in morality to men. Traditional patriarchal thought linked women with that which harms or threatens mankind. Nel Noddings sought to explain why women's voices had been mute in moral debate. She laid the groundwork for a critique of evil from the perspective of women.

In *Women and Evil* (1989), Nel Noddings discussed three forms of evil: "natural evil" (5–8), "cultural evil" (104–105), and "moral evil" (99–100). Natural evil refers to painful and harmful events that occur naturally, such as disease, earthquakes, storms, and death. Cultural evils are recognized within the culture in which they appear. Cultural evil includes all the harmful social practices that may be accepted or rejected in different times and places, such as poverty, racism, war, and sexism. Moral evil is the harm we do intentionally or negligently to another person to cause physical or psychic pain. Moral evil occurs when someone causes pain to another person, or when someone fails to relieve another's pain.

Nel Noddings (1989) identified pain, separation, and helplessness as the primary states of consciousness associated with evil. The most basic of these is pain. Separation and helplessness are also regarded as evil because psychic pain accompanies them. Moral evil exists in inducing, sustaining, or failing to relieve these conditions. Evil is real, and we need to understand and accept that the tendency toward evil is present in all of us. Daniel Taylor, in *The Healing Power of Stories*, noted:

> [Stories reinforce] the important truth that moral and immoral are valid categories and not just arbitrary names for personal opinions. . . . Good and evil genuinely exist and are knowable, and . . . the ability to distinguish between them is crucial to survival and to living well. The story affirms not only that good and evil are real but that they are tied to human conduct. *We* can act in ways that are good and in ways that are evil. And it matters which we do. (1996, 31–32)

An attitude and story of caring seeks to relieve human suffering inspired by the three forms of evil: natural, cultural, and moral.

Contemporary education has traditionally been guided by notions of optimism and progress. These views reflect "masculine" orientations designed to "overcome" evil. Nel Noddings, in *Women and Evil*, noted, "A primary purpose of education should be to reduce pain, separation, and helplessness by encouraging people to explore the nature of evil and commit themselves to continue the search for understanding" (1989, 229–230). She suggested approaching education from a perspective that advocates living sensitively with as little evil as possible. We reduce pain, separation, and helplessness by guiding others, assuming the role of teacher and learner. Such a vision points to Noddings's nonrelativistic and value-laden view of relational, caring education.

An Ethic of Caring

An ethic of caring is a story situated to counter evil—to provide an alternative set of options. Nel Noddings located the origin of ethical behavior in human affective response. She affirmed the work of Martin Heidegger (1962), who identified caring as "the very Being of human life" (Noddings 1992, 15). For Heidegger, caring includes "an attitude of solicitousness toward other living beings, a concern to do things meticulously, the deepest existential longings, fleeting moments of concern, and all the burdens and woes that belong to human life" (Noddings 1992, 15). These characteristics reflect Noddings's attitude of caring, central to her relational ethic.

Caring in Relation. Caring can not be articulated as a specific set of behaviors; caring is a way of being in relation with others. Nel Noddings (1984) explained to "care" (9–16) and to be "cared for" (19–21) involves two parties in relation. For a "one-caring" (30–58) and a "cared-for" (59–78) to be in relation, both persons must contribute to the relation. Something from the one-caring must be completed in the cared-for, while the cared-for looks for something that indicates that the one-caring holds regard for him or her. When one person cares for another, both persons are connected emotionally and empathically. The act of inspiring a friend with encouragement and support is only possible in mutual caring relation. Encouragement is motivated by affection and good will, and may only be received by a person who feels positively connected to the person who cares.

An ethic of caring involves reciprocity between persons in relation. When a person cares, he or she must consider the other's perspective, needs, and expectations. The essential elements of caring are a "commitment to act in behalf of the cared-for, a continued interest in his [or her] reality throughout the appropriate time span, and the continual renewal of commitment over this span of time" (Noddings 1984, 16). When one friend cares for another, she has his best interests at heart, remains involved in the story as appropriate, and continues her commitment to the friendship.

In caring, the one-caring views the situation from the perspective of both self and other. Nel Noddings refers extensively to the work of Martin Buber (1947/1965a), who calls this relational process "inclusion" (83–103). The one-caring views the situation from one's own perspective as well as the perspective of the cared-for. One-caring engages in "confirmation" of the cared-for (Buber 1947/1965a, 83–103). The one-caring recognizes the cared-for's potential self, and works with him or her to realize that possibility. One-caring receives the cared-for in relation, similar to the association between *I and Thou* (Buber 1958).

The one-caring must focus attention on, become mentally engrossed with, the cared-for to be in a relation of care. "The danger is that caring, which is essentially nonrational in that it requires a constitutive engrossment and displacement of motivation, may gradually or abruptly be transformed into abstract problem solving" (Noddings 1984, 25). Receiving the other means being with the other—not thinking of the other as an object. Each person is historically situated in a life story. The one-caring must be aware of the unique elements of the cared-for's situation; to ignore this uniqueness is to confuse caring with narcissism—which emphasizes one's own historical formation. The one-caring attempts to apprehend the reality of the other. When one cares, interest and attention are redirected from one's own reality to the reality of the other. The one-caring must view the reality of the cared-for as a possibility that could occur in one's own life. Caring occurs in relation with others. The one-caring cannot manufacture a single response and dole it out to cared-fors, assuming, as some clothing manufacturers do, that "one size fits all." To do so would violate the distinction between particular relational and traditional approaches to ethics and deny the other the act of caring. Nel Noddings rejects the "universalizability" (1984, 149) of caring. Universal caring would lead to replacing genuine caring with abstract problem solving. If a person does not focus on the cared-for, caring is absent because attention is instead focused on an abstract problem, not a human being.

There is, by nature of the relation, an inequality between the one-caring and the cared-for. This difference in status is situated in the cared-for's historical moment. The person who is "cared-for" (Noddings 1984, 19–21) needs assistance which the one-caring can offer. Caring is only complete when the act is fulfilled in both persons. While the one-caring may actually care, if the cared-for does not believe she or he holds regard for the other, the caring process remains incomplete—caring has only been partially actualized. For caring to be complete, the cared-for must recognize the one-caring's actions as genuine.

When the cared-for does not feel caring from his or her partner, he or she may respond nevertheless in an act of "ethical heroism" (Noddings 1984, 76), contribute to the caring relation. The one who is cared-for depends upon the one-caring. If the cared-for demands too much or ungraciously accepts care, the one-caring may become resentful and withdraw care.

Natural caring requires relation that emerges when we care out of love or spontaneous inclination. Ethical caring arises out of natural caring. Ethical caring does not depend upon following codes or principles, but upon the development of an ethical self framed by a story "in congruence with one's best remembrance of caring and being cared-for" (Noddings 1984, 49). The ethical self "is an active relation between my actual self and a vision of my ideal self as one-caring and cared-for" (Noddings 1984, 49). The one-caring recognizes a fundamental relatedness between self and other out of which a clearer self image emerges—an ethical self that can emerge only from caring for others.

Risks of Caring. Conflict and guilt are inescapable risks of caring. One-caring is directed both toward the other and self. Sometimes we want to care, but we do not. Perhaps we feel as though we should act in caring ways, but decline to do so. Nel Noddings (1984) cites the work of Paul Tillich, who "describes the anxiety of guilt as ontological. It transcends the subjective and objective. It is a constant threat in caring" (38). Viewing guilt as ontological implies that humans are story-laden people. Guilt cannot function without stories to serve as a guide. As such, guilt becomes a communicative reminder of the relationship between persons and narrative. Martin Buber would suggest that authentic or "existential guilt" (1965b/1966a, 121–148) is a healthy call to connection and a moral story. Buber recognized that "guilt is an essential factor in the person's relations to others: it performs the necessary function of leading him [or her] to desire to set those relations to rights" (Friedman 1965, 48). Buber wanted us to eliminate groundless "neurotic guilt" (Friedman 1965, 47–50). Noddings notes that if what induces guilt can be overcome by action, then one should act to reduce guilt. The one-caring must risk having the courage to offer care where appropriate, and to continue to care in spite of the inevitability of conflict and guilt.

An ethic of caring also implies a limit on one's obligation. Nel Noddings (1984) noted two criteria that govern our obligation to care: "the existence of or potential for present relation, and the dynamic potential for growth in relation" (86). We have an obligation to care if a relationship or the possibility of a relationship exists, and if there is growth potential in the relationship. The one-caring selects from among the endless demands of caring by referring to standards of behavior and custom within one's community. If the one-caring follows the general rules of one's community (assuming these rules are not seen as offensive), one is not likely to hurt others. However, if one behaves consistently and automatically by rules, one cannot be said to care. Caring is only possible by applying rules in dialogue with the person we care for in his or her own historical situation.

People must seek to nurture the "ethical ideal" (Noddings 1984, 120–124) in others. The ethical ideal strives to maintain and enhance caring. Nel Noddings's ethic of caring emerges from one's conception of one's ethical self as one-caring. Relatedness and commitment in spite of risk is central to the process of caring. Relational narratives contribute to our understanding of the self in relation to others. Carol Witherell and Nel Noddings assert that understanding the self-in-relation is "at the heart of education, healing, and social change" (1991a, 79). Cultural and personal stories reveal the nature of self-in-relation and uncover possibilities for ethical action.

Intuition and Interpersonal Reasoning

Nel Noddings suggests that the educational environment offers a context in which a relational story of caring may be told. "Intuition"

(Noddings and Shore 1984, 43–67) and "interpersonal reasoning" (Noddings 1991, 157–169) are both part of the learning process. Together they enable story-based critical thinking to occur, which is necessary for dialogue.

Intuitive Capacities. In *Awakening the Inner Eye: Intuition in Education* (1984), Nel Noddings and Paul J. Shore explore the role of intuition in learning, creating, expressing, and problem solving. Intuition is a way of knowing which expands our personal abilities; a story-framed education contributes to enhancing intuitive capacities.

Nel Noddings and Paul J. Shore (1984) discussed two important features of intuition: the "experience-enabling function" (49–50) and the "object-giving function" (49–50). The experience-enabling function of intuition makes experience, from which knowledge is constructed, possible. The experience-enabling function allows us to anticipate, organize, choose, and evaluate experiences. Without this function, we would not be able to experience the joys of nature, the excitement of completing a project, or the anticipation of communicating with a friend. The object-giving function refers to the role of intuition in people's ability to select objects, locate them in space and time, and separate them from other objects; it addresses the interaction of mind and object. For example, when listening to a friend, we separate his or her voice from outside noise and other sounds in the room. We also recognize words and interpret our friend's meaning and the intent of his or her expression; this recognition is a form of intuitive problem solving.

When a person seeks to resolve a problem, he or she does not need complete information or complete understanding; however, he or she must have the commitment to persevere until understanding occurs. Moral intuition provides the impulse to act toward another as the cared-for (Noddings 1984, 59–78). This form of intuition is directed by "the Will" (1984, 58–60), that aspect of self focused on survival and well-being. The Will reveals itself through our body as "force" (1984, 59), which may be directed toward understanding, feeling, expression, and creation. The Will supports and enables intuitive activity to exist as one moves about in the world. The Will is the impetus for intuition and reason. Our Will must be primarily concerned with human relationships. Relationships with others (subject-to-subject relation) must be more significant than contact with objects (subject-to-object contact).

Complementary to Reason. Intuition acts in complementary fashion with reason. While it is impossible to totally separate intuition from reason, we can identify episodes that are primarily intuitive and contrast these with episodes that are primarily analytic. Episodes that are primarily analytic are characterized by step-by-step procedures. In an analytic act, various stages comprise the task. If we are interrupted while engaging in an analytic act, we simply continue our task at the point we stopped. However, if we are interrupted in an intuitive task, we are unable to immediately identify where we were when we were interrupted, or even why we were at that point in the task. In an analytical mode, success is realized as an answer or result. In an intuitive mode, success is realized in achieving understanding in a given context.

Both intuition and reason are vital to the creation of a story. Viktor Frankl, in *The Doctor and the Soul* (1946/1973), recognized that our greatest desire is for life to have meaning. The desire for meaning is the beginning point for sharing stories. Sharing stories is a way to identify connections and relationships between things in past, present, and future experiences. Stories involve all the intuitive modes.

Intuitive modes are characterized by four features: "involvement of the senses, commitment and receptivity, a quest for understanding of empathy, and a productive tension between subjective certainty and objective uncertainty" (Noddings and Shore 1984, 69). First, intuitive activity involves "the senses" (Noddings and Shore 1984, 69–74) through immediate contact with the objects of our knowledge or feelings. In contacting an object intuitively, we constantly return to the object with all our senses—sight, hearing, touch, taste, and smell. When persons operate in an intuitive mode, they use recognized concepts or meaning structures to define the object. However, they return again and again to the object to define and redefine its meaning. Contact with the object directs and redirects intuitive thoughts, whereas an analytic thinker is directed by concepts previously attached to the object. For example, in the process of learning about a topic we engage ourselves by reading, listening, writing, and asking questions. We focus on all the nuances of the object of attention during the process of learning rather than preconceptions of the event or objects superfluous to the endeavor.

Second, intuitive activity requires "receptivity and commitment" (Noddings and Shore 1984, 74–80). As a person contacts an object intuitively, he or she is open to information provided by the senses, without judging or deciding about his or her relation to the object. The person is committed to receiving insight about the object. In learning, the learner must be committed to achieving understanding and be willing to exert the energy necessary to receive the insight he or she desires.

Third, intuitive activity is directed toward "understanding" (Noddings and Shore 1984, 80–87), empathy, or insight. In learning, when we understand something, we integrate that knowledge into our lives. An analytic approach divides the educational experience into various stages—going to class, taking notes (point one, point two, etc.), and leaving. The advent of online education has made educational experience available across geographic boundaries. While this technological approach to education is lauded as progressive, it offers an analytic approach to education. A person will need to learn to integrate information into his or her life when one focuses on stages of an experience—perhaps through more use of storytelling in the online environment. In an intuitive activity, once a person holistically understands information, he or she is able to apply that knowledge in everyday life. An intuitive approach to education yields increased understanding and praxis application of information in one's community.

Fourth, productive tension between "subjective certainty and objective uncertainty" (Noddings and Shore 1984, 87–89) occurs during intuitive activity. During intuitive activity, a person makes a decision to act (subjective certainty) while also experiencing uneasiness about the means for communicating subjective certainty (objective uncertainty). In returning to our educational example, intuitive activity is present when a person knows he or she wants to ask a question (subjective certainty)—yet the productive tension of how to word the question (objective uncertainty) is also present. Subjective certainty and objective uncertainty work together to result in greater understanding about the object of intuition. Intuition allows us to understand. When understanding is present, we can see how experiences interrelate in our lives.

Meaning and Story. Intuition is also affected by a person's search for meaning and understanding. If we recognize how events are connected in life, we are more likely to take intuition seriously. When things are connected they matter: "If nothing is connected, then nothing matters" (Taylor 1996, 2). Stories allow us to account for our experience, to understanding the meaning of events and how experiences are connected together. Nel Noddings and Paul J.

Shore (1984) believe intuition reveals meaning by interplay of the object and our ability to initiate meaning. Meaning is partially dependent upon the thing to which meaning will be attached. If the object is something with which we are familiar, our goal is to understand the object and its potential, along with its relation to other objects. Stories act as glue to organize events and meaning.

Story and dialogue lend power to educational experiences "because of their capacity to expand our horizons of understanding and provide rich contextual information about human actors, intentions, and experiences" (Witherell 1991, 84). Stories provide explanation that enables us to achieve understanding. Stories situate abstract concepts in a reality which is comprehendible.

Each person's life story is distinct from the life stories of others. And although we are separate, we are connected in caring, story-framed relationships with others. One of the authors recently attended several academic honors and commencement ceremonies, at which persons were recognized for their individual accomplishments. At each of the ceremonies, the speaker called students to recognize their connection with others who had made their educational experience possible. Each of the speakers sought to redirect the emphasis from an individual's story of success to the connection of caring relations that guided the formation of his or her story. Moral stories involve much more than "me" or "I." Meaning is story-shaped.

There is significant concern in education today about the development of critical thinking and logical reasoning skills. Many American students do not understand what they read, and can only apply their knowledge to the simplest kinds of problems. Nel Noddings asserted that the area of "interpersonal reasoning" (1991, 157–169) presents even greater challenges.

Norma Haan described interpersonal reasoning as "moral dialogue between agents who strive to achieve balanced agreement, based on compromise they reach or on their joint discovery of interests they hold in common" (1978, 303). In contrast to analytic reasoning, which proceeds step by step according to logical principles, interpersonal reasoning is open, flexible, and responsive. Interpersonal reasoning is guided by an attitude that values the relationship of interactants over any particular outcome, and is characterized by connection rather than separation and abstraction. Noddings provides a check on interpersonal reasoning with her focus on story. A story of caring informs the good life that guides a particular interaction—providing a background that informs caring action. Ethics rests within a story informed relationship. In this fashion, Noddings walks through the extremes of both universalism and relativism: stories provide a flexible third alternative framework.

Nel Noddings, in "Stories in Dialogue: Caring and Interpersonal Reasoning" (1991), identified the features of interpersonal reasoning, which include an attitude or solicitude of care, attention, flexibility, effort aimed at cultivating the relation, and a search for an appropriate response.

> A major aim of interpersonal reasoning is to identify a range of possible responses and to find a satisfactory mode of delivery for the response. In one sense, of course, the whole dialogue can be characterized as "address and response," but, in another sense, at least one party is often wrestling with the problem of how to respond. There is usually a range of responses that will be acceptable to the one who needs help. (Noddings 1991, 162)

An individual cultivates relation with both oneself and others in the process of interpersonal reasoning.

In *The Challenge to Care in Schools* (1992), Nel Noddings noted that interpersonal reasoning involves communicating, shared decision making, the ability to compromise, and the capacity to support each other in solving everyday problems. Currently, the educational system minimally addresses interpersonal reasoning. Yet Noddings is dedicated to the position that students need to learn

> how to sympathize and empathize with other people and to understand their own inclinations toward cruelty and violence. In addition to learning to communicate appreciatively with people of good will and effectively with people who may be untrustworthy, I want our children to examine the effects of their own lives on others. (1992, 55)

Noddings approaches interpersonal reasoning from a story of caring.

Educators can help students develop a capacity for interpersonal reasoning as teachers engage in activities of caring with students. Interpersonal reasoning is the decision-making function of the story of caring. For Nel Noddings, the crisis of caring is directly related to the neglect of interpersonal reasoning. People develop a moral orientation of caring through direct contact with those who need to be cared for and by hearing stories about the importance of caring. However, interpersonal reasoning may not always lead to ethical results. Two people may potentially make a decision that is morally bankrupt when the interests of others are considered. In addition, it is possible for two people who do not care for each other to cooperate to produce an evil result. Interpersonal reasoning is a necessary but not sufficient condition for ethical decision making.

In the process of interpersonal reasoning, we develop constructs or meaning structures that assist in understanding the situation of the cared-for. Noddings explained that if we are to understand others' behavior, we have to examine their "perceptions, purposes, premises, ways of working things out" (1990, 14–15), along with the context as it affects interaction. We learn about others as we encounter their "communities of memory" (Bellah, Madsen Sullivan, Swidler, and Tipton 1985, 152–155) stored in story. Memory makes caring possible when it frames a story about the ontological necessity of human caring.

Memory holds information which makes such reasoning possible. Stories are a way of knowing *and* a way of remembering. Daniel Taylor reminds us that:

> [W]ithout memory, knowledge is useless. . . . Memory reminds us where any particular nugget of knowledge comes from, how it was discovered, how it has been used, where it has worked and where it hasn't. And the best medium for such memories is story. Stories preserve memories best because they give them a shape that attracts the mind. (1996, 37)

We rely on background memories of our personal and collective past to assist us in the present; they offer guidance for foreground action.

One creates his or her life meaning by understanding, communicating, and living a story. Through sharing stories we "can penetrate cultural barriers, discover the power of the self and the integrity of the other, and deepen [our] understanding of [our] respective histories and possibilities" (Witherell and Noddings 1991b, 4). Diversity in community can be bridged through understanding the stories that shape the lives of others. As we share stories, they help shape our future experience. A person interprets one's life differently when he or she is exposed to different stories. Interpersonal reasoning seeks to identify the range of possible responses, select stories from among the appropriate responses, and respond to the other—further contributing to an ongoing story.

Historicality and Dialogic Civility

Nel Noddings's work examines how an attitude of caring can be employed within the educational environment. She grounds much of her discussion in Martin Buber's (1958) work.

I-Thou relation, which exemplifies interpersonal reasoning guided by intuitive experience, is inseparable from notions of caring and love. Respecting the other as Thou assists the process of teaching and learning. In genuine dialogue, teachers can present an effective world directed toward stretching students' experiences while also caring for students' development of a personal ethical ideal. Caring for the student in connection and understanding his or her perspective in dialogue opens opportunities for the student to learn to care for others.

There is no single method for establishing relations of trust and caring. There is no single standard to be applied across situations, instead, we assist others to better themselves—and in turn better ourselves. One who cares must attend to the other, feeling his or her energy extending toward the other's needs and projects. One's ability to care for and be cared for requires attention and time to develop. Caring is learned in relation with others through dialogue. The uncertainty of genuine dialogue can lead to new and fresh ways of exploring situations through interpersonal reasoning.

Nel Noddings's contribution to dialogic civility is an ethic of caring, situated in the context of education. Intuition and interpersonal reasoning are an important outgrowth of her ethic of caring. She invites us to renew the story of relational ethics by revisiting the issue of caring amid our hurried lives. We need only consider what life would be like without caring, to shore up our energy with renewed vigor and reach out to others. Noddings's view of caring is story based, not psychologically grounded. Noddings functions as a storyteller of caring and asks us to join, not as implementors, but as co-creators in an ongoing story that continues to both ground and change the nature of an interpersonal good life through dialogic civility. Noddings outlines a dialogic story-filled view of interpersonal interaction. She offers a background narrative of caring that guides, shapes, and focuses dialogic civility with self and other in interpersonal relation.

*C*hapter *T*hirteen

Robert Bellah

Re-Storying Broken Covenants

Community of Memory —

The decisions we are making and will make about the future of
our institutions will reshape us as moral beings. And as we
respond to challenge and change, our economic and governmental
institutions, like our families, schools, universities, churches, and
synagogues, will be crucially important — as the bearers of our collective memories and our cultural traditions, and as the expression of important, but often barely conscious, patterns of meaning
and self-definition. Perhaps no maxim can better provide guidance
than the Socratic admonition to "know thyself." To reflect on our
institutions will serve as a primary means toward growing self-
knowledge.

—Robert Bellah et al., *The Good Society*

Limits of Change —

Some critics of American society welcome this erosion of all normative order in the society and see it as a prelude to "revolution." I do not. Cynicism and moral anarchism, whether
expressed in crimes against persons and property by the dispos-
sessed or in self-interested manipulation by the better-off, are, if
I read modern history right, more likely a prelude to authoritarianism if not fascism. Those who would criticize all the accepted
conventions of our society — all the inherited obligations to family, friends, work and country — as "bourgeois" may be sowing bit-
ter seeds. A period of great social change always produces a cer-

tain amount of antinomianism and anarchism. But by that very token a time of great change is a time of great danger. Change can be, as anyone who reads the 20th century can see, for the worse as well as for the better.

—Bellah, *The Broken Covenant*

I ndividual freedom is the heart of the American Dream. However, when individual freedom moves to excessive individualism, a series of personal and societal problematics emerge, as outlined in *Habits of the Heart* (Bellah, Madsen, Sullivan, Swidler, and Tipton 1985). According to Robert Bellah, Richard Madsen, William M. Sullivan, Ann Swidler, and Steven M. Tipton, there are two competing parts of the American Dream: the pursuit of individual freedom and the search for community. Excessive individualism is the result of ignoring community, and a totalitarian sense of community misses the dialectic counterweight of the individual person. Bellah et al. (1985, 1991) and Maurice Friedman (1982b, 1983, 1984, 1985) recognize that our language in daily communication fosters and supports individualism while the notion of community has become a secondary consideration. "Therapeutic language" (Arnett 1997d, 149–160) centered on self-actualization perpetuates an emphasis on the individual over the community—leaving us to actualize only one half of the American Dream, the pursuit of individual freedom.

This chapter examines "therapeutic language" as a metaphor for the problem of pursuing community; therapeutic language lacks a narrative background to sustain the search for community. Therapeutic language works to describe the individual; only language contextualized within a community can provide the basis for the story life of a people. Bellah et al. reinforce the importance of narrative structures needed for community to be more than a mere collection of persons. They encourage a language that invites community in interpersonal interaction without relying on a psychologically based framework. The linguistic foundation for community is not the individual psyche, but the story-shaped life or *Habits of the Heart* of the people. The relevance of Bellah's writing to our understanding of dialogic civility is centered around his commitment to a story-laden view of community and a meaningful existence with others.

Introduction

In *Individualism and Commitment in American Life* (1987), Robert Bellah et al. connect the problem of therapeutic language to excessive individualism. The same message is at the center of work by Philip Rieff (1966/1987) and Richard Sennett (1976/1992, 1980). For Rieff, the "self" takes on a "sacred" tone in therapeutic language (1990, 355). He contends that the therapeutic linguistic framework has become normative within daily discourse.

> *The Triumph of the Therapeutic* first appeared twenty years ago. Ten years later, titling the book "prophetic," the editor of *The American Scholar* referred to the American "state of unconditional surrender" to the type. The surrender is no longer American. As Western culture continues to be Americanized, the therapeutic, in . . . triumph, has spread beyond these borders and even beyond Europe. (Rieff 1990, 351)

This normative focus on self has lessened people's commitment and imagination about the construction of human community. Excessive individualism has robbed some people of a story worth living beyond the immediate satisfactions of comfort, vanity, and status.

Robert Bellah et al. (1985, 1991), Maurice Friedman (1983), Philip Rieff (1966/1987, 1990), and Richard Sennett (1976/1992, 1980) have all suggested that we are currently confronted with a linguistic inability to invite community due to limitations arising from an overuse of therapeutic discourse. The inability to choose between individualism and community comes from a normative use of language based in self-expression and self-focus. Bellah et al. and others call us to be choice makers in interpersonal communication, which requires a linguistic system capable of nurturing and sustaining both individualism and community. Only in the process of choice making can community be meaningful. Our goal is to describe the limits of individualistic language for building community and to point to another choice, a story-formed sense of meaning in relational community.

Robert Bellah et al. (1985) assert that we are in a genuine dilemma: social evolution has progressed too far in a singular direction, resulting in an overemphasis on individualism. A return to pre-Enlightenment disregard for individual differences would result in intolerable discrimination and oppression. "The question, then, is whether the older civic and biblical traditions have the capacity to reformulate themselves while simultaneously remaining faithful to their own deepest insights" (Bellah et al., 1985, 144). We seem at an impasse of three options: individualism, return to feudal/small town status differentiation, or reassessment of old narrative structures. In light of these unpleasant options, some therapists have called for a greater sense of community. Yet the psychological/individual language of the trade undercuts their objective. Parents, like therapists, call for change—in this case a change in "values," only they are unsure what "values" are. We are caught in a profound ambivalence: we have praised individualism in America and now find it fighting us, not contributing to quality interaction. Our myths still tell us to struggle against an oppressive society, to keep the individual free. Yet we have a nagging sense that the individual can only prosper long term with others, in society, in relation. We are caught between yes and no in our response to individualism. The myth of the "single one" is powerful yet our sense of its fiction is dawning on us today.

From this historical standpoint of awareness of metanarrative decline and perhaps collapse, we ask the following question about Bellah's work: "How might a story-centered view of interpersonal community offer an alternative to therapeutic language and an individualistic orientation?" Interpersonal communication grounded in the overuse of therapeutic language misses a narrative connection—persons opting, perhaps unknowingly, for an individualistic orientation toward self.

The Practices of Identity

Habits of the Heart (Bellah et al. 1985) is not only a book title, but a metaphor for intellectual and cultural mores that sustain and undergird community. The term *habits of the heart* was coined by French social philosopher Alexis de Tocqueville, who published the first two volumes of *Democracy in America* in 1835.

> I have said earlier that I consider mores to be one of the great general causes responsible for the maintenance of a democratic republic in the United States.
> I here mean the term "mores" (*moeurs*) to have its original Latin meaning: I mean it to apply not only to "*moeurs*" in the

strict sense, which might be called the habits of the heart, but also to the different notions possessed by men [or women], the various opinions current among them, and the sum of ideas that shape mental habits.

So I use the word to cover the whole moral and intellectual state of a people. . . . I am only looking for the elements in them which help support political institutions. (Tocqueville 1835/1969, 287)

Like Tocqueville, Robert Bellah et al. (1985) used the phrase "habits of the heart" in a broad-based fashion, including the intellectual grounding that bonds people together.

The metaphor "habits of the heart" revolves in oxymoronic tension around two different "habits"—an emphasis on individualism and an emphasis on community. Of the two "habits," individualism is currently the strongest in our culture—and yet, persons crave community with others. In a sense our current habits of individualism are in contrast with a heart that longs for community. This acute ambivalence of self-reliance and community is not new. It is at the center of the American revolution. The tension between the individual and us was seen early on as key to American health by Alexis de Tocqueville. But he, like James Madison and Eugene Debs, wondered if we could keep the tension of opposing social goods in place. "They believed that the survival of a free people depends on the revival of a public virtue that is able to find political expression that works for the common good of the community, not just oneself" (Bellah et al. 1985, 271).

Individualism

Alexis de Tocqueville's nineteenth-century warning of the tendency of individualism to overwhelm community is consistent with Robert Bellah et al.'s (1985) conclusion in *Habits of the Heart*. The habit of individualism seems stronger than the habit of community in contemporary society, continuing to isolate us from one another. Bellah et al. recognized "individualism" (1985, 142–163) to be a concentration on oneself via self-growth, self-promotion, and self-concern. "Community" (Bellah et al. 1985, 191) suggests an appreciation of others with a desire to further the life of the collective group, not only oneself. Perhaps most important, these two approaches conceptualize meaning as arising from different places—in an individualistic orientation meaning emerges from oneself; in a story-based view of community meaning is given birth in a common life shared with others.

Robert Bellah et al. (1985, 1991) do not dichotomize individualism and community, however. Bellah recognizes the significance of both orientations. However, he and his associates note that contemporary society primarily emphasizes individualistic advancement; community is currently a secondary issue. Maurice Friedman stated a similar position:

> Many psychotherapists and psychologists who today recognize the essential importance of mutual relations between persons still see these relations largely as the function of the individual's becoming and the means to that end. As long as dialogue is entered *merely* as a means to the end of health, maturity, integration, self-expression, creativity, "peace of mind," "positive thinking," and richness of experience, it will not even produce those things. . . . The relation between persons takes place not only in the "I-Thou" of direct meeting but also in the "We" of family and community. . . . It is not only the fate of smaller and larger groups that depends upon the common speech-with-meaning. If man [or woman] does not recover the genuineness of existence as We, he [or she] may cease to exist at all. (1983, 29–32)

Friedman's general call to move from individual concern to community sensitivity is echoed in Bellah et al.'s *Habits of the Heart*, in which he laments the positive nature of some parts of the nineteenth century. Moral life, however flawed, was propelled by face-to-face encounters with others. Nineteenth-century society was guided by a common life of integrated economic, technical, and functional relationships. Yet today, to feel significant our first impulse is not toward relationship, but economic and technological competition against others. Meaningfulness is simply too quickly tied to self-absorption.

To illustrate the power of individualism and the desire for community without a proper language to sustain it, Bellah et al. tell the stories of many Americans, using four persons as "representative" examples.

One of their "representative" characters was Brian Palmer. Brian was a successful upper-echelon manager, who worked long hours and struggled to succeed in his career. "In many ways, Brian's is an individual success story. He has succeeded materially" (Bellah et al. 1985, 5). Brian, however, discovered that single-minded devotion to career was not enough. A divorce and the responsibility of children altered his perspective; he wanted a greater sense of community through involvement with his family. Robert Bellah et al. discovered, however, that when Brian was asked to justify his move from an individualistic to a community-oriented ethic he had difficulty doing so. According to the authors, Brian lacked the necessary vocabulary to fully nurture and sustain a community commitment.

> [Brian's] increased commitment to family and children rather than to material success seems strangely lacking in substantive justification. "I just find that I get more personal satisfaction from choosing course B over course A. It makes me feel better about myself. . . ." Despite the combination of tenderness and admiration he expresses for his wife, the genuine devotion he seems to feel for his children, and his own resilient self-confidence, Brian's justification of his life thus rests on a fragile foundation. Morally, his life appears much more coherent than when he was dominated by careerism, but, to hear him talk, even his deepest impulses of attachment to others are without any more solid foundation than his momentary desires. He lacks a language to explain what seem to be the real commitments that define his life, and to that extent the commitments themselves are precarious. (Bellah et al. 1985, 8)

Brian's story is significant in that a desire for community, without a story-based language to sustain it, has become the prototype rather than the exception in daily life.

The language of psychological individualism is so common and powerful in everyday speech that it overshadows the language of community. We require, but nevertheless seem to lack, an everyday language capable of transcending our own "radical individualism" (Bellah et al. 1985, 21). The dominance of this problem is reinforced by the commonality of individualistic communicative structure of therapeutic language in everyday communicative life.

Robert Bellah et al. is not surprised that humanistic psychology and a focus on the individual was so powerful a social force. Humanistic psychologists question and at time reject the significance of "external authority, cultural tradition, and social institutions. . . . The self in all its pristine purity is affirmed" (Bellah et al. 1985, 81). In defense of humanistic psychology, it was an extension of one part of the American Dream and the logical rejection of a class-oriented society. In some ways, humanistic psychology was yet another rebellion or Boston Tea Party against a narrative that was no longer appropriate for that historical moment—the conventions and rules from the previous era needed to go, replaced by self-rule! An American psychology naturally fought for the freedom of the individual self.

Therapeutic Limits

The connection between popular acceptance of humanistic psychology and individualism has permitted this "therapeutic vocabulary" and "therapeutic attitude" to become part of everyday language and meaning structures. According to Bellah et al., a therapeutic orientation or attitude increases individual autonomy, the pursuit of self-actualization, and a reluctance to sacrifice for another. Therapeutic language celebrates the individual.

> Social bonds are those based on the free choices of authentic selves. . . . The only valid contract is one based on negotiation between individuals acting in their own self-interest. . . . No binding obligations and no wider social understanding justify a relationship. It exists only as the expression of the choices of the free selves who make it up. And should it no longer meet their needs, it must end. (Bellah et al. 1985, 98–104)

Bellah et al., however, did not conceptualize the language of "therapeutic individualism" as necessarily generated from narcissism. They did not question the motivations of therapeutic practitioners, but rather critiqued a psychological language that sets limits on the possibilities of community. Robert Bellah et al. described a therapist, Margaret Oldham, as an example of this phenomenon. Margaret was motivated to help people. Her vocabulary, however, led to individualism, not community. Phrases such as "taking responsibility for oneself," and "self-reliance" lack lasting meaning in community-centered perspective (Bellah et al. 1985, 56).

The consequence of the "therapeutic language" of individualism combined with the individual roots of this culture result in a "culture of isolation" and, at best, a limited sense of community (Bellah et al. 1985, 285). Such an orientation is likely to define community as a "lifestyle," not as a commitment and service to others. An individualistic culture makes the idea of institutional support inaccessible. "In our life with other people we are engaged continuously, through words and actions, in creating and re-creating the institutions that make that life possible" (Bellah et al. 1991, 11). A concern for lifestyle encourages us to seek out other "like-minded" persons whose task is to enrich and reinforce one's own interests.

An ethical dilemma permeates the use of individualistic language for inviting community. In *Habits of the Heart* (1985) and *The Good Society* (1991), sociologists Robert Bellah et al. leave us with a clear message: too much individual concern limits the possibilities of community. Stories about "us" form communities, not demands to attend to "me" or "my" needs.

Robert Bellah et al. (1985) defined the terms "therapeutic contractualism" (128–130), "individualism" (142–163), and "community" (191) by exploring general societal trends and relying on broad-based commonsense definitions. The "therapeutic attitude" (123) for Bellah et al. is grounded around costs and benefits to the self:

> It is often difficult, working with the resource of popular therapeutic language, to give a full account of social and historical context. A therapist deeply concerned about the integrity of our lives and what threatens it, often has only an impoverished language in which to think about such issues. Asked about work that comprises a person's character, such as corporate bribery, one such therapist answers in utilitarian style that we have to "ask ourselves what it costs us." Then she adds that such costs are "cumulative." . . . Straining its logic to follow the trajectory of moral character over a lifetime, the language of costs and benefits can give us only a thin, quantitative facsimile of it. . . . Judgments of character as "self-esteem" and of action as what "works for me now" only dimly depict the meaning of work well done, a family well raised, and a life well lived, as if all such judgments were merely a matter of subjective feeling. (136–137)

"Therapeutic language" centered in the individual self is inadequate for the existence of community. Habits of the heart must emerge from the dialogue of relationship, not just from individual opinion—individual perspectives must be tested and modified in conversation with others.

A concern for community encourages communicating out of a genuine concern for others. The power of Robert Bellah et al.'s (1985) cultural critique is similar to that offered by Maurice Friedman (1985). Friedman recognized two languages within therapeutic language—one of individual self-actualization and the other of I-Thou and community. In popularizing the individual image of the self, a dialogically centered image of self can become lost. "One of the hardest obstacles to grasping [Martin] Buber's basic thesis that the self only becomes a self in its relationship to the Thou is our sense of individuality and self-awareness that persists when we are in relationship with others and when we are not" (Friedman 1977, 169).

Robert Bellah et al. provided a picture of "therapeutic language" grounded in individualism that leads from community to a one-sided view of the American Dream (individual fulfillment). They countered that Americans have not only one part of the American Dream, but two, the first of individual fulfillment and the second of community. These two values need to be held in dialectical tension for the full constructive impact of the American Dream to be part of daily societal life. Unfortunately, the American Dream is too often limited to a private dream about me, my success, and my ability to stand out and be noticed, leaving ordinary folk to fend for themselves. This dream drives many of us to move from rags to riches; such a vision is hard to release "even though it contradicts another dream that we have—that of living in a society that would really be worth living in" (Bellah et al. 1985, 285). The dream of community is possible through a story-informed view of interpersonal communication with others that Bellah et al. called a "community of memory" (1985, 152). Such a memory is tied to institutions, public virtues, and the stories we tell about the good life. We do not own a "community of memory"—we participate in it with others.

Community is not just consideration for the moment of individual interests. Community is an attitude of long-range concern for the generations prior to and following our own. A "community of memory" (1985, 152–155) has a history, a story told collectively at different times in order to provide a memory or live tradition to which one can belong. An understanding of oneself is rooted not just in individual accomplishment, but in a loyalty and commitment to a people. "Where history and hope are forgotten and community means only the gathering of the similar, community degenerates into lifestyle enclave" (Bellah et al., 1985, 154). An individualistic vocabulary is inadequate for building and promoting a community-based understanding of interpersonal communication.

Characters of Modern Life

Much of the recent insight of Robert Bellah is grounded in the scholarship of Alasdair MacIntyre. In *After Virtue* (1981/1984), MacIntyre outlines the significance of a character type in communicating meaning within a tradition.

> With what I have called *characters* it is quite otherwise; and the difference arises from the fact that the requirements of a *character* are imposed from the outside, from the way in which others regard and use *characters* to understand and to evaluate themselves. With other types of social role the role may be adequately specified in terms of the institutions of whose structures it is a part and the relation to those institutions of the individuals who fill the roles. In the case of a *character* this is not enough. A *character* is an object of regard by the members of the culture generally or by some significant segment of them. He [or she] furnishes them with a cultural and moral ideal. Hence the demand is that in this type of case role and personality be fused. Social type and psychological type are required to coincide. The *character* morally legitimates a mode of social existence. (MacIntyre 1981/1984, 29)

The cultural requirements for MacIntyre's understanding of characters involves imposition from the outside, representing a cultural and moral ideal. In essence, "*characters* . . . are those social roles which provide a culture with its moral definitions" (MacIntyre 1981/1984, 31).

Alasdair MacIntyre connects the characters of modern life to "emotivism" (1981/1984, 30)—behavior guided by personal preference. In *After Virtue,* MacIntyre outlines three major characters: "Rich Aesthete," "Manager," and "Therapist" (1981/1984, 30). These figures of modern culture often go uncontested; they are the icons of a good life in a culture lacking roots and a clear sense of direction. The main characters that Bellah et al. outline are pointed to in MacIntyre's (1981/1984) primary character representations of this historical moment.

The most powerful characters in the modern culture are the manager and therapist. Often the language of one is adapted by the other in a historical time of self-centered evaluation—"How does this decision impact me?" Bellah contends that the manager and the therapist define much of twentieth-century American culture. The social basis of individualistic capitalism dominates local economic forms and our interaction with one another. Both the manager and the therapist seem hostile to older ideas of moral order— the manager challenges the former owner/leader and the therapist challenges the priest/pastor. "[T]he effects of this managerial and therapeutic understanding are not always benign; it does not all succeed, even by its own standards. Indeed, the very term *therapeutic* suggests a life focused on the need for cure. But cure of what?" (Bellah et al. 1985, 47). A cure from an old moral order which was not perfect, but not necessarily more problematic than the empowered self of today. Success is too often and too quickly defined as "liberation and fulfillment of the individual. . . . [I]t enables the individual to think of commitments—from marriage and work to political and religious involvement—as enhancements of the sense of individual well-being rather than as moral imperatives" (Bellah et al. 1985, 47). *Habits of the Heart* are not simply exchanged and rejected quickly; yet the manager and the therapist push for a functional view of life—"Does it work for me?" Such a perspective is quite different than the question, "What does it mean for us?"—which asks for a response available in a story- and narrative-laden perspective. Like Alasdair MacIntyre, Bellah is concerned about a language of virtue, no longer able to command our attention and bind us together.

Central Concepts in Robert Bellah's Work

Robert Bellah invites readers into a moral story of significant power and importance about the quality of our communicative lives together. He places his understanding of story within a social science tradition interested in understanding the forest, not just the trees, around us.

A social science concerned with the whole of society would, as we have said, have to be historical as well as philosophical. Narrowly professional social science has given us valuable information about many aspects of contemporary society, but it often does so with little or no sense of history. Social historians have been ingenious in giving us information about the past that is often only slightly less rich than that discovered by social scientists about the present. Yet what we need from history, and why the social scientist must also, among other things, be a historian, is not merely comparable information about the past, but some idea of how we have gotten from the past to the present, in short, a narrative. Narrative is a primary and powerful way by which to know about a whole. In an important sense, what a society (or a person) is, is its history. So a Habermas or . . . MacIntyre gives us his story about how modern society came to its present pass. Such stories can, and must, be contested, amended, and sometimes replaced. (Bellah et al. 1985, 302)

Bellah contends that an individualistic language, "therapeutic language," lacks a story foundation. He seeks a language that will hold "us" together; a language that bonds. He challenges a language that took us even further into individualism, a focus upon the self and, of course, away from our moorings in community. We view Bellah as a social science story teller with a twofold task. First, he tells us a problematic story, and then he begins to offer an alternative story in its place.

Broken Covenants

Robert Bellah is concerned that therapeutic language supporting evermore individualism has become an oppressive ideology. The ideology of therapeutic language within the culture pulls people apart rather than pointing to the importance of the common good. Robert Bellah, in *Beyond Belief: Essays on Religion in a Post-Traditionalist World*, stated his concern about ideological structures that dictate their message in the form of problematic stories:

[People] are not oppressed by armies and unfair economic systems alone. They are also oppressed by dead ideologies which can be locked into personalities and societies and program them on a course of fatal disaster, often in the name of "realism" and "necessity." Under these conditions we have need more than ever for the dreamers of dreams and the seers of visions. Freedom of the imagination, the ability to live in many realities at once, may be our strongest weapon in the struggle for human liberation. (1970, xx)

Movement into rigid ideological structures and *Beyond Belief* (Bellah 1970) is the problematic story that Bellah calls us to understand. He suggests that for many therapeutic language is not only beyond belief, but beyond challenge.

Working dialectically, Robert Bellah calls us to remember that we cannot live without narrative structures; he simply wants to keep narrative structures open, away from ideological abuse. First, he points to the danger of misusing narratives. Second, he reminds us not to abandon a narrative too quickly, simply because it is enacted in a questionable fashion. He provides us with yet another important metaphor, the notion of a *Broken Covenant* (1975) to hold in dialectical tension with *Beyond Belief* (1970). The problem of self-focus coupled with the absence of a story pointing to the importance of reaching out to the other in dialogue permeates Bellah's project. He recognizes the value of a narrative view of life, even when narratives are misused. He calls us to both recognize and then reconstruct within the historical needs of today in *The Broken Covenant* (Bellah 1961/1975).

Robert Bellah reminds us that not all covenants are lived in perfect fashion, but one must be wary of eliminating our commitment to covenants just because of their flaws. We can try to improve broken covenants, but we need to be wary of turning our backs on them too quickly. Perhaps Bellah sensed a historical shift—one in which the story of narrative critique is so strong that narrative covenants are simply ignored or responded to with deep routine cynicism; as if the metaphor of *Beyond Belief* (1970) took on such power that the constructive contribution of belief in a narrative system no longer seems possible in a postmodern culture.

The experience of becoming a routine cynical spotter of broken covenants invites reliance upon therapeutic language and focus upon the self. People's disillusion with American institutions begins to shift focus from "us" and what "we" can build to "me" and what possessions "I" own.

A tendency to rank personal gratification above obligation to others correlates with a deepening cynicism about the established social, economic, and political institutions of society. A sense that the basic institutions of society are unjust and serve the interests of a few at the expense of the many, is used to justify the inapplicability of moral obligations to one's self. (Bellah 1975, x)

With an unreflective cynical smugness people begin to confuse the good life with their ability to spot a flaw in an important narrative structure and thereby protect their self-focus. Spotting broken covenants is not a substitute for a productive life that works to support a covenant's commitments.

A covenant calls for collective responsibility to a narrative structure that is meant to guide, not dictate, the actions of a people. When one gives up completely on a narrative covenant he or she is but one step away from inserting routine cynicism and ultimate anarchy into community life.

Struggling with deep unreflective cynicism and the normative nature of emotivism led Alasdair MacIntyre to write *After Virtue* (1981/1984). Attention to the same concern propelled Robert Bellah to call attention to two different responses to broken covenants. The first response is emotivism or the excessive use of therapeutic language that grounds life within the solitary self. The second response, however, is constructive—our task is to rebuild broken covenants on the soil of our historical moment.

The Declaration of Independence, the Bill of Rights, and the Fourteenth Amendment to the Constitution have never been fully implemented. Certainly the words "with liberty and justice for all" in the Pledge of Allegiance are not factually descriptive. But while I can understand the feeling . . . that such hypocritically employed documents should be rejected, I would follow the course of [insisting] . . . they be fulfilled. If they have never been completely implemented, neither have they been entirely without effect. If the liberty they protect is largely negative, largely a defense against encroachment, it is still the indispensable condition for the attainment of any fuller freedom. (Bellah 1961/1975, 151)

Our responsibility is to work to ground, construct, rework, and support broken covenants in the realities of today. Bellah asks us to be builders, not simply people who recognize the limitations and the flaws of what is given in this historical moment.

Robert Bellah sees us living in a time of a "broken covenant," which is open to hope, but limited by individualistic language. His concern with therapeutic language is that it is inappropriately applied to public contexts. He is not opposed to therapy, but to the overgeneralization of the power and use of therapeutic language. We are not critical of "therapeutic language" in general, but rather of a particular form of therapeutic language that promotes the individual self over a dialogical self. An emphasis on dialogue is central for a community-based understanding of interpersonal communication.

Tacit Understanding of a Problematic Story

Clearly, Robert Bellah et al. understand the problem of a therapeutic language story. Bellah et al. suggest that tacit recognition of this problem is emerging within the culture at large. Within contemporary society, many people experience the broken covenant with the therapeutic project: "I know something is wrong. I want community, but I feel so alone. With so much emphasis on communication and the language of therapy, why do I feel as if something is still missing from my life?"

Therapeutic language has us look for jobs or careers that permit us to express ourselves, which is quite different than being "called" (Bellah et al. 1985, 69) to the narrative of a profession.

> In a calling, by contrast, one gives oneself to learning and practicing activities that in turn define the self and enter into the shape of its character. Committing one's self to becoming a "good" carpenter, craftsman, doctor, scientist, or artist anchors the self within a community practicing carpentry, medicine, or art. It connects the self to those who teach, exemplify, and judge these skills. It ties us to still others whom they serve. (Bellah et al. 1985, 69)

Bellah and associates point to a tacit concern that many sense — our psychologically based language simply does not promote a story-based sense of community. The task of those hoping to offer a story-laden voice to the twenty-first century is to provide an alternative way to both express and ground communicative community. Bellah et al. began such an effort in *The Good Society* (1991).

Communicative Background—The Common Good

In a time of postmodern consciousness, Robert Bellah is even more convinced that a communicative background needs to guide our handling of personal and societal differences. He would not reject the postmodern assertion that we no longer have agreement on virtue structures that can frame a narrative for us. However, we believe he would approach this problem dialectically: he would first state that such an era exists and then acknowledge the task to co-constitute a communicative background or narrative that can guide difference and lack of agreement. His project is to find a narrative background that can offer guidance without dictating.

The following outlines the basic nature of Robert Bellah et al.'s *The Good Society* (1991) project:

> What is missing in this American view of society? Just the idea that in our life with other people we are engaged continuously, through words and actions, in creating and re-creating the institutions that make life possible. This process is never neutral but is always ethical and political, since institutions (even such an intimate institution as the family) live or die by ideas of right and wrong and conceptions of the good. (11–12)

Bellah does not presuppose that we will come to a view of a societal good without argument and debate. He is confident that argument over a general theme of a good society can at least give us direction. We suggest that the language of Sissela Bok's "minimalist" (1995, 9) set of values is akin to Bellah et al.'s (1991) concern.

Robert Bellah et al.'s minimalist set of hopes or expectations from society are the following. First, that persons would be committed to a notion of a good society. Second, that people would recognize the need for a continuing argument in defining what such a reality would be in each historical era. Third, that our use of individualistic language and focus on self needs to be complemented by a renewed sense of the importance of institutions in our lives. These three expectations frame a "community of memory" (1985, 152–155). Finally, Bellah et al. are interested in a "politics of generativity" (1991, 276)—we simply need to be concerned with those that will come after us. Life, for Bellah, is not to be hoarded and spent on oneself alone.

Inviting Community

Robert Bellah et al. (1985) provided a number of solutions promoting the invitation of human community in their last chapter, "Transforming American Culture." Their solutions are primarily related to structural societal changes. However, throughout *Habits of the Heart* (1985) they identified three important ideas for developing a language to invite community in interpersonal communication.

First, community does not rest primarily on feelings, but rather on a commitment to story-centered values that bond people together. In short, we need to reverse the implications of the following quotation:

> The objectified moral goodness of Winthrop obeying God's will or Jefferson following nature's laws turns into the subjective goodness of getting what you want and enjoying it. Utility replaces duty; self-expression unseats authority. "Being good" becomes "feeling good." . . . Given this individualistic moral framework, the self becomes a crucial site for the comparative examination and probing of feelings that result from utilitarian acts and inspire expressive ones. (Bellah et al. 1985, 77–78)

Robert Bellah et al. indicated the need for a language tied to something beyond individual feelings, such as Eugene Eubanks's "moral dimension of communication" (1980, 297–312) and Richard Weaver's (1948) pursuit of the Ideal. But Bellah et al. set ideals in the historicality of the community, not in a Platonic ideal. They do not suggest that a language centered on the self and feelings is wrong—they just want an individualistic vocabulary to be secondary to an emphasis on story-guided values that bond people together.

Second, relationship cannot be considered the most important term in communication from a community perspective. Story-guided values, not just positive feelings and utility, are needed to bond relationships.

> The limitation for millions of Americans who remain stuck in this duality in one form or another is that they are deprived of a language genuinely able to mediate among self, society, the natural world, and ultimate reality. Frequently, they fall back on abstractions when talking about the most important things. They stress "communication" as essential to relationships without adequately considering what is to be communicated. They talk about "relationships" but cannot point to the personal virtues and cultural norms that give relationships meaning and value. (Bellah et al. 1985, 237)

The implication is that a community-sensitive language of interpersonal communication views relationships as a byproduct (rather than the goal) of a common life together. Robert Bellah et al. are not averse to relationship—relationship is simply a secondary emphasis that emerges as a result of a community story that contains a vocabulary of commitment, sacrifice, loyalty, and principle.

Finally, the language of interpersonal communication sensitive to community is grounded in a "community of memory." Developing a language that is sensitive to community takes time and a willingness to commit oneself to a community long enough to embrace the stories and dramas that bind the people together. In our culture, the dream of individual success requires the person to uproot community to find success. William Whyte (1956/1957), in *The Organization Man*, described mobility, not community, as the trademark of this lifestyle. Instead of movement, Robert Bellah et al. suggested a willingness to become part of the drama or story, to become a participant in the "community of memory" (1985, 152). Their suggestion is similar to Walter Fisher's (1984) connection of story or narrative with involvement in public moral argument. Bellah et al. seek a vocabulary that grounds one's story in community, not just individual pursuits.

Historicality and Dialogic Civility

This chapter raises significant issues for advancing our understanding about the philosophy of interpersonal communication from a dialogic civility perspective. Robert Bellah et al. (1985) suggest that in light of the current strength of individualistic vocabulary and in a spirit of dialectic, it may be time to turn to a story-guided or "community of memory" (1985, 152) view of community—not as the total answer, but as counterweight to the status quo in discussions of interpersonal communication grounded in the metaphor of self. How might a story-guided community-sensitive language base for interpersonal communication be described? We suggest a language of community is possible using dialogic civility as a metaphor and background narrative for interpersonal discourse.

Robert Bellah et al. (1985, 1991) do not suggest that an individualistic approach to interpersonal communication is wrong. However, from a standard of ethical choice making, an individualistic approach is problematic if a story-guided community-based approach to interpersonal communication is not available; there needs to be a choice. Clearly, the implications of grounding commitment to significant stories as a narrative background for interpersonal communication needs further exploration. Perhaps the most important "language" horizon before us lies in the pursuit of community. We depend on language for community: "What we cannot imagine and express in language has little chance of becoming a sociological reality" (Bellah et al. 1991, 15). Bellah suggests that our responsibility is to present the possibility of linguistic choice before those who unreflectively assume the merits of individualistic language; such an educational commitment to choice can only enrich our study and practice of interpersonal communication. Bellah points to a dialogic civility that calls for community, open analysis of broken covenants, and a willingness to work to repair the broken nature of fragile narrative structures.

Robert Bellah calls for public discourse about the good society; he calls for dialogic civility as the communicative means to ground the effort. Bellah critiques the limits of individualistic psychological language. He reminds us of a story-guided "community of memory," and he offers hope in simply stating that all is not lost. We have taken the wrong communicative path, but repair, healing, and health only require a change of direction and our willingness to carve out new paths together to create a "community of memory" worthy of guiding us in the twenty-first century. In a world in which too many people, working too quickly, take too much pride in outlining broken covenants, Bellah calls us to roll up our sleeves, pitch in, be a part of the effort to fix the broken and discover the needed for "us." In so doing, we will find meaning in life by contributing to a "community of memory" that will sustain others when they take up the task in the middle of a story worth living. Our goal is to make visible a community of memory that is even more responsive and more inclusive of our diverse society.

Part III

Dialogic Civility

Part III organizes our story about dialogic civility. We offer the term as a metaphor, but the entire interpretive work is an effort to tell a story about public respect between persons that genuinely meets our historic moment in dialogue and civility. Dialogic civility is deeply grounded in historicality and the conviction that genuine meeting makes possible change and alteration.

Just as we do not reject cynicism, but caution against routine cynicism, we do not reject a deconstructive hermeneutic; we simply want to offer an additional option. Dialogic civility is situated in a constructivist hermeneutic, calling us to public respect as we work to co-constitutively discover the minimal communication background assumptions necessary to permit persons of difference to shape together the communicative terrain of the twenty-first century. Perhaps if enough people began to communicate out of a narrative background of dialogic civility, the story of communication in the twenty-first century would be one that guided difference, diversity, and discourse under the arm of respect and caring for the other.

Chapter Fourteen

The Interpersonal Praxis of Dialogic Civility

The Praxis of Narrative—

What then is the relation of our narrative understanding to this practical understanding? The answer to this question governs the relationship that can be established between the theory of narrative and that of action, in the sense given this term by English-language analytic philosophy. This relationship, in my view, is a twofold one. It is a reaction of presupposition and of transformation.

On the one hand, every narrative presupposes a familiarity with terms such as agent, goal, means, circumstance, help, hostility, cooperation, conflict, success, failure, etc., on the part of its narrator and any listener. In this sense, the minimal narrative sentence is an action sentence. . . . In the final analysis, narratives have acting and suffering as their theme. . . . There is no structural analysis of narrative that does not borrow from an explicit or an implicit phenomenology of "doing something."

> —Paul Ricoeur, *Time and Narrative, Vol. 1*

A Web of Stories—

Because women's sphere of activity has traditionally been and still today is so concentrated in the private sphere in which children are raised, human relationships maintained and traditions handed down and continued, the family's experience has been more attuned to the "narrative structure of action" and the "standpoint of the concrete other." Since they have had to deal with concrete individuals, with their needs, endowments, wants and abilities, dreams as well as failures, women in their capacities as primary caregivers have had to exercise insight into the claims of the particular. In a sense the art of the particular has been their domain, as has the "web of stories," which in Hannah Arendt's words constitutes the who and the what of our shared world.

　　　　　　　　　　　　　—Seyla Benhabib, *Situating the Self*

"A web of stories" from diverse interpersonal voices point us to this concluding and beginning[1] juncture—a public background narrative to interpersonal communication grounded in dialogic civility that embraces the dialectic of cynicism and hope in the praxis of everyday discourse with others. This concluding chapter unifies the theoretical insight of Part I, "Interpersonal Praxis: From Communicative Crisis to Narrative Action," with concepts from authors outlined in Part II, "Interpersonal Voices." This final chapter suggests the importance of dialogic civility as both a metaphor for respect in public discourse and a narrative background for interpersonal communication tied to this historical moment.

This final chapter outlines a public narrative of respect pointed to by interpersonal voices of authors highlighted in this work. In a postmodern era of routine cynicism a critical tension exists in everyday communication. When a hermeneutic of suspicion becomes normative, we too quickly question all narrative structures. On the other hand, a desire for security in an environment of insecurity can lead us to mistakenly attempt to resurrect old metanarratives; such a world is unlikely to return. As we accept the postmodern reality of metanarrative collapse, we recognize the importance of diversity awareness, appreciation, interaction, and respect for the other and suggest there is a pragmatic need for "humble narratives" (Arnett 1997b, 44–45) to guide us. This chapter points to a humble narrative of respect for the other in the public communicative arena not as the answer, but as one contribution to an ongoing conversation about human beings working constructively with one another. In this chapter we flesh out what the respect for the other that dialogic civility necessitates might look

---

[1] It is impossible to talk about narrative without using language of action which denotes a beginning and continuing openness to change. Once language moves to more inflexible prose the spirit of narrative—which is open to participation and change—is shed for the ideological security of an *a priori* sense of conviction.

like, as we move interpersonal voices to the question of our post-modern era.

This concluding interpretive essay is grounded in an awareness of the dangers of routine cynicism, and deep respect for persons and the uniqueness of the historical situation. In this chapter we explore "What web of metaphorical significance might constitute a public narrative of dialogic civility" and "Why is such a public communicative narrative historically appropriate in an age of diversity and difference?" The web of metaphorical significance centers our theory and is derived from the contributions of authors recognized in Part II.

From Privatized to Public Discourse

This work centers on a basic presupposition: interpersonal communication from a privatized, therapeutic, feeling perspective has exhausted itself. In this historical moment, it is appropriate to examine a public framework for interpersonal communication. Philip Rieff's work (1966/1987) acknowledged the triumph of the therapeutic world view over the religious metanarrative, but the victory also brought decay and collapse for the victorious therapeutic paradigm. Just as a powerful country can embrace ruin by overextending its military reach beyond its economic infrastructure, overextension of private therapeutic discourse into the public realm has, ironically, weakened the hold that therapeutic discourse has on daily interpersonal communication.

In everyday discourse and interaction, there is increasing commonsense questioning of the historical appropriateness of privatized emotive approaches to interpersonal communication; such a communication style is no longer appropriate for the public arena and is perceived by some as simply dysfunctional. When nontraditional students who are employed in the workplace hear a critique asserting the inappropriate use of therapeutic discourse in public settings they almost stand and cheer. One student stated, "I am so happy to be in this class. I have had the conviction for a number of years that the communication 'stuff' we have been taught in many of our seminars is no longer working in our company, but I wondered if it was just my lack of insight that was causing me to miss something." These students understand that an emotive workplace is an exhaustive place to spend a day. Instead of discussing how to get a task done, the communication moves too quickly to how one feels about the task and how one feels in general. How one feels about what has happened in one's private life is often considered legitimate data to govern workplace decisions. The blurring of public and private life has been pushed too far. Instead of offering a sense of humanity to the workplace, emotive exhaustion and self-centered conviction has too frequently been invited into daily discourse.

Our effort is clearly not to salvage the therapeutic paradigm but to move interpersonal discussion to another sphere—public life. Our goal for public interpersonal communication is not intimacy, but civility. We seek a narrative of dialogic civility that offers a commitment to keeping the conversation going in an age of diversity, change, and difference. All interpersonal communication relationships can benefit from a foundation of civility; in addition, some relationships can be nourished by intimate communicative exchange. A foundation of civility, not intimacy, however, should define public interpersonal communication. Intimacy is a byproduct of in-depth relationships that cannot and should not be expected or demanded in public interpersonal discourse with others at school, in the workplace, or in public social gatherings such as church or any form of social agency. Intimacy in interpersonal exchange is to be prized and cherished, not demanded.

We suggest that there is a vital and important place for interpersonal communication in the public domain—guided by the metaphor of civility, not intimacy, self, or feelings. A major contribution of the Enlightenment was the opening of public space.

With much scholarly material pointing to the limitations of the Enlightenment, Richard Bernstein's argument is even more powerful. He simply reminds us that there is a place for public verification of evidence in the public sphere; the confusion of private and public discourse puts at risk this positive contribution of the Enlightenment to public dialogue. Privatized/emotive discourse leads us to an interpersonal "dark age" where power and similarity guide the notion of community, not public discourse. . . . When multiple private positions are at odds and each is taken unknowingly into the public arena, the contribution of the Enlightenment, bringing into the open ideas that can be publicly verified and examined ceases, is ignored and left unused. We put at risk the best of the Enlightenment contribution to open and free discourse when the public domain is entered with private narrowness.

Community with an interest in diversity requires a commitment to public discourse. If we are to outline what some of us can and cannot tolerate, many of us generally have a more gracious spirit at a public level than in our own private lives. (Arnett 1997b, 43)

Diversity appreciation requires ignoring the impulse to judge an idea on the basis of our own private predispositions. The task of dialogic civility is to find ways to govern public interpersonal discourse, recognizing that private/emotive positions are unlikely to move the discourse in a positive direction. Only "I," not "we," have access to "my" private view of truth; dialogic civility is based on a co-constitutive, public discourse model that we frame together.

Our thesis in this final chapter is similar to that which Jean Bethke Elshtain pointed to in *Democracy on Trial*—the public domain needs to be reclaimed.

A politics of displacement is a dynamic that connects and interweaves public and private imperatives in a way that is dangerous to the integrity of both. It is more likely for a politics of displacement to take hold when certain conditions prevail. First, established public and private, secular and religious institutions and rules are in flux, and people have a sense that the center does not hold. Second, there are not clearly established public institutions to focus dissent and concern. Third, and finally, private values, exigencies, and identities come to take precedence in all things, including public involvement as a citizen.

This, clearly is the world we are now in. But note that *private* here does not refer to our need to preserve certain relationships and institutions but rather to that diminished universe of one: me and my fleeting angers, resentments, sentiments, and impulses. (1993/1995, 40–41)

Our task should not be to "diminish the universe" of interpersonal discourse by limiting the parameters of interpersonal communication to the private/intimate domain. On the contrary, we seek to ground part of interpersonal communication in the public domain, in a background narrative of dialogic civility.

A Minimal Foundation for Dialogic Civility

We contend that respect for the other is a basic building block for a public narrative of dialogic civility. A public narrative of dialogic civility suggests an agreed-upon communicative convention about respect for the other and our relational responsibility in an interpersonal relationship. Our perspective is grounded in a pragmatic goal of keeping the conversation going in our postmodern era of virtue contention. Our task is to co-construct communicative agreement; we cannot presuppose its existence. Postmodernity suggests that presupposed agreement does not exist; however, we contend that conversation about ways to work constructively with one another are essential as we support both diversity and uniqueness without falling prey to emotivism and narcissism.

Sissela Bok's notion of *Common Values* (1995) reminds us of minimal values that are important to a public narrative of dialogic civility: "These three categories of moral values—the positive duties of mutual care and reciprocity; the negative injunctions concerning violence, deceit, and betrayal; and the norms for certain rudimentary procedures and standards for what is just—go into what P. F. Strawson has referred to as a 'minimal interpretation of morality'" (16). We add a fourth category to Bok's suggestions—commitment to "keeping the conversation going" (Rorty 1979, 378), out of recognition that many issues need more conversation and dialogue. Basic respect for the other calls us to live in caring reciprocity, limit violence, and find agreed-upon ways to define the notion of justice. We begin communicative life with a commitment to a background of dialogue that embraces patience, persistence, and public discourse rooted in respect for the other.

Respect for the other cannot be assumed, taken for granted, or demanded for oneself without a commitment to the other. Dialogic civility begins with a set of public discourse assumptions about the notion of the other. Our goal is to work with the other in such a fashion as to "keep the conversation going" (Rorty 1979, 378), permitting us to find momentary agreement on issues of mutual consequence. We need to keep the other in the conversation.

We begin with the assumption that respect for the other is a pragmatic necessity in a postmodern and metanarrativeless culture. Respect for the other is the keystone to a public narrative of dialogic civility. Being disrespectful is likely to drive the other from the discourse, not engage the other in conversation that will guide the communicative outcome. The notion of respect can be exemplified in communicative interaction in the following manner. First, in any communicative event both self and other are present, but the communicative direction needs to be guided mutually by the other and the self. Focusing solely on self can too easily eventuate in narcissism. Concern for the other calls for a public commitment beyond me. Second, dialogic civility assumes that life is lived in dialectic. Granted, there are people so concerned about the other that they should be encouraged to take care of the self. But, in this historic moment, this is not the general problem society faces in a therapeutic culture focused on the metaphor of self. The twenty-first century calls for diversity awareness, often placing respect for the other at odds with a self-oriented communicative metaphor. Third, dialogic civility suggests a minimal commitment to a public reciprocal respect for the other out of a pragmatic communicative need to keep the conversation going. Such respect is needed as we keep the conversation going between persons of difference and in a time of lack of agreement about metanarrative structures.

A public life places demands on us to reach beyond ourselves. In this historical moment, metaphors of self and self-actualization must now be significantly tempered with metaphors of the other and respect for the other (Arnett, in press). Life lived in this concrete moment calls for dialectical correctives when we discover excess in action. Excessive use of the self metaphor has led us to a dead end—the other has become simply a pragmatic historical necessity in a era of diversity, difference, and lack of metanarrative guidance.

Concern for the other connects us to the world of civic space—public space—not privatized discourse. Public space is the world of limits, wariness about absolutes, calls to compromise, sociability, and concern for "us" that includes self and other. This civic space is not a place of perfection or a place of interpersonal grace that permits discourse to take place—it is realistic space grounded in the failings of human life. Although Plato would not be happy in such a compromised sphere of discourse, Aristotle's notion of *phronesis* (1985, 1141a20–1142a) fits here. Such a civic place is not utopian; in fact it is based on the knowledge that "virtue without limits becomes terror" (Elshtain 1993/1995, 123). Thus, we seek to connect respect to a public space, seeking not a utopia, but a realm where interpersonal discourse involves more than "me," more than the "self."

Clearly dialogic civility is not value free. In a postmodern culture, it is necessary when possible to make one's "standpoint"

(Wood 1992, 12–18) known in a public arena. Jurgen Habermas (1983) works at establishing rules and procedures for discourse ethics in a postmodern culture. He realizes that we must make such rules public. A public set of rules or guidelines provides a background out of which communication can take place in a time of metanarrative absence. The concepts that guide our story about dialogic civility are public, civil, ongoing conversation, and dialectical awareness of the historical interplay of self and other, crisis and responsibility, and tradition and change. Those that point to such a public form of interpersonal discourse are the storytellers that we consider historically needed in the twenty-first century. Dialogic civility in the public arena is tied to the conviction that keeping the conversation going in a confused age is our best hope for finding "humble narratives" that will guide us with care through the twenty-first century.

Respect and Civility

An investigation of public discourse necessitates locating metaphors that take us out of a privatized view of interpersonal discourse and suggest public implications of communicative action. Thus, we consider it historically appropriate to shift from use of the term respect to the concept of civility. Respect is often associated, though not exclusively, with private discourse. The notion of civility brings a clear public perception to awareness. *Webster's New Collegiate Dictionary* defines civility as "training in the humanities [and] a polite act or expression" (1974, 204). Civility has been associated with communicative behavior that offers a sense of grace to the other—space to live and communicate. "In your face" communication is not associated with civility. Our support is for a communicative style that is pragmatically more likely to "keep the conversation going" (Rorty 1979, 378) than a communicative exchange that verbally attacks the other. A more aggressive communicative style is still needed upon occasions, as Franklyn S. Haiman outlined in "The Rhetoric of the Streets" (1967). In this historical moment, however, if we are to embrace diversity, we need to hear one another and keep a conversation going through civil discourse. In short, civility in common usage has fewer attitudinal and psychological implications associated with privatized discourse and more easily moves us to awareness and discussion in the public arena.

Our call for a public narrative of dialogic civility is more modest than trying to convert people's private attitudinal presuppositions toward a sensitivity of the other; we do not emphasize the inner workings of the psyche or attitudes of the communicators. We are searching for basic guidelines that can assist our interaction in the public arena. As important as respect is, we consider civility to be a more appropriate term in this historical moment—due to its clear public connections. Our task is to offer a "humble narrative" (Arnett 1997b, 44–45) of dialogic civility—proposing a pragmatic public effort to keep the conversation going by the manner in which we address, listen, and respond to the other.

Dialogic civility suggests that we want to keep public discourse alive to assist "us" "through the practice of public conversation and joint action" (Bellah et al. 1991, 169). Robert Bellah and his colleagues, in *The Good Society* (1991), reminded us that the good life is most often lived through institutions, not just through "me." Dialogic civility suggests that much of our interpersonal discourse has a purpose beyond "me"—a goal to assist institutions in providing a ground for a meaningful life for those involved. Colleges, churches, families, local to international governments, and even long-term friendships are all institutions that we create and maintain through public interpersonal discourse.

Harold Barrett (1991) reminds us that the struggle for a civil discourse is not new and was part of Alexis de Tocqueville's concern about excessive individualism that took us from public commitments to an unduly focused private agenda. To respect the other calls for civility and an awareness of individuality in public space. Excessive concern about the self moves us from civility to individualism and to eventual narcissism.

In America today, the strongest cultural force conflicting with civility is *individualism*: the extreme of self-interest. To be sure, various manifestations of individualism have been in evidence in the nation for a long time. Recall that during his visit in the early 1800's Alexis de Tocqueville became concerned about its negative effect on social relations in America. But, before proceeding, let's remind ourselves that individualism is not individuality. The latter, a quality distinguishing one person from another, is socially useful—even a mark of civility, e.g., as representing strength of will, courage, responsibility, independence and a spirit of freedom. No, individualism is something different: a doctrine or personal aberration enforcing the assumption that the individual and not society is the dominant consideration or end. In a philosophic sense, it is solipsistic, the self being the gauge of existence. In terms of social philosophy, individualism is narcissistic dogma: my principle, myself. (Barrett 1991, 152)

Dialogic civility is an interpersonal reminder of a historically grounded public assumption that basic respect for the other is pragmatically needed as we continue to understand and work with difference in an era of diversity, change, and narrative debate. The focus on self is dialectically necessary for some, but in general social terms such an emphasis has moved into the excess of individualism and narcissism leaving behind the productive ground of individuality.

Civility and the Other

Dialogic civility works to keep conversation going that seeks to enrich a life lived meaningfully through others—persons, institutions, places of work, and long-term friendships. Robert Bellah et al. (1985) reminds us that the other, whether a person or an institution, needs to be part of our lives. The other calls us to reach out beyond ourselves. In our lives happiness is found in life with the other.

[F]ew have found a life devoted to "personal ambition and consumerism" satisfactory, and most are seeking in one way or another to transcend the limitations of a self-centered life. If there are vast numbers of a selfish, narcissistic "me generation" in America, we did not find them, but we certainly find the language of individualism, the primary American language of self-understanding, limits the way in which people think. (Bellah et al. 1985, 290)

Our task is to offer an interpersonal vocabulary that points us toward the public, the other, the intentional nature of life as "experience of." This pragmatic turn to the metaphor of the other requires us to be dialectically wary of the metaphor of self in this historical moment.

Kenneth Gergen's *The Saturated Self* (1991) outlines how the romantic and modern view of self is no longer appropriate in a post-modern culture. The notion of relatedness, not isolation and self is a guiding principle—"the emphasis shifts from self to relationship" (Gergen 1991, 157). Gergen compares the postmodern person to a restless nomad without the stability of self. We move in a different interpretive frame and suggest that postmodernity offers an incred-ible opportunity for people to rework and reground their lives in narratives that emerge out of conversation and involvement with others—persons and institutions.

When we are not on sure ground, we need to pragmatically keep the conversation going (civility) and we need to pragmatically protect our conversational partners (the other). The conviction of a postmodern culture is that talk with another can reveal narrative structures as communicative background that can guide us in this historical moment. The notions of civility and the other take us from insensitivity and meism to the opportunities that "we" can locate together. Pragmatically, we suggest that the metaphors of civility and other need to guide us in this historical moment.

A Call for Dialogic Civility

One of the authors sat in an administrative meeting with another professor of communication and the chairperson of an applied sci-ence area. The topic of discussion was the difficulty of teaching stu-dents in a service course designed for applied science students. Arrogance, demands, impatience, anger, and even temper tantrums were common in their classroom behavior. Three faculty over a three-year period had been run out of the classroom by these stu-dents; the faculty refused to ever teach the course again. Our task was to figure out why the course over a three-year period with dif-ferent instructors had been so problematic for both teachers and students. For the first time in our university careers we were met with a sobering realization: "No one wants to teach these students!"

As we explored this unique case we found the students' lack of respect for the teachers as fundamental to the teachers' negative assessment of the class. We found it interesting to note that all three teachers who had been run out of this particular classroom were considered good and in one case outstanding in other settings.

Clearly, we were interested in the question, "What makes the quality of communicative life between the students and the instructor in this course so negative?" Our answer after much investigation and conversation centered on the students' communicative focus of attention. The students were interested in grades. They learned through practice with other instructors that being abrasive paid dividends. They pointed to classes where student learning outcomes were measured by "objective" tests covering applied science facts and application. They noted that in some courses, a published grade distribution list "objectively" stated where they stood among their peers.

In the communication course under question, however, much of the grading was not through "objective" tests, but in the form of "subjective" essays. The students had no "objective" data to trust and not enough experience with the discipline of communication to know when a good to outstanding teacher was actually in their midst. The students simply had limited experience with a "subjective" grading method and with "situational" or "contextual" definitions of communicative competence.

The students were comfortable with the practice of objective grading by instructors; the students made judgments about good teaching unreflectively without considering the paradigmatic differences in subjective and objective or qualitative and quantitative learning. In unreflective practice we act because we are accustomed to engaging in a particular action without weighing alternative possibilities. When these students were thrust into the communication course, they entered a situation that disrupted their unreflective communicative practice. The students could no longer rely upon past practices that they had come to expect and equate with a high quality course. A complaint could no longer in "practice" be stopped by referring to an "objective" test with a clear distribution of grades.

The lack of student effort to treat the instructor with respect was a common theme that we had to address. The students appeared to feel no need to be respectful to a communicator seemingly incapable of talking their language—a language of "objective" justification. Students unleashed blame and anger on instructors in an uncivil fashion; disrespect toward an instructor considered to be a communicative alien was seemingly acceptable behavior. Respect was to be reserved for those more like "me"—meaning they practiced a similar form of communication—"objective justification." When students met an alien "other" who was seemingly unable to communicate with "objective" justification, they engaged in behaviors of intimidation, lack of respect, and outbursts in class, which seemed "appropriate" to them. The students saw as alien any communicator working from a different set of paradigmatic guidelines for communicative competence.

At this point in the meeting the three administrators were left with two options: first, the course could be changed to only "objective" tests or second, the faculty could help students learn how to handle the "subjective" world of "contextual" communicative claims and actions that can make or break a career that requires communicative flexibility and constructive teamwork. In this case all the students were headed to an applied science career that offered interpersonal service to others as well as science knowledge at an assistant level. We chose to pursue the second option of introducing these "objective" communicators to the world of communicative ambiguity and interpersonal imprecision in order to, hopefully, advance their future job prospects, which clearly require not only command of science "facts," but an ability to work in the "subjective" world of interpersonal communication that involves "me" and the "other."

The administrators decided that introducing "difference" in grading was analogous to tolerating and respecting "difference" in communicative styles. We cannot, nor should we expect the other to always be like us—such expectation is the psychological error of projection. The question for us was "How do we introduce an appreciation and a respect for difference?" For us, subjective grading offered students a learning opportunity for working with people of diverse paradigmatic backgrounds.

Generally, change is best invited in an additive, rather than a substitutional fashion. Thus, our goal was to affirm the importance of "objective justification" in communication as the students learned basic applied science issues, and additionally to ask the students to understand when to permit a more "subjective" form of communication to guide interaction with the "other." Giving students the communicative flexibility to walk from one communicative style to another necessitated an awareness of the limits of unreflective "practice" and the importance of praxis—theory-informed action.

Using the language of this work, praxis is communicative action performed thoughtfully out of a knowing narrative structure that offers background guidance for communicative foreground action. We decided to offer a course with a clear narrative base that provided background guidance for why communicative style flexibility is essential—to be successful in the workplace. We wanted to use this communicative problem as an opportunity for students to encounter a communicative background that permits respect for the other and guides understanding as one works with people using different communicative styles.

Our analysis and discussion resulted in the formation of a course centered in a narrative background around a basic human concern—respect for the other. We titled the course, "Communication and Professional Civility." In the language of this work, professionalism is a contextual narrative, communication is the speech act directed toward another, and civility is a metaphor reminding us to offer an interpersonal voice grounded in a basic sense of respect for the other. We wanted to offer a narrative structure to counter the student's unreflective self-centered and intimidating focus. The aim of this book is similar—to offer a metaphor of dialogic civility that reminds us of the importance of the other, not just our own needs; reminding us of respect for the other, translated in a public language as civility. When such a metaphor is given communicative life by many people and directs their lives, it begins to take on narrative significance.

In the example above, our educational process sought to encourage the teacher to respect the student and the student to offer a similar civil gesture. Such a public narrative agreement regarding public respect for the other cannot be assumed in a routinely cynical culture willing to use intimidation to enhance one's own position at the disadvantage of the other. Public interpersonal discourse must include a sense of respect, which has civility as communicative background for an interpersonal exchange.

From Unreflective Practice to Praxis

Offering a narrative alternative to unreflective practices of a culture is not done quickly. The first step in moving out of an unreflective framework is to understand communicative practices that go unexamined in everyday life. The second step is to reflect upon the historically problematic nature of those practices. Most practices were not originally problematic, however, if they are used when a historically appropriate need is no longer present they become problematic. We move to a dysfunctional stage when a practice continues that no longer addresses the historical needs of a given moment. When we recognize the practice and its lack of connection to the historical moment, we can then work to discover a new communicative praxis—theory-informed action—that is sensitive to the historic needs of a given era. When one realizes that a given practice is not appropriate for a historic moment, an invitation to narrative praxis exists. A praxis alternative must be grounded in both why and how; the why refers to the limited nature of a practice and how counters the practice with a guiding narrative—communicative praxis (Schrag 1986). As Leslie A. Baxter and Barbara M. Montgomery, in *Dialogues and Dialectics* (1996), remind us, praxis involves social actors, a genuine situated social life, historicality, concrete practices, and knowing choice. Praxis is the act of real people in real life making real choices that have consequence and importance for their own lives and the lives of those around them.

Using the above scheme of practices, problematics, and praxis, we understand our communicative situation to have developed in the following way. First, early interpersonal authors connected an alternative to a sole focus on information to a therapeutic model in communication that was primarily grounded in the self. This model was one of the first efforts to address the pragmatic implications of how a life could be guided in a time of metanarrative decline. This effort was historically appropriate at that time—remnants of narrative life could be drawn into dialogue with one's own unique view of the world in that given situation. In that moment, the self was story-informed, not narcissistic. Our communicative practices were dependent upon beginning recognition of metanarrative decline and unknowing reliance upon remnants of that narrative as the self tried to make sense out of the emerging changes.

The problematic, however, was given birth after the historical ability of the self to draw upon narrative remnants declined—at that juncture, we had Philip Rieff's *Triumph of the Therapeutic* (1966/1987) without a "community of memory" (Bellah et al. 1985, 152) gleaned from formerly taken-for-granted narrative structures. Carl Rogers and Abraham Maslow are part of a first pragmatic effort to address the loss of a metanarrative. Rogers's self theory and Maslow's science about the self offer a temporary answer. Rogers pointed to a great character who has enough courage to listen to experience in the midst of metanarrative decline. In a time in which people were "talked at," he listened. He showed us that public life need not be grounded only in command. Public life requires us to listen and respond to the other. In a time of change, Maslow sought additive change that did not destroy the other, but offered synthesis, growth, and building. The public life of a scientist in the creation of new theories need not always be substitutional nor an act of destruction of what has come before. Creation can be grounded in additive change.

The problem with their effort is that they tried to construct a biologically informed dialogue model, primarily out of philosophical and counseling practices. The self, in this form, becomes the biological spokesperson for the innate impulses toward constructive behavior. The dialogue is biologically driven and is centered on a premise that the innate nature of a person is neutral or fundamentally good. The focus on self was a historical extension of the American focus on the individual. As Howard Kirschenbaum stated of Rogers's work, he was "as American as apple pie" (1979, 138). The problematic was the power of a scientific language coupled with speculation and good ol' fashioned American optimism placed in the self. While a biological model makes sense from the historical moment from which it was constructed, it is much more difficult to accept such a view in an era in which we are more likely to equate Rogers's and Maslow's sense of optimism as historically limited.

The second wave of interpersonal voices that we examined in this work begin to more closely address our understanding of this postmodern era characterized by a quandary of direction, which we term a *crisis-informed dialogue*. In these cases the dialogue addresses the concrete human situation that is central to the lived experience of the writer. In an era in which public political life upheld collectivism and individualism as polar options, Martin Buber chose the metaphor of the between to remind us of the importance of both self and other. In a time in which exclusion was normative, Carol Gilligan made public space available for woman's voice. Gilligan introduced the voice/inclusion of woman into the public discussion about the moral development of the human being. Paulo Freire's sensitivity to the oppressed in autocratic Brazil led him to understand that at times interpersonal exclusion is preferrable to inclusion with muted voice. As an educator, he outlined an understanding of historically appropriate face saving. In a world of public animosity and consistent dispute, Sissela Bok calls for minimal values that offer a common ground in the celebration of diversity that is central for the twenty-first century. Viktor Frankl's experience of suffering in Nazi concentration camps draws us out of self-preoccupation into the public domain of finding meaning in the midst of disruption. Such an insight is most appropriate in meta-narrative decline and possible collapse. Note that in each case communicative hope is not placed primarily with the individual, but in the action that answers the communicative crisis in which one is grounded. The needed response in a historical moment of metanarrative decline is in dialogue with the crisis that addresses one's life at that specific moment. A problem (problematic) with this form of dialogue emerges when one begins to manufacture crises where they do not really exist. When false crisis propels action, we no longer find meaning in the unique situation before us. Instead, we locate meaning in the midst of our own self-constructed drama.

Finally, we find a *story-informed dialogue* in the interpersonal voices examined in this work—an effort to bring the reader into conversation with an important story. Nel Noddings continues to make public space for the ontological significance of an interpersonal ethic of caring, necessary for a significant relational existence. In a time that publicly called for more attention to the notion of community but did so with psychological and individualistic language, Robert Bellah reminds us of a language of commitment to institutions and to others who are communities of memory for our habits of the heart. He also asks us to have the courage to meet and address broken covenants. Flawed narratives need our assistance, not just condemnation. Neither writer asks us to embrace a metanarrative, but to broaden our narrative horizons as we consider important questions that are appropriate for the historic drama of our time. Each in his or her own way is pointing us to part of the human story that needs to be included, from minimal agreement on values to the importance of human community to the inclusion of difference. Questions of moral education from a feministic perspective, a tale about the importance of minimal common values, and how our *Habits of the Heart* (Bellah et al. 1985) are impacted by an individualistic culture are stories that bring us into dialogue in the public sphere.

The work of Carl Rogers and that of Abraham Maslow leave us looking for answers responsive to the self, to deal with the beginning of metanarrative decline. Martin Buber, Carol Gilligan, Paulo Freire, Sissela Bok, and Viktor Frankl invite us to see the power of the moment of crisis, while Nel Noddings and Robert Bellah call us to listen to the stories of others. The dialogue of biology (self), the dialogue of crisis, and the dialogue of story all seek to inform us, but differently, and each is helpful in its given historical moment. Yet each can become problematic if an unreflective dialogic practice is "inappropriately" followed in the "wrong" historical moment. Dialogic civility is a praxis alternative to our common historical problematic.

Our Historical Problematic

We contend that the communicative problem before us results from living in postmodernity and attempting to use an industrial metaphor as our guide. As we share with students, communication can be understood in three major eras with three central metaphors: communication in an agrarian era is grounded in the metaphor of place, communication in the industrial era centers around the metaphor of self, and communication in the postmodern era or information age is marked by the metaphor of narrative or story. In each of the above, the sense of location or place in which communication is centered is primary. In an agrarian era, the sense of place is physical. In the words of Walter Brueggemann, it is *The Land* (1977). In an industrial era, we were transplanted, moved off the place called home and sent into an urban life in search of employment. In this less secure place, the self could be counted upon—not the owners of production. Finally, in a postmodern era in which the metanarrative structures are no longer in place and we are long past an agrarian perspective, we need to re-place the exhausted metaphor of the self. In this case, the new place becomes the "humble narrative" (Arnett 1997b, 44–45) or a philosophical sense of home. However, if one confuses the decline of metanarratives with the absence of all narratives, we are left with trying to make the focus on self the appropriate answer for every historical moment.

In each era, people look for wisdom and guidance in different places. Both the dialogue of biology of the self and the dialogue of crisis presume that a narrative remnant can assist the self or the self in genuine crisis to find its way. However, in a postmodern era of further narrative decline we cannot count upon narrative remnants to guide ourselves or the other. Our historical moment is dialogically informed by stories we tell one another in our time of narrative confusion. We do not reject any of the above ways of informing dialogue between persons; each has its place historically; each addresses different questions—the first beginning with the metaphor of self, the second with the metaphor of crisis, and the third with the metaphor of story.

Working within the notion of story, we suggest the historically based need for a dialogue of civility that takes the notion of respect in a time of diversity to the public domain and keeps the conversation going. Dialogic civility is a background story that can inform our interpersonal discourse with the other. Similar to the lack of dialogic civility in the classroom, we are suggesting a narrative why to people who may not necessarily see the importance of being civil to another in the public domain of occasional interaction.

We recognize there are both "good" and "bad" narratives. However, our only hope of countering "bad" narratives is to offer different ones in their place. For us, a "bad" background narrative for interpersonal communication is one that does not seriously address the historical moment in which the discourse is taking place. To counter a "bad" narrative, one must first offer a speech act: one must state a position, then have that position assume the dynamics of a good story—which include main characters, drama, and direction. The characteristics of a narrative emerge when large numbers of people begin to believe the speech act spun as a story. A narrative is a corporate act, embraced by multiple people; a story can be told by a single person. Civil dialogue renews a democratic spirit, enables reexamination of the public domain, diminishes exhaustion from the blind alley of a privatized therapeutic age, responds to the pragmatic need for procedural guidelines in a postmodern age, and, finally, offers a pragmatic hope that civility will permit us to keep a conversation going. In the process of civil dialogue, answers to difficult struggles about differences can be located and discussed together.

In this historical moment, we need to resist two temptations: attending only to the self and taking pride in recognizing one crisis after another, pointing out situational limitations without attempting to overcome them. We need to attend to the other and respond to this situation in a historically appropriate fashion. As a friend stated, "I am growing tired of those who take such pride in seeing crises and problems and stroking themselves for their insight. We need human beings willing to roll up their sleeves and respond to problems in ways that seek to alleviate crises. We need those who know that it is not just 'me,' but 'us'—self and other—that make the intentional connection of life meaningful."

We offer a counternarrative to the routine cynicism and narcissism that has been part of our communicative landscape for too long. Ironically, such a set of communicative problems can be partially tied to a view of communication that centered on the self in a different historical era. We have pointed to metaphors of self and crisis as problematic. We do not mean to imply that they are not helpful in appropriate historical situations—however, when self and crisis are used unreflectively they become problematic. Not every concern should center around the self and not every event in life is a crisis. When such terms become part of a landscape of linguistic banality, we lose the ability to attend to the self and pay genuine attention to crisis when historically necessary. Thus, we do not reject these terms, but suggest that they must dialectically take a back seat to the metaphors of the other and responsibility in this communicative moment. In this era, it is difficult for most of us to forget the self and ignore a crisis. We are self-preoccupied and too eager to call attention to crises and problems. With such action in place, dialectical reminders to attend to the other and to have respond-ability are crucial for dialogic engagement to take place.

We are suggesting the importance of a communicative background of respect that addresses a "generalized other" (Benhabib 1992, 158) in order to meet and address the "concrete other" (Benhabib 1992, 159). The generalized other calls for a general set of characteristics and the concrete other calls for our flexibility in being responsible to the unique individual person in the historical moment. The generalized other and the concrete other impact the communicative event in being called to "confirm not only your *humanity* but your human *individuality*" (Benhabib 1992, 158). The dialectic of the generalized other (part of a communicative narrative background) and genuine response to the concrete other (listening and response to the concrete moment) is central to the narrative of dialogic civility. People need to take a minimal set of common values into discourse with the other—common values that embody human respect for the other as we listen with serious intent to the other.

We advocate a dialogic civility lived out in the praxis of discourse and action. Calvin Schrag points toward this dialectical model of a "new humanism" (1986, 214), which we place in more pragmatic discourse terms, dialogic civility. Using Schrag's (1986) insights, we offer dialogic civility as a public alternative to humanism in this historical moment.

So what is the destiny of humanism? Foucault may be right in his prediction that man [or woman] as an invention of recent date will soon be erased like a face drawn in sand at the edge of the sea; but this besiege soon to be erased is but a portrait composed of modern philosophical constructs. In the restored portrait of man [or woman] as decentered subjectivity, sketched on the terrain of communicative praxis, a new humanism [dialogic civility] begins to unfold. This new humanism [dialogic civility] no longer promises invariant def-

initions of a foundational subject, but instead moves about in
a hermeneutical play of perspectival descriptions of the life of
discourse and action. (Schrag 1986, 214)

We point to a dialogic civility that is not foundational but sugges-
tive and responsive to the demands of the historical moment in the
midst of human discourse and action. Respect for the other suggests dialogic civility with pragmatic discourse consequences—it
keeps the conversation going. Out of communicative praxis emerges
a conversational necessity—if respect for the other is ignored the
chances of the discourse opening new horizons are minimal, if not
non-existent. Interpersonal communication needs public, other, and
respond-ability as dialectical companions to private, self, and crisis
discernment. Techniques are driven by an a priori evaluation of
what is needed or required in a given situation. Narratives only
guide; they do not dictate. Thus, a good narrative must carry within
it contradictions (dialectical tension) in order to appropriately
address the needs of a given historical moment.

Practical Philosophy of Dialogic Civility

A practical philosophy begins with a problem. Ours began with
awareness of metanarrative decline and routine cynicism. First,
we chose a philosophical stance from which to approach our communicative situation: we selected historicality and dialogue as
foundational for our work. We then framed dialogic civility as a
narrative goal for our inquiry and framed metanarrative decline
and routine cynicism as the driving rationale for a background
narrative of dialogic civility. We explored the voices of authors
looking for key concepts that might link our historical moment to
the narrative of dialogic civility. These concepts act as metaphors
connecting historicality and narrative (Arnett, in press).

Metaphor is a form of linguistic implementation that provides a
unique response to a given historical moment, while also being
guided by a communicator's narrative framework. Metaphor is a dialogic medium between narrative and historical situation; it points
the communicator in a direction that is appropriate for the historical
moment, while also being directed by the historical moment. Narrative background and historicality influence our understanding and
choice of metaphor. Metaphorical utterance and narrative discourse

are enfolded in a vast poetic sphere. The historical situation and the bias of one's narrative standpoint guide metaphor selection.

Linguistic choices refer beyond what is visibly perceptible. Language allows communicators to construct referential expressions by relying on abstract terms that are commonly used and understood.

> This semantic dynamism, proper to ordinary language, gives a "historicity" to the power of signifying. New possibilities of signifying are opened up, supported by meanings that have already been established. This "historicity" is carried by the attempt at expression made by a speaker who, wanting to formulate a new experience in words, seeks something capable of carrying his [or her] intention in the network of meanings he [or she] finds already established. Thanks to the very instability of meaning, a semantic aim can find the path of its utterance. Therefore, it is always in a particular utterance . . . that the sedimented history of assembled meanings can be recovered in a new semantic aim. (Ricoeur 1975/1977, 298)

Narrative provides the interpretive context for understanding metaphorical significance of communication concepts and action. Numerous narratives compete for connection to the historical moment. In addition, the same metaphor can be used by different narratives to guide communicative action—which is why dialogue is necessary to understand the other in our postmodern age. A web of metaphors that reach out to the other in an act of co-creation can begin to center a theory of interpersonal communication and provide practical reasons for action.

In a narrative of dialogic civility there is not one metaphor, but several we have gleaned from the authors we have discussed. These multiple metaphors form a "web of metaphorical significance" (Arnett 1988, 153–157) that connect the narrative of dialogic civility with our historical moment of cynicism and metanarrative decline. Individually, these metaphors connect the historical moment and guiding narrative, collectively they form the narrative content of dialogic civility.

Our web of metaphorical significance connects historical concerns of metanarrative decline and routine cynicism with public background narrative of dialogic civility. Metaphors carry double duty. Individually they connect action, collectively they frame the narrative vision. With such linguistic power, it is clear that metaphors should be chosen with care.

The following list of metaphors frames the "web of metaphorical significance" of dialogic civility, acting individually as implementers and collectively as narrative guide. Material earlier in these chapters attributes author origination.

- *Listening* to the other and the historical moment
- *Additive change* when possible; avoiding the impulse of domination
- *Between* as a reminder of the life of relationships, not just "me"
- *Voice / inclusion* calling for presence and attentiveness
- *Historically appropriate face saving* that suggests the importance of keeping the person in the conversation
- Finding *meaning in the midst of narrative disruption* that allows us to survive and often prosper in times of change
- An *ethic of care* pointing us to a life in relational service, not just functional survival or narcissistic seeking of comfort and aid from someone else
- A *community of memory* tied to ideas, people, and institutions that require our participation
- A willingness to meet *broken covenants* head on, not denying their brokenness, while finding ways to repair, change and alter a historically recognized flaw or limitation

Metaphors individually implement and guide a person's action; collectively they form a story about dialogic civility that becomes a value system that shapes interaction with others. Interpersonal communication is not value free. Discourse can be guided by unreflective practices or the praxis of knowing theory and action, in this case, dialogic civility. As we enact this web of metaphors in communication with others, we bring into action interpersonal praxis which addresses this historical moment with a sense of realistic hope.

Conclusion—Dialogic Civility

The historical face of dialogic civility is based in change and a willingness to address the problems that impact human development in a given period of time within the public arena. Dialogic civility exists wherever there is genuine effort to offer public change within a conversational context that seeks not violence, but concern for the other and calls for responsible action.

The effort to bring conversation to the public arena and to call one into responsibility to the other is not, of course, a novel idea. People used dialogic civility to call religion to accountability when religion became so institutionally concerned that the person was without a champion. Dialogic civility was a central feature in opening the doors of the Enlightenment. Inquiry, openness, new ideas, and exploration were given support by a focus on the human spirit that no longer saw all the answers in institutions. This country is based upon dialogic civility as a conversational ideal. Jefferson understood the dialectical of dialogic civility for his historical moment—the focus on the individual and the call to concern for the common good. The individual must keep a people free from tyranny and be the same person who works with others to "unite in common efforts for the common good" (Jefferson 1987b, 28). The human spirit of the individual was necessary to break the chains of inflexible institutions and essentially an aristocratic cast system. He wanted an aristocracy not based upon blood line, but rather one based on virtue and talent. "There is no artificial aristocracy, founded on wealth and birth, without either virtue or talents" (Jefferson 1987a, 33). He wanted a public system of merit that could replace an aristocratic world view based upon birthright and wealth. Dialogic civility works to invite the other into the conversation within the public domain where ideas can be evaluated for their virtue and their merit, not their connections to others.

Alasdair MacIntyre, in *After Virtue* (1981/1984), warns of a time without a common virtue structure. But it was Alexis de Tocqueville (1835/1969) who first pointed to such a concern in his distinction between individuality and individualism. Thomas Jefferson, like Alexis de Tocqueville, understood that the focus on the individual is vital, but can fall into what de Tocqueville termed "individualism" (1835/1969, 506). In working to keep institutions from being oppressive, a self-oriented focus (individualism) as an extreme dialectical response may also become problematic. Equating truth with the self in any historical situation is the home of "emotivism" (MacIntyre 1981/1984, 6–22) and "narcissism" (Lasch 1978/1979). Dialogic civility works to keep both institutions and persons concerned about the other as discourse is lived out in the public domain.

We offer a narrative structure that is a "web of metaphors" pointing to a larger narrative—the importance of the other. A narrative is like a philosophical sense of community; it connects us to people, ideas, values, and ways to address real conflicts and struggles. We come to terms with life decisions with a benchmark of those who have come before us and responded to life in ways that made sense and offered insight.

Students asked one of the authors to define a dialogic civility view of interpersonal communication with full knowledge that work as diverse as that of Carl Rogers, Martin Buber, and Sissela Bok are placed in a dialogic framework by the author. The author's response guided the major contribution of this book: "A dialogic civility approach to interpersonal communication is not a technique or a rigid philosophy. It is what Sissela Bok has called common values about the process of communication that conceptualize communication as more than the processing of information and even more than information and relationship, but goes so far as to place a value-laden tone to processing information and relationship in such a fashion as to enhance the notion of respect for the other, even in disagreement."

Our story about dialogic civility is summarized as follows:

1. Interpersonal communication must reclaim the public domain as the major part of communicative interaction in an age of diversity.

2. Respect in the public domain requires a term that reminds us of the public arena—dialogic civility.

3. Dialectical responsiveness calls us to attend to the metaphors of other and responsibility as historically needed emphases in a time of excess emphasis on self and crisis.

4. Dialogic civility keeps the conversation going in a postmodern culture that lacks metanarrative agreement.

5. Dialogic civility embraces a "web of metaphorical significance" that both points to implementation and collectively provides a guiding story for interpersonal interaction. The "web of metaphorical significance" includes listening to the other and the historical moment, additive change that avoids the impulse of domination, "between" as a reminder of the life of relationships, voice/inclusion calling for communicative presence, using historically appropriate face

saving, finding meaning in the midst of narrative disruption, adhering to an ethic of care, connecting to a community of memory, and a willingness to find ways to mend broken covenants.

6. When this "web of metaphorical significance" appropriately addresses a given historical moment and people begin to affirm its relevance, a narrative form of guidance is given birth. A narrative has main characters (a "web of metaphorical significance"), a direction (public respect), and a history (continuing efforts to meet metanarrative decline), and it begins to assume the place of a common (agreed upon) communicative background. At this juncture, a narrative of dialogic civility begins to guide communicative action.

Dialogic civility is ultimately a reminder that life is best lived with concern for self, other, and sensitive implementation with the historical moment, while consistently reminding us that our communicative actions have public consequences that shape the communicative lives of many people. Narratives begin with one voice that makes enough sense that others begin a similar practice. They begin as a speech act, take the form of a story, and when people begin to be collectively guided by a given story, a narrative is given birth. When a story becomes corporate, a narrative structure or communication background is given life. We outlined a story about dialogic civility. Together, we can nurture the narratives that will shape our conversation together in a civil fashion, inviting dialogue among persons of difference in the public sphere of our interpersonal lives together—offering interpersonal hope in the face of routine and unreflective cynicism.

W orks Cited

Abbagnano, Nicola. "Humanism." *The Encyclopedia of Philosophy.* Ed. Paul Edwards. New York: Macmillan, 1967. 69–70.

Adler, Alfred. *The Practice and Theory of Individual Psychology.* Trans. P. Radin. 1929. London: Routledge and Kegan Paul, 1964.

Allport, Gordon. Preface. *Man's Search for Meaning: An Introduction to Logotherapy.* By Viktor Frankl. 1959. New York: Pocket Books, 1974. vii–xiii.

Anderson, Rob. "Dialogue I: Phenomenological Dialogue, Humanistic Psychology, and Pseudo-Walls: A Response and Extension." *Western Journal of Communication* 46 (1982): 344–357.

Anderson, Rob, and Kenneth N. Cissna. *The Martin Buber-Carl Rogers Dialogue: A New Transcript With Commentary.* Albany: SUNY Press, 1997.

Anderson, Rob, Kenneth N. Cissna, and Ronald C. Arnett. *The Reach of Dialogue: Confirmation, Voice and Community.* Cresskill, N.J.: Hampton, 1994.

Arendt, Hannah. *On Revolution.* New York: Viking Press, 1963.

Aristotle. *Nichomachean Ethics.* Trans. Terence Irwin. Indianapolis: Hackett, 1985.

———. *On Rhetoric: A Theory of Civic Discourse.* Trans. George A. Kennedy. New York: Oxford University Press, 1991.

Arnett, Ronald C. "Commencement Address for Professional Studies Degree." Duquesne University Commencement. Pittsburgh, Pa. August 5, 1995.

——. *Communication and Community: Implications of Martin Buber's Dialogue.* 1986. Carbondale: Southern Illinois University Press, 1997a.

——. "Communication and Community in an Age of Diversity." *Communication Ethics in an Age of Diversity.* Ed. Josina M. Makau and Ronald C. Arnett. Urbana: University of Illinois Press, 1997b. 27–47.

——. *Dialogic Education: Conversation About Ideas and Between Persons.* 1992. Carbondale: Southern Illinois University Press, 1997c.

——. "Existential Homelessness: A Contemporary Case for Dialogue." *The Reach of Dialogue: Confirmation, Voice, and Community.* Ed. Rob Anderson, Kenneth N. Cissna, and Ronald C. Arnett. Cresskill, N.J.: Hampton, 1994. 229–245.

——. "Interpersonal *Praxis*: The Interplay of Religious Narrative, Historicality, and Metaphor." *Journal of Communication and Religion* 21 (1998): 141–163.

——. "The Responsibility of a Duquesne Education." Duquesne University Saturday College Commencement. Pittsburgh, Pa. August 3, 1996a.

——. "Rogers and Buber: Similarities, Yet Fundamental Differences." *Western Journal of Communication* 46 (1982): 358–372.

——. "Technicians of Goodness: Ignoring the Narrative Life of Dialogue." *Responsible Communication: Ethical Issues in Business, Industry, and the Professions.* Ed. James J. Jaksa and Michael S. Pritchard. Cresskill, N.J.: Hampton, 1996b. 339–355.

——. "Therapeutic Communication: A Moral *cul de sac.*" *The Dilemma of Anabaptist Piety: Strengthening or Straining the Bonds of Community.* Ed. Stephen L. Longenecker. Camden, Me.: Penobscot Press, 1997d, 149–160.

——. "Toward a Phenomenological Dialogue." *Western Journal of Speech Communication* 45 (1981): 201–212.

Ayres, Joe. "Four Approaches to Interpersonal Communication: Review, Observation, Prognosis." *Western Journal of Speech Communication* 48 (1984): 408–440.

Barnlund, Dean C. "A Transactional Model of Communication." *Foundations of Communication Theory.* Ed. Kenneth K. Sereno and C. David Mortensen. New York: Harper and Row, 1970. 87–94.

Barrett, William. *The Death of the Soul.* New York: Doubleday, 1986.

——. *The Illusion of Technique: A Search for Meaning in a Technological Civilization.* 1978. New York: Doubleday, 1979.

——. *Rhetoric and Civility: Human Development, Narcissism, and the Good Audience.* Albany: SUNY Press, 1991.

Bateson, Gregory. *Steps to an Ecology of Mind.* New York: Ballantine, 1972.

Baxter, Leslie A., and Barbara M. Montgomery. *Relating: Dialogues and Dialectics.* New York: Guilford Press, 1996.

Belasco, James. *Teaching the Elephant to Dance: Empowering Change in Your Organization.* New York: Crown, 1990.

Belenky, Mary Field, Blythe Clinchy, Nancy Goldberger, and Jill Tarule. *Women's Ways of Knowing: The Development of Self, Voice, and Mind.* New York: Basic Books, 1986.

Bellah, Robert. *Beyond Belief: Essays on Religion in a Post-Traditionalist World.* New York: Harper and Row, 1970.

——. *The Broken Covenant: American Civil Religion in Time of Trial.* 1961. New York: Seabury, 1975.

Bellah, Robert N., Richard Madsen, William M. Sullivan, Ann Swidler, and Steven M. Tipton. *The Good Society.* New York: Knopf, 1991.

——. *Habits of the Heart: Individualism and Commitment in American Life.* Berkeley: University of California Press, 1985.

——. *Individualism and Commitment in American Life: Readings on the Theme of Habits of the Heart.* New York: Perennial Library, 1987.

Benhabib, Seyla. *Situating the Self: Gender, Community, and Postmodernism in Contemporary Ethics.* New York: Routledge, 1992.

Benhabib, Seyla, and Fred Dallmayr. *The Communicative Ethics Controversy.* Cambridge, Mass.: MIT Press, 1990.

Berlo, David. *The Process of Communication.* New York: Holt, Rinehart, and Winston, 1960.

Bertalanffy, Ludwig von. *Modern Theories of Development.* New York: Oxford University Press, 1933

Boase, Paul. *The Rhetoric of Christian Socialism.* New York: Random House, 1969.

——. *The Rhetoric of Protest and Reform, 1878–1898.* Athens: Ohio University Press, 1980.

Bok, Sissela. *Common Values.* Columbia: University of Missouri Press, 1995.

——. *Lying: Moral Choice in Public and Private Life.* 1978. New York: Vintage Press, 1979.

———. *Secrets: On the Ethics of Concealment and Revelation.* 1983. New York: Vintage Press, 1984.

———. *A Strategy for Peace: Human Values and the Threat of War.* New York: Pantheon Books, 1989.

Bonhoeffer, Dietrich. *Ethics.* 1949. New York: Macmillan, 1955.

———. *Life Together.* New York: Harper and Row, 1954.

Bormann, Ernest. *The Force of Fantasy: Restoring the American Dream.* Carbondale: Southern Illinois University Press, 1985.

Bronowski, Jacob. *Science and Human Values.* New York: Harper and Row, 1956.

Brown, Charles T., and Paul W. Keller. *Monologue to Dialogue: An Exploration of Interpersonal Communication.* 2nd ed. Englewood Cliffs: Prentice-Hall, 1973.

Brown, Lyn Mikel, and Carol Gilligan. *Meeting at the Crossroads: Women's Psychology and Girls' Development.* Cambridge, Mass.: Harvard University Press, 1992.

Brueggemann, Walter. *Hopeful Imagination: Prophetic Voices in Exile.* Philadelphia: Fortress Press, 1986.

———. *The Land: Place as Gift, Promise, and Challenge in Biblical Faith.* Philadelphia: Fortress Press, 1977.

Buber, Martin. "Autobiographical Fragments." *The Philosophy of Martin Buber.* Ed. Paul A. Schilpp and Maurice Friedman. LaSalle, Ill.: Open Court, 1967a. 3–32.

———. *Believing Humanism.* 1967b. New York: Simon and Schuster, 1969.

———. *Between Man and Man.* 1947. New York: Macmillan, 1965a.

———. "Hope for This Hour." *The Human Dialogue: Perspectives on Communication.* Ed. Floyd W. Matson and Ashley Montagu. New York: Free Press, 1967c. 306–312.

———. *I and Thou.* 2nd ed. Trans. Walter Kaufmann. New York: Charles Scribner's Sons, 1958.

———. *Israel and the World: Essays in a Time of Crisis.* 1948. New York: Schocken Books, 1976.

———. *The Knowledge of Man: A Philosophy of the Interhuman.* 1965b. New York: Harper and Row, 1966a.

———. *Meetings.* LaSalle, Ill.: Open Court, 1973.

———. *Pointing the Way.* Trans., Ed., Maurice S. Friedman. 1957. New York: Schocken Books, 1974.

———. "Replies To My Critics." *The Philosophy of Martin Buber.* Ed. Paul A. Schilpp and Maurice Friedman. LaSalle, Ill.: Open Court, 1967d. 689–746.

———. *The Way of Response: Martin Buber; Selections From His Writings.* Ed. Nahum N. Glatzer. New York: Schocken Books, 1966b.

Callahan, Daniel, and Sissela Bok, eds. *Ethics Teaching in Higher Education.* New York: Plenum Press, 1980.

Camus, Albert. *Resistance, Rebellion, and Death.* 1960. Trans. Justin O'Brien. New York: Vintage Books, 1974.

Cervantes Saavedra, Miguel de. *The History of Don Quixote de la Mancha.* New York: E. P. Dutton, 1909.

Cohen, Herman. *The History of Speech Communication: The Emergence of a Discipline, 1914–1945.* Annandale, Va.: Speech Communication Association, 1994.

Cooley, Charles Horton. *Social Process.* 1918. Carbondale: Southern Illinois University Press, 1966.

Davis, Kathy. "Toward a Feminist Rhetoric: The Gilligan Debate Revisited." *Women's Studies International Forum* 15 (1992): 219–231.

Derrida, Jacques. "The Ends of Man." *After Philosophy: End or Transformation?* Ed. Kenneth Baynes, James Bohman, and Thomas McCarthy. Cambridge: MIT Press, 1987. 119–158.

Douville, Linda M. "The Power of Hope." *American Journal of Nursing* 94.12 (1994): 34–36.

Duncan, Ronald, ed. *Gandhi: Selected Writing.* New York: Harper and Row, 1972.

Ellul, Jacques. *The Humiliation of the Word.* Grand Rapids, Mich.: William B. Eerdmans, 1985.

———. *The Technological Society.* New York: Knopf, 1964.

Elshtain, Jean Bethke. *Democracy on Trial.* 1993. New York: Basic Books, 1995.

Erikson, Erik. *Childhood and Society.* New York: W. W. Norton, 1950.

Eubanks, Eugene. "Reflections on the Moral Dimension of Communication." *Southern Speech Communication Journal* 45 (1980): 297–312.

Farrell, Thomas B. *Norms of Rhetorical Culture.* New Haven: Yale University Press, 1993.

Farson, Richard. "Carl Rogers: Quiet Revolutionary." *Carl Rogers: The Man and His Ideas.* Ed. Richard I. Evans. New York: E. P. Dutton, 1975. xxviii–xliii.

Fisher, Walter R. "Narrative as a Human Communication Paradigm: The Case of Public Moral Argument." *Communication Monographs* 51 (1984): 1–22.

Foucault, Michel. *Power / Knowledge: Selected Interviews and Other Writings.* New York: Pantheon Books, 1980.

Frankl, Viktor. *The Doctor and the Soul.* 1946. New York: Vantage Books, 1973.

———. *Man's Search for Meaning: An Introduction to Logotherapy.* 1959. New York: Pocket Books, 1974.

———. *Psychotherapy and Existentialism: Selected Papers on Logotherapy.* New York: Simon and Schuster, 1967.

———. *The Unheard Cry for Meaning: Psychotherapy and Humanism.* 1977. New York: Simon and Schuster, 1978.

———. *The Will to Meaning: Foundations and Applications of Logotherapy.* New York: New American Library, 1969.

Freire, Paulo. *Cultural Action for Freedom.* 1970. Cambridge: Harvard Educational Review, 1988.

———. *Education for Critical Consciousness.* 1969. New York: Continuum Press, 1996a.

———. *Letters to Christina: Reflections on My Life and Work.* New York: Routledge, 1996b.

———. *Pedagogy of Hope: Reliving Pedagogy of the Oppressed.* 1992. Trans. Robert R. Barr. New York: Continuum Press, 1996c.

———. *Pedagogy of the Oppressed.* 1970. Trans. Myra Bergman Ramos. New York: Seabury, 1974.

———. *The Politics of Education: Culture, Power, and Liberation.* Trans. Donaldo Macedo. South Hadley, Mass.: Bergin and Garvey, 1985.

Freud, Sigmund. *New Introductory Lectures on Psycho-Analysis.* Trans. W. J. H. Sprott. New York: W. W. Norton, 1933.

———. "The Origin and Development of Psychoanalysis." *American Journal of Psychology* 21 (1910): 181–218.

———. *Psychopathology of Everyday Life.* 1900. New York: Macmillan, 1914.

———. *Three Essays on the Theory of Sexuality*. 1905. Trans. James Strachey. New York: Basic Books, 1962.

Friedman, Maurice. *The Confirmation of Otherness in Family, Community, and Society*. New York: The Pilgrim Press, 1983.

———. *Contemporary Psychology: Revealing and Obscuring the Human*. Pittsburgh: Duquesne University Press, 1984.

———. *The Healing Dialogue in Psychotherapy*. New York: Jason Aronson, 1985.

———. *The Human Way: A Dialogic Approach to Religion and Human Experience*. Chambersburg, Pa.: Anima Books, 1982b.

———. "Introductory Essay." *The Knowledge of Man*. By Martin Buber. Ed. Maurice Friedman. New York: Harper and Row, 1965. 11–58.

———. "The Self and the World: Psychologism and Psychotherapy in Martin Buber's *I and Thou*." *Review of Existential Psychology and Psychiatry* 15 (1977): 163–172.

———. *Martin Buber: The Life of Dialogue*. 1955. Chicago: University of Chicago Press, 1976.

———. *Martin Buber's Life and Work: The Early Years 1878–1923*. New York: E. P. Dutton, 1981.

———. *Martin Buber's Life and Work: The Later Years 1945–1965*. New York: E. P. Dutton, 1983b.

———. *Martin Buber's Life and Work: The Middle Years 1923–1945*. New York: E. P. Dutton, 1983a.

———. *Touchstones of Reality: Existential Trust and the Community of Peace*. 1972. New York: E. P. Dutton, 1974.

Gadamer, Hans G. *Dialogue and Dialectic: Eight Hermeneutical Studies on Plato*. New Haven: Yale University Press, 1980.

———. *Reason in the Age of Science*. Cambridge, Mass.: MIT, 1981.

———. "Text and Interpretation." Trans. Dennis J. Schmidt and Richard E. Palmer, *Dialogue and Deconstruction*, Ed. Diane P. Michelfelder and Richard E. Palmer. Albany: SUNY Press, 1989, pp. 21–51.

———. *Truth and Method*. 1960. New York: Crossroad, 1986.

———. *Hermeneutics, Tradition, and Reason*. Trans. Georgia Warnke. Stanford: Stanford University Press, 1987.

Gadotti, Moacir. *Pedagogy of Praxis: A Dialectical Philosophy of Education*. New York: The University of New York Press, 1996.

Geertz, Clifford. *The Interpretation of Cultures.* New York: Basic Books, 1973.

Geiger, Henry. "Introduction." *The Farther Reaches of Human Nature.* 1971. By Abraham H. Maslow. New York: Viking Press, 1973. xv–xxi.

Gergen, Kenneth J. *The Saturated Self: Dilemmas of Identity in Contemporary Life.* New York: Basic Books, 1991.

Gilligan, Carol. "Exit-Voice Dilemmas in Adolescent Development." *Mapping the Moral Domain: A Contribution of Women's Thinking to Psychological Theory and Education.* Ed. Carol Gilligan, Janie Victoria Ward, and Jill McLean Taylor with Betty Bardige. Cambridge, Mass.: Harvard University Press, 1988a. 141–158.

——. "Hearing the Difference: Theorizing Connection." *Hypatia* 10.2 (1995): 120–128.

——. *In a Different Voice: Psychological Theory and Women's Development.* Cambridge, Mass.: Harvard University Press, 1982.

——. "In a Different Voice: Women's Conception of the Self and of Morality." *Harvard Educational Review* 47 (1977): 481–517.

——. "Preface: Teaching Shakespeare's Sister: Notes from the Underground of Female Adolescence." *Making Connections: The Relational Worlds of Adolescent Girls at Emma Willard School.* Ed. Carol Gilligan, Nona P. Lyons, and Trudy J. Hanmer. Cambridge, Mass.: Harvard University Press, 1990a. 6–29.

——. "Prologue." *Making Connections: The Relational Worlds of Adolescent Girls at Emma Willard School.* Ed. Carol Gilligan, Nona P. Lyons, and Trudy J. Hanmer. Cambridge, Mass.: Harvard University Press, 1990b. 1–5.

——. "Prologue: Adolescent Development Reconsidered." *Mapping the Moral Domain: A Contribution of Women's Thinking to Psychological Theory and Education.* Ed. Carol Gilligan, Janie Victoria Ward, and Jill McLean Taylor with Betty Bardige. Cambridge, Mass.: Harvard University Press, 1988b. vii–xxxiv.

——. "Remapping the Moral Domain: New Images of Self in Relationship." *Mapping the Moral Domain: A Contribution of Women's Thinking to Psychological Theory and Education.* Ed. Carol Gilligan, Janie Victoria Ward, and Jill McLean Taylor with Betty Bardige. Cambridge, Mass.: Harvard University Press, 1988c. 3–19.

——. "Women's Psychological Development: Implications for Psychotherapy." *Women, Girls, and Psychotherapy: Reframing Resistance.* Ed. Carol Gilligan, Annie G. Rogers, and Deborah L. Tolman. Binghamton, N.Y.: Harrington Park Press, 1991. 5–31.

Gilligan, Carol, and Jane Attanucci. "Two Moral Orientations." *Mapping the Moral Domain: A Contribution of Women's Thinking to Psychological Theory and Education.* Ed. Carol Gilligan, Janie Victoria Ward, and Jill McLean Taylor with Betty Bardige. Cambridge, Mass.: Harvard University Press, 1988. 73–86.

Gilligan, Carol, Lyn Mikel Brown, and Annie G. Rogers. "Psyche Embedded: A Place for Body, Relationships, and Culture in Personality Theory." *Studying Persons and Lives.* Ed. A. I. Rabin, Robert A. Zucker, Robert A. Emmons, and Susan Frank. New York: Springer Publishing, 1990. 86–147.

Gilligan, Carol, Annie G. Rogers, and Deborah L. Tolman. "Introduction." *Women, Girls, and Psychotherapy: Reframing Resistance.* Ed. Carol Gilligan, Annie G. Rogers, and Deborah L. Tolman. Binghamton, N.Y.: Harrington Park Press, 1991. 1–3.

Gilligan, Carol, and Grant Wiggins. "The Origins of Morality in Early Childhood Relationships." *Mapping the Moral Domain: A Contribution of Women's Thinking to Psychological Theory and Education.* Ed. Carol Gilligan, Janie Victoria Ward, and Jill McLean Taylor with Betty Bardige. Cambridge, Mass.: Harvard University Press, 1988. 111–138.

Glendon, Mary Ann. *Rights Talk: The Impoverishment of Political Discourse.* New York: Free Press, 1991.

Goldfarb, Jeffrey C. *The Cynical Society: The Culture of Politics and the Politics of Culture in American Life.* Chicago: University of Chicago Press, 1991.

Goldstein, Kurt. *The Organism.* New York: American Book Co., 1939.

Greene, Maxine. "Foreword." *Stories Lives Tell: Narrative and Dialogue in Education.* Ed. Carol Witherell and Nel Noddings. New York: Teachers College Press, 1991. ix–xi.

Gurstein, Rochelle. *The Repeal of Reticence.* New York: Hill and Wang. 1996.

Haan, Norma. "Two Moralities in Action Contexts: Relationship to Thought, Ego Regulation, and Development." *Journal of Personality and Social Psychology* 36 (1978): 285–305.

Habermas, Jurgen. *Legitimation Crisis.* Trans. Thomas McCarthy. 1973. Boston: Beacon Press, 1975.

———. *Moral Consciousness and Communicative Action.* Cambridge, Mass.: MIT Press, 1983.

Haiman, Franklyn S. "Democratic Ethics and the Hidden Persuaders." *The Quarterly Journal of Speech* 44 (1958): 385–392.

———. "A Re-examination of the Ethics of Persuasion." *Central States Speech Journal* 3 (1952): 5–10.

———. "The Rhetoric of the Streets: Some Legal and Ethical Considerations." *Quarterly Journal of Speech* 53 (1967): 99–114.

Harding, Sandra. *Whose Science? Whose Knowledge? Thinking from Women's Lives*. Ithaca, N.Y.: Cornell University Press, 1991.

Hartsock, Nancy. "The Feminist Standpoint: Developing the Ground for a Specifically Feminist Historical Materialism." *Discovering Reality: Feminist Perspectives on Epistemology, Metaphysics, Methodology, and Philosophy of Science*. Ed. Sandra Harding and Merrill B. Hintikka. Boston: Reidel, 1983. 283–310.

———. *Money, Sex, and Power: Toward a Feminist Historical Materialism*. Boston: Northeastern University Press, 1985.

Hauerwas, Stanley. *A Community of Character: Toward a Constructive Christian Social Ethic*. Notre Dame: University of Notre Dame Press, 1981.

Hauerwas, Stanley, and David Burrell. *Truthfulness and Tragedy: Further Investigations in Christian Ethics*. Notre Dame: University of Notre Dame Press, 1977.

Heidegger, Martin. *Being and Time*. Trans. John MacQuarrie and Edward Robinson. New York: Harper and Row, 1962.

Herder, Johann Gottfried. *Against Pure Reason: Writings on Religion, Language, and History*. Trans. and Ed. M. Bunge. Minneapolis: Fortress, 1993.

———. *Outlines of a Philosophy of the History of Man*. Trans. T. Churchill. 1800. New York: Bergman Publishers, 1966.

Hirschman, Albert. *Exit, Voice, and Loyalty: Responses to Decline in Firms, Organizations, and States*. Cambridge, Mass.: Harvard University Press, 1970.

Hoffer, Eric. *The True Believer: Thoughts on the Nature of Mass Movements*. New York: Harper and Row, 1951.

Horton, Myles, and Paulo Freire. *We Make the Road by Walking: Conversations About Education and Social Change*. Ed. Brenda Bell, John Gaventa, and John Peters. Philadelphia: Temple University Press, 1990.

Hughes, Robert. *Culture of Complaint: The Fraying of America*. Oxford: Oxford Press, 1993.

Hugo, Victor. *Les Miserables*. 1862. New York: Fawcett Premier, 1961.

Hunter, James D. *Before the Shooting Begins: Searching for Democracy in America's Culture War.* New York: Free Press, 1994.

Husserl, Edmund. *Ideas: General Introduction to Pure Phenomenology.* 1931. London: Collier Books, 1969.

Jefferson, Thomas. "Aristocracy and Liberty." *Individualism and Commitment in American Life: Readings on the Themes of Habits of the Heart.* Ed. Robert N. Bellah, Richard Madsen, William M. Sullivan, Ann Swidler, and Steven M. Tipton. New York: Perennial Library, 1987a. 32–38.

———. "First Inaugural Address." *Individualism and Commitment in American Life: Readings on the Themes of Habits of the Heart.* Ed. Robert N. Bellah, Richard Madsen, William M. Sullivan, Ann Swidler, and Steven M. Tipton. New York: Perennial Library, 1987b. 27–31.

Jung, Carl. *Collected Papers on Analytical Psychology.* Trans. Constance E. Long. London: Baillere, Tindall, and Cox, 1922.

———. *Analytical Psychology.* New York: Moffat Yard, 1916.

Kanter, Donald, and Philip H. Mirvis. *The Cynical Americans: Living and Working in an Age of Discontent and Disillusionment.* New York: W. W. Norton, 1989.

Kelley, William, and Andrew Tallon. *Readings in the Philosophy of Man.* 2nd ed. 1967. New York: McGraw-Hill, 1972.

Kerber, Linda K., Catherine C. Greens, Eleanor E. Maccoby, Zella Luria, Carol B. Stack, and Carol Gilligan. "On *In a Different Voice*: An Interdisciplinary Forum." *Signs* 11 (1986): 304–333.

Kirschenbaum, Howard. *On Becoming Carl Rogers.* New York: Delta, 1979.

Kirschenbaum, Howard, and Valerie Land Henderson. *Carl Rogers: Dialogues.* Boston: Houghton Mifflin, 1989.

Koestler, Arthur. *Darkness at Noon.* Trans. Daphne Hardy. 1941. New York: Bantam Books, 1972.

Kohlberg, Lawrence. "The Development of Modes of Thinking and Choices in Years 10 to 16." Diss. University of Chicago, 1958.

———. "Moral Stages and Moralization: The Cognitive-Developmental Approach." *Moral Development and Behavior: Theory, Research, and Social Issues.* Ed. Thomas Lickona. New York: Rinehart and Winston, 1976. 31–53.

———. *The Philosophy of Moral Development.* San Francisco: Harper and Row, 1981.

————. *The Psychology of Moral Development: Essays on Moral Development, 2.* San Francisco: Harper and Row, 1984.

————. "Stage and Sequence: The Cognitive-Development Approach to Socialization." *Handbook of Socialization Theory and Research.* Ed. David A. Goslin. Chicago: Rand McNally, 1969. 347–380.

Korzybski, A. *Science and Sanity: An Introduction to Non-Aristotelian Systems and General Semantics.* 1933. New York: Science Press, 1948.

Kroeger-Mappes, Joy. "The Ethic of Care vis-a-vis The Ethic of Rights: A Problem for Contemporary Moral Theory." *Hypatia* 9.3 (1994): 108–131.

Kuhn, Thomas. *The Structure of Scientific Revolutions.* Chicago: University of Chicago Press, 1962.

Kurtz, Paul, ed. *Humanistic Manifestos I and II.* 1933. Amherst, N.Y.: Prometheus Books, 1973.

Lapham, Lewis. *The Wish for Kings: Democracy at Bay.* New York: Grove Press, 1993.

Lasch, Christopher. *The Culture of Narcissism: American Life in a Time of Diminishing Expectations.* 1978. New York: W. W. Norton, 1979.

————. *The Minimal Self: Psychic Survival in Troubled Times.* New York: W. W. Norton, 1984.

————. *The True and Only Heaven: Progress and Its Critics.* New York: W. W. Norton, 1991.

————. *The Revolt of the Elites and the Betrayal of Democracy.* New York: W. W. Norton, 1995.

Lee, Harper. *To Kill a Mocking Bird.* New York: J. B. Lippincott, 1960.

Levinas, Emmanuel. *Time and the Other.* 1947. Pittsburgh: Duquesne University Press, 1987.

Lippmann, Walter. *The Public Philosophy.* Boston: Little, Brown and Co., 1955.

Lorde, Audre. *Sister Outsider: Essays and Speeches.* Freedom, Cal.: Crossing Press, 1984.

Luijpen, William. *Phenomenology and Metaphysics.* Pittsburgh: Duquesne University Press, 1965.

Lyotard, Jean-Francois. *The Differend: Phrases in Dispute.* Trans. George Van den Abbeele. Minneapolis: University of Minnesota Press, 1988.

MacIntyre, Alasdair. *After Virtue: A Study in Moral Theory.* 1981. Notre Dame: University of Notre Dame Press, 1984.

Makau, Josina, and Ronald C. Arnett, eds. *Communication Ethics in an Age of Diversity.* Urbana: University of Illinois Press, 1997.

Maslow, Abraham H. *The Farther Reaches of Human Nature.* New York: Viking Press, 1971.

——. *Motivation and Personality.* 3rd ed. 1954. New York: Harper and Row, 1970a.

——, ed. *New Knowledge in Human Values.* 1959. Chicago: H. Regnery, 1970b.

——. *The Psychology of Science: A Reconnaissance.* 1966. Chicago: Henry Regnery, 1969.

——. *Religion, Values, and Peak-Experiences.* 1964. New York: Viking Press, 1970c.

——. *Toward a Psychology of Being.* 2nd ed. 1962. New York: D. Van Nostrand Co., 1968.

Matson, Floyd. *The Broken Image.* New York: Braziller, 1964.

May, Rollo. *Power and Innocence: A Search for the Sources of Violence.* 1972. New York: Dell, 1976.

Nichols, Marie Hochmuth. "When You Set Out For Ithaka . . ." *Central States Speech Journal* 28 (1977): 145–156.

Niebuhr, Reinhold. *The Irony of American History.* New York: Charles Scribner's Sons, 1952.

Noddings, Nel. *Caring: A Feminine Approach to Ethics and Moral Education.* Berkeley: University of California Press, 1984.

——. *The Challenge to Care in Schools: An Alternative Approach to Education.* New York: Teachers College Press, 1992.

——. "Constructivism in Mathematics Education." *Constructivist Views on the Teaching and Learning of Mathematics.* Ed. Robert B. Davis, Carolyn A. Maher, and Nel Noddings. Reston, Va.: National Council on Teachers of Mathematics, 1990. 7–19.

——. *Philosophy of Education.* Boulder: Westview Press, 1995.

——. "Stories in Dialogue: Caring and Interpersonal Reasoning." *Stories Lives Tell: Narrative and Dialogue in Education.* Ed. Carol Witherell and Nel Noddings. New York: Teachers College Press, 1991. 157–170.

——. *Women and Evil.* Berkeley: University of California Press, 1989.

Noddings, Nel, and Paul J. Shore. *Awakening the Inner Eye: Intuition in Education.* New York: Teachers College Press, 1984.

Nouwen, Henri J. M. *The Wounded Healer*. 1972. New York: Doubleday, 1979.

Piaget, Jean. *The Moral Judgment of the Child*. 1932. New York: Free Press, 1965.

Polanyi, Michael. *Personal Knowledge*. Chicago: University of Chicago Press, 1958.

———. *The Study of Man*. Chicago: University of Chicago Press, 1959.

Rapoport, Anatol. "Strategy and Conscience." *The Human Dialogue: Perspectives on Communication*. Ed. Floyd W. Matson and Ashley Montagu. New York: Free Press, 1967. 79–96.

Ricoeur, Paul. *The Rule of Metaphor: Multi-disciplinary Studies in the Creation of Meaning in Language*. Trans. Robert Czerny with Kathleen McLaughlin and John Costello. 1975. Toronto: University of Toronto Press, 1977.

———. *Time and Narrative, Vol. 1*. 1983. Chicago: University of Chicago Press, 1984.

Rieff, Philip. *The Feeling Intellect: Selected Writings*. Chicago: University of Chicago Press, 1990.

———. *The Triumph of the Therapeutic: Uses of Faith after Freud*. 1966. Chicago: University of Chicago Press, 1987.

Rogers, Carl. *Becoming Partners: Marriage and its Alternatives*. New York: Dell Publishing, 1972.

———. *On Becoming a Person: A Therapist's View of Psychotherapy*. Boston: Houghton Mifflin, 1961.

———. *Client-Centered Therapy*. 1951. Boston: Houghton Mifflin, 1965.

———. *Freedom to Learn*. Columbus: Charles E. Merrill Publishing, 1969.

———. "A Human Science." *The Carl Rogers Reader*. Ed. Howard Kirschenbaum and Valerie Land Henderson. Boston: Houghton Mifflin, 1989. 259–295.

———. *A Way of Being*. Boston: Houghton Mifflin, 1980.

Rogers, Carl, and Barry Stevens. *Person to Person: The Problem of Being Human*. 1967. New York: Simon and Schuster, 1972.

Rorty, Richard. *Philosophy and the Mirror of Nature*. Princeton: Princeton University Press, 1979.

Sartre, Jean-Paul. *Being and Nothingness: An Essay on Phenomenological Ontology*. Trans. Hazel E. Barnes. New York: Washington Square Press, 1953.

Sauvage, Micheline. *Socrates and the Human Conscience.* Trans. Patrick Hepburne-Scott. New York: Harper, 1961.

Scannell, Margie L. "Mrs. C. . . . Numerous Medical Problems Only Made Her Stronger." *Gastroenterology Nursing* 16.3 (1993): 131–132.

Schrag, Calvin O. *Communicative Praxis and the Space of Subjectivity.* Bloomington: Indiana University Press, 1986.

———. *The Self After Postmodernity.* New Haven: Yale University Press, 1997.

Schultz, Emily A. *Dialogue at the Margins: Whorf, Bakhtin, and Linguistic Relativity.* Madison: University of Wisconsin Press, 1990.

Sennett, Richard. *Authority.* New York: Knopf, 1980.

———. *The Fall of Public Man.* 1974. New York: W. W. Norton, 1992.

Sherif, Muzafer. "Superordinate Goals in the Reduction of Intergroup Conflicts." *American Journal of Sociology* 63 (1958): 349–356.

Shor, Ira, and Paulo Freire. *A Pedagogy for Liberation: Dialogues on Transforming Education.* New York: Bergin and Garvey, 1987.

Sinclair, Upton. *The Jungle.* 1905. New York: The New American Library, 1960.

Skinner, B. F. (Burrhus Frederic). *Beyond Freedom and Dignity.* New York: Knopf, 1971.

Spielberg, Steven, dir. *Schindler's List.* Universal City Studios, Inc., 1993.

Spitzack, Carole. *Confessing Excess: Women and the Politics of Body Reduction.* Albany: SUNY Press, 1990.

Stewart, David, and Algis Mickunas. *Exploring Phenomenology.* Chicago: American Library Association, 1974.

Stewart, John. *Beyond the Symbol Model: Reflections on the Representational Nature of Language.* Albany: SUNY Press, 1996.

———. *Bridges Not Walls: A Book About Interpersonal Communication.* Reading, Mass.: Addison-Wesley, 1973.

———. *Bridges Not Walls: A Book About Interpersonal Communication.* 2nd ed. Reading, Mass.: Addison-Wesley, 1977.

———. *Bridges Not Walls: A Book About Interpersonal Communication.* 3rd ed. New York: Random House, 1982.

———. *Bridges Not Walls: A Book About Interpersonal Communication.* 4th ed. New York: Random House, 1986.

———. *Bridges Not Walls: A Book About Interpersonal Communication.* 5th ed. New York: McGraw-Hill, 1990.

———. *Bridges Not Walls: A Book About Interpersonal Communication.* 6th ed. New York: McGraw-Hill, 1994.

———. *Bridges Not Walls: A Book About Interpersonal Communication.* 7th ed. New York: McGraw-Hill, 1995a.

———. "Interpretive Listening: An Alternative to Empathy." *Communication Education* 32 (1983): 379–391.

———. *Language as Articulate Contact: Toward a Post-Semiotic Philosophy of Communication.* Albany: SUNY Press, 1995b.

Stewart, John, and Carole Logan. *Together: Communicating Interpersonally.* 4th ed. New York: McGraw-Hill, 1993.

Stone, Isador F. *The Trial of Socrates.* Boston: Little, Brown and Co., 1988.

Sykes, Charles J. *Dumbing Down Our Kids: Why American Children Feel Good About Themselves But Can't Read, Write, or Add.* New York: St. Martin's Griffin, 1995.

Taylor, Charles. *The Ethics of Authenticity.* Cambridge, Mass.: Harvard University Press, 1991.

Taylor, Daniel. *The Healing Power of Stories: Creating Yourself Through the Stories of Your Life.* New York: Doubleday, 1996.

Thatcher, V. S., ed. *The New Webster Encyclopedic Dictionary of the English Language.* 1965. Chicago: Consolidated, 1969.

"This Does Not Happen Here." *Newsweek* 1 May 1995: 24–27.

Tocqueville, Alexis de. *Democracy in America.* 1835. Trans. George Lawrence. Ed. J. P. Mayer. Garden City, N.Y.: Anchor Books, 1969.

Toffler, Alvin, and Heidi Toffler. *War and Anti-War: Survival at the Dawn of the 21st Century.* Boston: Little, Brown and Co., 1993.

Tracy, David. *Plurality and Ambiguity: Hermeneutics, Religion, and Hope.* Chicago: University of Chicago Press, 1987.

Vico, Giambatista. *On Humanistic Education: Six Inaugural Orations, 1699–1707.* Trans. Giorgio A. Pinton and Arthur W Shippee. Ithaca: Cornell University Press, 1993.

Voltaire, Francois Marie Arouet de. *Candide.* 1962. New York: Washington Square Press, 1966.

Wallace, Karl R. "Education and Speech Education Tomorrow." *The Quarterly Journal of Speech* 36 (1950): 177–183.

———. "An Ethical Basis of Communication." *Communication Education* 4 (1955): 1–9.

———. "A Glance Ahead at the Field of Speech." *The Quarterly Journal of Speech* 30 (1944): 383–387.

———. "The Substance of Rhetoric: Good Reasons." *The Quarterly Journal of Speech* 49 (1963): 239–249.

Warnke, Georgia, trans. *Hermeneutics, Tradition, and Reason.* By Hans G. Gadamer. Stanford: Stanford University Press, 1987.

Watson, John B. *Psychology, From the Standpoint of a Behaviorist.* Philadelphia: J. B. Lippincott Co., 1919.

Watzlawick, Paul, Janet Beavin, and Don Jackson. *Pragmatics of Human Communication: A Study of Interactional Patterns, Pathologies, and Paradoxes.* New York: W. W. Norton, 1967.

Weaver, Richard. *Ideas Have Consequences.* Chicago: University of Chicago Press, 1948.

Webster's New Collegiate Dictionary. Ed. Henry Bosley Woolf. Springfield, Mass.: G and C Merriam Co., 1974.

Weil, Simone. *The Need for Roots: Prelude to a Declaration of Duties Towards Mankind.* 1952. New York: Routledge and Kegan Paul, 1987.

White, Kenneth W. "Hans-Georg Gadamer's Philosophy of Language." *Interpretive Approaches to Interpersonal Communication.* Ed. Kathryn Carter and Mick Presnell. Albany: SUNY Press, 1994. 83–114.

Whyte, William. *The Organization Man.* 1956. New York: Doubleday, 1957.

Wiesel, Elie, and Philippe de Saint-Cheron. *Evil and Exile.* Notre Dame: Notre Dame University Press, 1990.

Witherell, Carol. "The Self in Narrative: A Journey Into Paradox." *Stories Lives Tell: Narrative and Dialogue in Education.* Ed. Carol Witherell and Nel Noddings. New York: Teachers College Press, 1991. 83–95.

Witherell, Carol, and Nel Noddings. "Narrative and Notions of the Self and the Other." *Stories Lives Tell: Narrative and Dialogue in Education.* Ed. Carol Witherell and Nel Noddings. New York: Teachers College Press, 1991a. 79–81.

———. "Prologue: An Invitation to Our Readers." *Stories Lives Tell: Narrative and Dialogue in Education.* Ed. Carol Witherell and Nel Noddings. New York: Teachers College Press, 1991b. 1–12.

Wood, Julia T. "Different Voices in Relationship Crises: An Extension of Gilligan's Theory." *American Behavioral Scientist* 29 (1986): 273–301.

———. "Gender and Moral Voice: Moving From Woman's Nature to Standpoint Epistemology." *Women's Studies in Communication* 15 (1992): 1–24.

———. *Relational Communication: Continuity and Change in Personal Relationships*. Belmont, Cal.: Wadsworth, 1995.

———. *Who Cares?: Women, Care, and Culture*. Carbondale: Southern Illinois University Press, 1994.

Index

Abbagnano, Nicola, 53, 305
action: dialogical theory of, 167; disconnected from language, 17–19; thoughtful, 211–215. See also meaning, in action; moral, action; responsibility, for actions; wisdom, of action
Adler, Alfred, 87, 305
Adorno, Theodor, 51
agrarian age, 215, 227. See also metaphor, of place
Allport, Gordon, 60, 209, 305
American Dream, 94–95, 256, 262, 264
Anderson, Rob, 84, 91, 305
Arendt, Hannah, 56, 113, 280, 305
Aristotle, 8, 44, 54, 66, 121, 139, 229, 241, 285, 305
Arnett, Ronald C., 8, 12, 16, 46, 49, 52, 57, 76, 84, 91, 135, 137, 146, 179–180, 194, 214, 219, 228, 256, 280, 283, 285, 287, 296, 299–300, 305–306
Attanucci, Jane, 153, 313
Augustine, 207
authenticity, 145–146
Ayres, Joe, 39, 306

bad faith, 16, 116, 184
Barnlund, Dean, 31, 306

Barrett, Harold, 228, 287–288
Barrett, William, 62, 172, 306–307
baseball, 58–60, 133, 222–223
Bateson, Gregory, 57, 307
Baxter, Leslie A., 293, 307
Baynes, Kenneth, 51
Beavin, Janet, 214, 321
being-in-the-world, 132
Belasco, James, 36, 307
Belenky, Mary, 22, 307
Bellah, Robert, 5, 15, 49, 58, 63–64, 66, 85, 101, 122, 252, 255–274, 287–288, 293, 295, 307
Benhabib, Seyla, 4, 47, 52, 56, 76, 85, 184, 280, 298, 307
Berlo, David, 30, 307
Bernstein, Richard, 113, 191, 282
Bertalanffy, Ludwig von, 105, 307
between, 129–130; horizon of, 130–132; nature of, 132–136
Bible, 56, 63, 258
Bildung, 29, 41, 54
blind faith, 210
Boase, Paul, 46, 307
Bohman, James, 51
Bok, Sissela, 5, 189–206, 271, 284, 295, 303, 307–309
Bonhoeffer, Dietrich, 92, 210, 308
Bormann, Ernest, 95, 308
broken covenant. See covenant

323

Bronowski, Jacob, 105, 308
Brown, Charles, 91, 308
Brown, Lyn Mikel, 149, 153–154, 158–159, 162, 164–165, 308, 313
Brueggemann, Walter, 206, 296, 308
Buber, Martin, 5, 8, 15, 16, 27, 32, 40, 45, 49, 62, 73, 84, 91, 98–99, 127–147, 176, 186, 209, 244–246, 253, 264, 294–295, 303, 308–309
Burrell, David, 237, 314

Caligula, 205
Callahan, Daniel, 201, 205, 309
Camus, Albert, 210, 309
care: ethic of, 243–246; in relation, 243–245; responsibility to, 155, 164; risks of, 245–246; story of, 238–239, 243
Cervantes Saavedra, Miguel de, 14, 309
change: additive, 109–110, 112–113; communicative, 30–31; limits of, 255; substitutional, 110, 112, 123. *See also* narrative, change; science, additive approach to, change
character: great, 62, 84, 143; of modern life, 265–266
Churchill, Winston, 47
Cissna, Kenneth, 84, 91, 305
civility, 6, 55, 71; foundation for, 284; and the other, 288–289. *See also* dialogic civility; other, civility and the; respect, civility
Clinchy, Blythe, 22
Cohen, Herman, 15, 309
collectivism, dangers of, 129
common: center of discourse, 128–129; good, 271–272; ground, 52–53, 59; sense, 43–46; values, 203–204. *See also* interpersonal, commonplaces
communication: basic forms of, 143–145; gender differences in, 149–150; process, 31; without ethical coherence, 194–197. *See also* crisis, of communication; interpersonal, communication
community: inviting, 272–273; of memory, 273; *sensus communis*, 43, 44, 54. *See also* story, based view of community
concentration camps, 24, 60, 209, 212, 229, 294
confirmation of otherness, 40–41. *See also* other
connection: disconnection, 158–160; re-connection, 160–161
Cooley, Charles Horton, 44, 309
courage, 228–229
covenant: broken, 267–270; new, 14
crisis: of adolescence, 158–162; of communication, 214, 294–295; of ethics, 191, 197; of exclusion, 151; of illiteracy, 169; informed dialogue, 294; manufactured, 16, 295; of meaning, 208; trivialization of, 16. *See also* moral, crisis
critical: consciousness, 182–184; thinking, 185
culture of silence, 180–181
cynicism, 22–23; and hope, 23–25; routine, 12–15, 20–22; situationally appropriate, 12, 17

Dallmayr, Fred, 76, 307
Darman, Richard, 119
Davis, Kathy, 151, 309
Debs, Eugene, 259
democracy, 14–15, 46–48, 258–259, 269; Athenian, 113, 117
Derrida, Jacques, 85, 309
dialectic: of cynicism and hope, 25–28; dance, 161–162; of good and evil, 209; of individual and community, 44, 55, 234, 256; practical, 41–43; of tradition and change, 62
dialogic: limits, 38–39; perspective, 39–41; view of narrative, 38. *See*

also dialogue; education, dialogic; self, dialogic; voice, dialogic

dialogic civility, 277, 301–304; call for, 289–292; minimal foundation for, 284–286; narrative of, 282, 286–287; new humanism, 298–299. *See also* historicality, and dialogic civility; limits, undergird dialogic civility; philosophy, practical

dialogue, 32, 39, 55, 143–145, 184–186; and crisis, 79, 125–229; genuine, 143–145; phenomenological, 46; and self, 79, 81–123; and story, 79, 231–275; technical, 143–145. *See also* public, dialogue; monologue

diversity, 6, 9, 12, 14, 50, 252

Douville, Linda, 229, 309

Duncan, Ronald, 228, 309

education: additive, 110–111; banking concept of, 181–183; dialogic, 8, 169, 171–172, 219; doubting model of, 22; liberating, 167; moral, 205, 239–241; purpose of, 122–123, 184; relational, 246; task of teacher, 137–138, 173. *See also Bildung*; hope, education provides; interpersonal, pedagogy; saving face, of a learner

Elshtain, Jean Bethke, 14, 283, 285, 309

Eliot, T. S., 62

Ellul, Jacques, 18, 138, 147, 172, 309

emotivism, 55, 62–63

empathy, 98–99

Enlightenment, 49, 113, 282–283, 302; pre-, 257

enthymeme, 139

entitlement, 100, 172, 186

Erasmus, 141

Erikson, Erik, 152, 309

ethical: bias, 55–56; coherence, 194–197; commitment, 54; self, 101

ethics, 15; communicative, 184; discourse, 286; minimalist, 197, 204; and postmodernity, 193–194; of rights, 155; relational, 234–235, 239; revolutionary, 202; re-storying, 235–241; traditional, 235–237. *See also* care, ethic of; crisis, of ethics; justice, ethic of; narrative, ethic

Eubanks, Eugene, 272, 309

evil, 111, 209; forms of, 242–243; impulse, 68; reducing, 242–243; states of consciousness associated with, 242

exclusion, 154

experiential knowing, 83, 114

faith, 68, 141

Farrell, Thomas, 51, 309

Farson, Richard, 87, 310

Fisher, Walter, 47, 49, 66, 273, 310

focus: of attention, 127, 132–134, 145; on connection, 150; dereflection, 225; hyperreflection, 223; on life, 142; paradoxical intention, 225; on self, 142

Foucault, Michel, 85, 298, 310

Frankl, Viktor, 5, 23, 24, 25, 60, 207–229, 248, 294–295, 310

freedom, 223

Freire, Paul, 5, 167–187, 240, 294–295, 310–311, 314, 319

Freud, Sigmund, 87, 154, 224, 310

Friedman, Maurice, 15, 40, 41, 99, 135, 246, 256–257, 260, 264, 311

friend, 18

Fromm, Erich, 73

Gadamer, Hans-Georg, 3, 17, 29, 30, 39, 41, 42, 43, 54–55, 142, 185, 212, 311

Gadotti, Moacir, 172, 311

Gandhi, Mahatma, 228

Geertz, Clifford, 204, 312
Geiger, Henry, 111, 312
Gergen, Kenneth, 194–195,
    288–289, 312
gestalt, 57, 96
Gilligan, Carol, 5, 149–166,
    294–295, 308, 312–313, 315
Glatzer, Nahum, 32
Glendon, Mary Ann, 73, 313
Goebbels, Joseph, 205
Goethe, 207
Goldberger, Nancy, 22
Goldfarb, Jeffrey, 11, 23, 313
Goldstein, Kurt, 104, 313
gossip, 201
Greene, Maxine, 233, 313
Greens, Catherine, 151, 315
guilt: existential, 246; implies story-
    laden people, 245; neurotic, 246
Gurstein, Rochelle, 65, 313

Haan, Norma, 250, 313
Habermas, Jurgen, 47, 184, 267,
    286, 313
habits of the heart, 258–259,
    263–264
Haiman, Franklyn, 46, 286,
    313–314
Harding, Sandra, 165, 314
Hartsock, Nancy, 165, 314
Hasidic: tales, 137; teachers, 25
Hauerwas, Stanley, 15, 49, 66, 237,
    314
health: psychological, 111–114, 121,
    150. *See also* interpersonal,
    health
Heidegger, Martin, 239, 243, 314
Henderson, Valerie Land, 93, 315
hermeneutic: constructivist, 277;
    deconstructive, 18, 277; philo-
    sophical, 30, 42, 64, 212
Hirschman, Albert, 164, 314
historical: bias, 42, 43; conscious-
    ness, 29; grounding, 92–93;
    moment, 34–38; problematic,
    296–299; situatedness, 29

historicality, 31–32; and dialogic
    civility, 100–102, 122–123,
    146–147, 164–166, 186–187,
    204–206, 227–229, 253,
    273–275; historicity, 300. *See
    also* dialogue, and crisis, and
    self, and story
Hitler, Adolph, 47, 73, 208
Hoffer, Eric, 113, 314
Holocaust, 25, 27
Hoover, J. Edgar, 22
hope, 8, 12, 23–28, 189; and opti-
    mism, 51; education provides,
    109; false, 104; within limits,
    25–28. *See also* narrative, hope
horizon of significance, 6–7, 27–28
Horkheimer, Max, 51
Horton, Myles, 170, 314
Hughes, Robert, 195–196, 314
Hugo, Victor, 21, 314
human organism: innate wisdom
    of, 97–98
humanism, 53–54
humanistic psychology, 53, 84, 110,
    261–262
humility, 170
Hunter, James, 11, 315
Husserl, Edmund, 132–135, 315

I-it, 140–141
I-Thou, 42, 99, 135, 140–141, 244,
    253, 260, 264
ideological: meaning structures, 53;
    thought, 69
ideology, 38, 181, 267; of intimacy, 50
identity, 258–266
inclusion, 154; and conflict of
    attachment, 160; limits of,
    175–179; and voice, 164
individualism, 259–262
industrial age, 215. *See also*
    metaphor, of self
information age, 215. *See also*
    metaphor, of story
intentionality, 132–133, 135, 140,
    143

interpersonal: commonplaces, 46–50; communication, 7–8; health, 114–115; pedagogy, 170–179; praxis, 43–46; reasoning, 246–252; relationship, 98–100; rootlessness, 6, 15; suspicion, 15–17. *See also* narrative, ethic; therapeutic, model of interpersonal communication

intuition, 246–252: complementary to reason, 248–249; intuitive capacities, 247. *See also* moral, intuition

Jackson, Don, 214, 321
James, William, 228
Jaspers, Karl, 216
Jefferson, Thomas, 272, 302, 315
Jung, Carl, 87, 315
justice, 155–156; ethic of, 165

Kafka, Franz, 68
Kanter, Donald, 13, 22, 315
Keller, Paul, 91, 308
Kelley, William, 132, 315
Kennedy, John F., 47, 105
Kennedy, Robert, 47
Kerber, Linda, 151, 315
King, Martin Luther, Jr., 47, 189
Kirschenbaum, Howard, 83–84, 87, 93, 96, 294, 315
Koestler, Arthur, 202, 315
Kohlberg, Lawrence, 150, 152–154, 315–316
Korzybski, A., 64, 316
Kroegor Mappes, Joy, 151, 154, 163, 316
Kuhn, Thomas, 105, 316
Kurtz, Paul, 56, 316

Lapham, Lewis, 118–119, 316
Lasch, Christopher, 12, 16, 19, 26, 35, 45, 52, 59, 69, 77, 93, 142, 187, 302, 316
Lee, Harper, 71, 316
Levinas, Emmanuel, 76, 316

limits, 39, 41, 45; historical, 59, 64; limitedness, 43; transcend, 112; undergird dialogic civility, 39. *See also* change, limits of; dialogic, limits; hope, within limits; inclusion, limits of; story, limits of; therapeutic, limits
Lippmann, Walter, 71–73, 316
listening: to the historical moment, 38, 41; to the other, 91–92, 301
Litt, Theodor, 43
Logan, Carole, 40, 320
logotherapy, 23, 60, 208, 211, 216, 218–220
Lorde, Audre, 153, 316
loyalty, 201–202
Luijpen, William, 132, 316
Luria, Zella, 151, 315
lying, 197–200
Lyotard, Jean-Francois, 85, 316

Maccoby, Eleanor, 151, 315
MacIntyre, Alasdair, 15, 19, 49, 51, 60–62, 64, 66–67, 85, 184, 265–267, 269, 302, 316
Madison, James, 259
Madsen, Richard, 5, 15, 49, 63, 101, 252, 256, 307
Makau, Josina, 12, 317
Maris, Roger, 58
Marx, Karl, 172
Maslow, Abraham, 5, 87, 103–123, 150, 293, 295, 317
Matson, Floyd, 105, 317
May, Rollo, 23, 317
McCarthy, Thomas, 51
McGwire, Mark, 59
meaning, 226; in action, 213; choosing, 224–227; discovering, 221–223; existential vacuum, 227; in suffering, 208; intersubjective, 132; and story, 249–252; tripod of, 221–222. *See also* logotherapy; narrative, carrier of meaning; responsibility, in meaning discovery; story, meaning

mentor, 118, 122, 145, 185, 219–220, 238–239
metanarrative, 7, 52, 54; decline, 62–64
metaphor, 6, 299–301; of place, 296; of self, 5, 296; of story, 5, 296; therapeutic, 64–71; web of metaphorical significance, 300–301, 303–304. *See also* agrarian age, industrial age; information age; therapeutic, metaphor
Mickunas, Algis, 133, 319
Mirvis, Phillip, 13, 22, 315
monologue, 143–146. *See also* dialogue
Montgomery, Barbara M., 293, 307
moral, 19; action, 161, 234; conflict, 161; crisis, 77, 150; cul de sac, 306; decision-making, 149, 154, 155; development, 150–151, 155, 157, 166; ecology, 63–64; intuition, 247; judgment, 150; reasoning, 150; self, 150; theory, 155, 164–165; voice, 149–150, 153. *See also* story, moral; voice, moral
morality, 162, 235; of care, 162–164
motivation, human, 117–121

narcissism, 142, 172, 187, 302
narrative, 6–7; background, 57–61; bad, 181, 210, 297; carrier of meaning, 210–211; change, 95; decline, 85; destruction, 128; development process, 182, 297; ethic, 74–78; good, 210, 297; guidance, 19, 77, 86, 147; hope, 51; humble, 52, 194, 280, 286–287, 296; praxis of, 279; public, 52, 55–56, 59, 63, 71–74; remnants, 89, 101; of science, 104, 109; sickness, 181–182; structure, 53–57. *See also* dialogic civility, narrative of; respect, narrative of; responsibility, narrative of

narrow ridge, 73, 129, 142
Nichols, Marie Hochmuth, 46, 317
Niebuhr, Reinhold, 196, 317
Nietzsche, Friedrich, 60, 119, 208
Nixon, Richard, 85
Noddings, Nel, 5, 101, 233–253, 295, 317, 321
noema, 133
noesis, 133
Nouwen, Henri, 112, 318
Nuremberg Trials, 85

ontological blindness, 213
openness, 176, 192, 201
optimism, 20–21; false, 25, 208; frail, 77; pragmatic, 86; unmet, 152; undue, 8, 75; unrealistic, 21, 35. *See also* hope, and optimism
other, 76–77; affirming the, 173–175; civility and the, 288–289; concern for the, 205; otherness, 41, 134–135; turning to the, 98–100. *See also* listening, to the other; respect, for the other; standpoint, of the other

partisanship, pathology of, 201–202
peace, 201–203
peak-experience, 121–122
Peters, R. S., 93
phronesis, 44, 46, 57, 285
philosophy: practical, 299–301; public 71–74. *See also* narrative, public
Piaget, Jean, 152, 154, 318
place. *See* metaphor, of place
Plato, 285
play, 142
pleasure principle, 224
poetic, communicative, 140–142
Polanyi, Michael, 105, 318
postmodernity, 193–194, 199
pot of gold, 136–137

power, 127
practice, 6; to praxis, 292–295; of
    identity, 258–259
pragmatic spiritualism, 216–218
praxis, 6, 171–173. *See also* inter-
    personal, praxis; narrative,
    praxis of; practice, to praxis;
    understanding, praxis as ground
    for
privacy, 200–201
public, 202; dialogue, 75, 77, 150;
    discourse, 74, 281–283; domain,
    66, 303; good, 71–72; virtue, 7,
    19. *See also* narrative, public;
    respect, public

Rapoport, Anatol, 107, 318
Reagan, Ronald, 119
relational neglect, 239
relationship, 98–100; grounded car-
    ing, 161. *See also* interpersonal,
    relationship
Renaissance: Italian, 53; Western,
    54
respect, 52–56; civility, 286–288;
    for the other, 74, 191, 285,
    287–288, 292; public, 7, 8, 173,
    277, 303; deserved, 118; narra-
    tive of, 280–281
responsibility: call to, 70, 302; for
    actions, 71; narrative of, 69;
    political, 183; in meaning dis-
    covery, 217; social, 15. *See also*
    care, responsibility to
rhetorical overreach, 22
Ricoeur, Paul, 42, 279, 300, 318
Rieff, Philip, 30, 64–65, 67–69, 257,
    281, 293, 318
Robinson, James, 21
Rogers, Annie, 149, 153, 162, 313
Rogers, Carl, 5, 83–102, 104, 110,
    151, 293–295, 303, 318
Roosevelt, Franklin Delano, 47
rootlessness. *See* interpersonal,
    rootlessness
Rorty, Richard, 284, 286, 318

Saint-Cheron, Philippe de, 25, 27,
    212, 321
Sartre, Jean Paul, 16, 116, 184, 318
Sauvage, Micheline, 116, 319
saving face, 169, 171, 173, 301; of a
    learner, 172–173, 184–185
Scannell, Margie, 229, 319
science: additive approach to,
    change, 108–110; value-laden,
    105–108, 112, 123; of self, 104;
    of values, 111; story of, 122. *See
    also* narrative, of science;
Schrag, Calvin, 44, 194, 293, 298,
    319
Schultz, Emily, 44, 319
secrets, 200–201
self, 96–97; actualization, 117–121,
    223–224; dialogic, 99, 102, 105,
    110, 122–123; esteem, 117–121;
    in service to the other, 111–112,
    224, 228; reflection, 187; serving
    bias, 17. *See also* metaphor, of
    self; moral, self
Sennett, Richard, 17, 49, 50, 65,
    257, 317
service, 224; call to, 111; signifi-
    cance found in, 137. *See also*
    self, in service to the other
Sherif, Muzafer, 77, 319
Shor, Ira, 5, 171, 173, 319
Shore, Paul J., 247–250, 317
Sinclair, Upton, 198, 319
Skinner, B. F., 87, 319
Socrates, 18, 116–117
Spielberg, Steven, 154, 319
Spitzack, Carole, 158, 319
Stack, Carol, 151, 315
Stalin, Joseph, 47
standard bearer of excellence,
    121–122
standpoint, 155; of the other, 279;
    theory: 56, 165, 192
Stevens, Barry, 86, 98–99, 101, 318
Stewart, David, 133, 319
Stewart, John, 3, 39–40, 42, 91,
    319–320

Stone, Isidor F., 117, 320
story, 6–7, 233, 235–236; bad, 46, 47, 69–70, 208; based view of community, 260, 270; laden culture, 100; filled wisdom, 101; good, 70; guidance, 136–139; guided values, 272–274; limits of, 147; meaning, 249–252; missing, 237–238; moral, 49, 86, 134, 250; problematic, 270–271; telling, 154; value-laden, 104; web of, 279–280. *See also* caring, story of; ethics, re-storying; meaning, and story; metaphor, story of; science, story of
Stout, Jeffrey, 51
Strawson, P. F., 284
suffering, 218–221
Sullivan, William, 5, 15, 49, 63, 101, 252, 256, 307
Swidler, Ann, 5, 15, 49, 63, 101, 252, 256, 307
Sykes, Charles, 88, 320

Tallon, Andrew, 132, 315
Tarule, Jill, 22
Taylor, Charles, 27, 74–75, 77, 320
Taylor, Daniel, 236–239, 242, 249, 252, 320
technicians of goodness, 146
technique mentality, 138
Thatcher, V. S., 13, 320
theory informed action. *See* praxis
therapeutic: attitude, 263; cul de sac, 50; culture, 62–64, 67, 69; language, 64–67, 256, 267–270; limits, 262–265; metaphor, 64–67; model of interpersonal communication, 30; triumph of, 68. *See also* metaphor, therapeutic
Third Reich, 139
Tillich, Paul, 245
Tipton, Steven, 5, 15, 49, 63, 101, 252, 256, 307

Tocqueville, Alexis de, 94–95, 258–259, 287, 302, 320
Toffler, Alvin, 215, 320
Toffler, Heidi, 215, 320
Tolman, Deborah, 162, 313
Tracy, David, 51, 76, 320
tragic triad, 222–223
transcendental ego, 135
trust, 84–85, 92, 101, 129; existential trust, 15; existential mistrust, 15–16, 27, 40; loss of, 16, 85, 88; of one's voice, 165
tyranny, of intimacy, 50

unconditional positive regard, 98–99
understanding, 3, 31, 39, 249; praxis as ground for, 44
unity of contraries, 142–143, 209, 212

values: human, 103–105, 116–117; minimal, 204, 271; moral, 284. *See also* common, values; science, value-laden, of values; story, guided values, value-laden
Vico, Giambatista, 43, 44, 54, 320
Voltaire, Francois Marie Arouet de, 202–203, 320
voice, 301, 303; dialogic, 168, 177; losing one's, 153–160; moral, 153–157; muted, 161, 242, 294; psychological, 155–156; relational, 150–151, 161; woman's, 149, 153, 155. *See also* inclusion, and voice; trust, of one's voice; moral, voice

Wallace, Karl, 46, 320–321
Warnke, Georgia, 30, 321
Watson, John B., 87, 321
Watzlawick, Paul, 214, 321
Weaver, Richard, 272, 321

web of metaphorical significance, 300–301, 303–304
Weil, Simone, 3, 233, 321
whistleblowing, 201
White, Kenneth, 42, 321
Whyte, William, 273, 321
Wiesel, Elie, 25, 27, 212, 321
Wiggins, Grant, 153, 313
Winthrop, John, 272

wisdom: of action, 138. *See also* human organism; story, filled wisdom
Witherell, Carol, 235, 240, 246, 250, 252, 321
Wood, Julia, 40, 44, 151, 153, 155–157, 161, 163, 165–166, 192, 286, 321–322
wounded healer, 112